QUICK AND EASY

VeganSlowCooking

641.5636
KEL

More Than 150 Tasty, Nourishing Recipes
That Practically Make Themselves

Carla Kelly

THE EXPERIMENT
NEW YORK

QUICK AND EASY VEGAN SLOW COOKING: *More Than 150 Tasty,*
Nourishing Recipes That Practically Make Themselves

The Experiment
260 Fifth Avenue
New York, NY 10001-6408
www.theexperimentpublishing.com

This book contains the opinions and ideas of its author. It is intended to provide helpful and informative material on the subjects addressed in the book. It is sold with the understanding that the author and publisher are not engaged in rendering medical, health, or any other kind of personal professional services in the book. The author and publisher specifically disclaim all responsibility for any liability, loss, or risk—personal or otherwise—that is incurred as a consequence, directly or indirectly, of the use and application of any of the contents of this book.

The Experiment's books are available at special discounts when purchased in bulk for premiums and sales promotions as well as for fundraising or educational use. For details, contact us at info@theexperimentpublishing.com.

Library of Congress Cataloging-in-Publication Data

Kelly, Carla, 1971–
  Quick and easy vegan slow cooking : more than 150 tasty, nourishing recipes that practically make themselves / Carla Kelly.
     p. cm.
  Includes index.
  ISBN 978-1-61519-043-0 (trade pbk.) — ISBN 978-1-61519-145-1 (ebook) 1. Vegan cooking.
2. Vegetarian cooking. 3. Electric cooking, Slow. 4. Quick and easy cooking. 5. Cookbooks.
I. Title. II. Title: More than 150 tasty, nourishing slow cooker recipes that practically make themselves.
  TX837.K37 2011
  641.5'636—dc23
                     2011032919

ISBN 978-1-61519-043-0
Ebook ISBN 978-1-61519-145-1

Cover design by Susi Oberhelman
Cover photograph of vegan soup © Stockfood | Ellert
Author photograph by Karen Jackson
Text design by Pauline Neuwirth, Neuwirth & Associates, Inc.

Manufactured in the United States of America
Distributed by Workman Publishing Company, Inc.
Distributed simultaneously in Canada by Thomas Allen and Son Ltd.
First published April 2012
10 9 8 7 6 5 4 3 2 1

For sticking by me,
Supporting me,
Loving me,
Giving me hugs,
Even when I was the crabby, stressed-out, still-in-my-pajamas-
on-the-computer-at-noon me.
For my family, as always: "more than the world."

Contents

To Serve With

Welcome

WHILE WRITING MY first book, *Quick and Easy Vegan Bake Sale* (The Experiment, 2011), I found myself with very little time on my hands to cook dinner. However, I still wanted to put something healthy and warming on the table, meals I could feel good about serving. I developed a range of one-dish recipes that used very little by way of pots and pans (who can face all that washing up?) but still used loads of vegetables and quality vegan protein. These morphed, over time, into many of the recipes in this book.

If you don't yet own *VBS* (as I fondly refer to it), we may need to be introduced.

Hi, I'm Carla; pleased to meet you. I'm happily married with two wonderful children, who (unfortunately) are still a lot less adventurous than I am when it comes to savory food. I'm originally from New Zealand and now reside in beautiful British Columbia, Canada. I came here after living in Queensland, Australia, and Edinburgh, Scotland. I'm also vegan. I came to veganism slowly but have been vegan for more than seven years, and I'm still going strong.

For my recipe creations I draw inspiration from my background, from food I grew up with and loved, experienced along the way, or just became interested in. I like to experiment—to put flavors together and draw from the results. My food philosophy is simple: I believe food tastes best when it's shared—with friends and family, with laughter and love.

When I put it to my team of wonderful recipe testers (volunteers who try out the recipes and provide online feedback while the recipes are still in development to ensure they work

perfectly) that the next book was to be a slow cooker book, their responses were interesting. You see, I'd never thought too much about slow cooking, and I was surprised at how many of them had. A few people didn't have slow cookers and weren't interested in getting one so weren't able to continue with testing. Others had them in the past but either gave them away through lack of use or didn't bother replacing them when they stopped working; they were a minority. Most were excited to be able to use their slow cooker more and even recommended friends and family members as testers. I found more and more people who loved their slow cookers but hardly used them.

I guess vegans do have a bit of a love affair with their slow cookers, but it seems to be a long, slowly simmering (excuse the pun) feeling that gets forgotten every now and then. People often associate the slow cooker with slowly braised cuts of tough meat, and not many slow cooker books focus specifically on vegan (or even vegetarian) recipes. If you are an experienced vegan hoping to "up the heat" of your love affair with your slow cooker, I hope this book will help! If you're new to veganism and afraid of losing your favorite slow-cooked meals, you too will find much to enjoy: plenty of classics and bean-packed delights, and if you want to venture into the lands of seitan, TVP, tempeh, and less common grains, I've got recipes for them too!

But this isn't a book *just* about slow cooking: As I was developing these recipes, I found that I would often come home (to a house that smelled as if it were heaven!) and throw together a conventionally made side dish to go with whatever I had bubbling away. In To Serve With (page 211), you'll find some of these conventionally made recipes that are either super quick and easy or items that can be made ahead and that store well. I've given suggestions from To Serve With for pairing with recipes in other chapters.

The focus in this book is definitely savory—main dishes, starters, and the like—seasonal, varied, and tasty. These are meals you'll want to welcome you home, meals you'll look forward to and plan to make again and again. You may find yourself wondering why it took so long to realize how much you really do love your slow cooker!

I haven't given recipes using the slow cooker as a vehicle for baking or for making breakfasts or desserts. You can do all those things (and more) in the slow cooker, but for this book, I want to feed you nutritious, tasty, savory food. In the pages that follow you'll find easy to make, easy to cook, nourishing, and comforting dishes that are suitable for every season, every occasion, and every taste. I hope you enjoy preparing them as much as I have making them for you.

Quick and Easy Slow Cooking?

At this point you would be forgiven for scratching your head and wondering about this obvious oxymoron. How can something that cooks for six or eight hours be quick and easy? The answer is as simple as it is logical. It's all about the preparation time and the actual active cooking time—not so much of the first, and very little of the second. Slow-cooking preparation is just quick and easy in the morning (or the evening before) instead of in the evening when you're looking for dinner. You're already in the kitchen for breakfast, so allow a little extra time before you rush out the door (yes, unfortunately, you may have to set the alarm 15 minutes earlier) so at the end of the day, when you have less energy and really can't face the idea of cooking, dinner is waiting for you.

The time commitment you make in advance leads to a very quick and easy dinner when you are ready to serve. In many cases you can take the lid off the slow cooker and transfer its ingredients immediately to bowl or plate, and thence to tummy! Even when you have to perform additional steps to get the food ready for the slow cooker, there is nothing longer than 45 minutes required (and many of the longer preparation times include hands-off time). Sometimes the additional steps can be completed well in advance of starting the slow cooker, with the ingredients held in the fridge until needed. Therefore, the actual *active* cooking time, which is the cooking outside the slow cooker, is given in the preparation time noted in the recipes. Sometimes active cooking time is even divided time: you do part of the preparation early in the process and part later. Occasionally there will be a small amount of active cooking at the end of the slow cooking time

(thickening a sauce, for example), but this really is minimal, and the fact remains that dinner is ready when you want it, is very convenient, and is very "quick and easy."

Why Use a Slow Cooker?

What benefits are there to me? What makes a slow cooker so wonderful? Here's my list. I'm sure you'll find your own reasons to add to this too!

CAN BE LOWER IN FAT

Case in point: I did a count of the slow-cooker recipes in this book (not including those in To Serve With and Basic Recipes) and found that out of 117 recipes there are 68 that contain no added oil—a whopping 58 percent. Of the remaining recipes, many use just a tablespoon of oil for an entire dish that serves a minimum of four (and sometimes up to eight). If there is still too much oil for your preference, adjust the amount to suit. You could sauté with less oil or with a vegetable stock when precooking your aromatics.

CAN BE HEALTHY

The recipes are not only lower in fat but also, in the main, full of fiber-containing beans, antioxidant-rich vegetables, and protein-rich soy foods.

BONUS TIME

When making a set-and-forget dinner, you are freed up and released from the kitchen so you can do other things, like take a long soak in the tub or update your Facebook status. Or, perhaps, even go to work.

ORGANIZATION

You'll need to plan ahead for meals, which leaves you more time for more important things like friends and family. You may be so pleased with the extra time you save through organizing that this habit will spill out into other areas of your life.

WORKS WELL WITH MENU PLANNING

You'll know in advance what is needed to start the slow cooker on any given day. This knowledge can save you time at the grocery store, preparation time, and money spent both on groceries and on that late-day takeout splurge—dinner is already ready.

MONEY SAVING

I haven't done the math, but especially if you're using dried beans, seasonal local vegetables, and grains bought in bulk, slow cooking ends up being a fairly economical way of feeding yourself and your family.

COMPLETELY COHESIVE FLAVORS

The long cooking time allows flavors to completely mingle—even without an initial sauté to soften the aromatics. Whatever flavors and nutrients leach out of the food are incorporated into the dish. You're not throwing away nutrition or flavor with the cooking liquid.

GREAT FOR A CROWD

Slow cooking is an easy way of making (and keeping warm) a large quantity of food with little stress. Lowering stress levels is always a positive! You can take a dish in your slow cooker to an event and plug it in to keep the food warm the whole evening. If you're attending (or hosting) a vegan potluck, these recipes are sure to impress.

EVERYONE CAN DO IT

The instructions for many of these recipes are chop, put in the slow cooker, stir, and set—which even the most kitchen challenged among us shouldn't find too hard to complete. For the novice as well as for the more experienced cook, slow cookers are a wonderful way to do it all yourself.

MINIMAL EFFORT REQUIRED

For those days when you are feeling under the weather, you can still get a healthy warming dinner on the table. Slow-cooked soups are especially good on the days when you're not feeling great.

CLEANS UP EASILY

Even cooked-on gunk usually wipes off after a soak in hot water—and most inserts are dishwasher safe. (If you do have a slow cooker that sticks more than you like, spray with a little nonstick spray prior to filling and you'll find cleanup is even easier.)

LEFTOVERS

Slow cooker recipes usually make enough to ensure you have leftovers. You can freeze them for the day when you're cooking on the spur of the moment. Pull a leftover meal out of the freezer, defrost, reheat, and—*voilà!*—dinner is on the table.

THE SMELL

It's glorious to walk in the door after a stressful day and be enveloped by the wonderful aroma of goodness! Smell may be the biggest plus of all.

Getting Started with Your Slow Cooker

Working with your slow cooker to create delicious meals, ready when you want them, is not hard if you take note of my handy hints.

PLAN

Read the recipes in advance, make notes of what you want to make when (creating a daily and/or weekly menu plan), and ensure you have all the ingredients.

Count back from the time you want to eat to decide when to start cooking, factoring in preparation times as listed in recipes.

PREPARE

Ensure all ingredients are in the form specified in the recipe (e.g., "soaked," "chopped," "thawed," etc.).

If asked to fill the slow cooker in a specific order and not stir, then please do so—items that need longer cooking will be at the bottom.

In most instances the slow cooker will be filled between one-half and three-quarters full.

COOK

Use the specified temperature setting. If pressed for time, you may cook on HIGH for about half the time recommended for cooking on LOW, although flavors generally won't develop as well.

Periodically turn the insert during the cooking time, if at all possible, to move the insert off any "hot spot."

Be flexible: Not every slow cooker will cook at exactly the same rate.

Add additional stock (¼ cup at a time and stirred in) and increase the cooking time by half-hour increments if the contents seem too thick before being fully cooked.

To extend the cooking time by an hour or so, prepare everything in advance and hold in the fridge overnight to chill. Place in the slow cooker still chilled, and it will have to come to room temperature in the slow cooker before it can start cooking.

Lift the lid and stir the dish in the last half of the cooking time only, and make sure the lid is off for as short a time as possible.

BE SAFE

Check the manual that comes with your model for specific safe usage requirements. Some inserts cannot be used chilled, on the stovetop, or under the broiler, while others can.

Always touch and move the heated insert wearing kitchen mitts to protect your hands from burns. Take care with the outer casing, as this, too, may be hot.

Do not immerse the outer casing in water: The electrical systems could get wet and become faulty, or even give you an electric shock.

Never leave the cord dangling over the counter, where it may get caught up and pull the slow cooker over.

Don't start the slow cooker if you've just taken the insert out of the fridge; let it come to room temperature first to avoid cracking.

Limit the time you leave food on the WARM setting to no longer than 2 hours. Not only may the food dry out, it may not be kept hot enough to retard bacterial growth.

Do not use the slow cooker to reheat previously cooked food, as the food will not get hot quickly enough to kill bacteria.

STORE AND REHEAT LEFTOVERS

Cool your portioned slow cooker meals to room temperature in shallow containers so the food cools quickly, minimizing time for any bacterial growth.

Once completely cool, cover and transfer to the fridge or freezer. Remember to label any food going into the freezer with the name and date of cooking. As a general rule, store food in the fridge for up to 5 days and in the freezer for up to 3 months.

Slow cooker meals get better over time as the flavors meld and develop. Reheat leftovers completely in the microwave, a saucepan, or the oven at 375°F, until piping hot. Don't refreeze, and don't reheat more than once.

Check the chapter introductions for more ideas for using up leftovers.

CLEAN

The inserts and lids are generally dishwasher safe (check the booklet for your model), but they can be hand-washed very quickly anyway. Ensure very hot water is used to remove any possible bacteria.

Wipe the outer casing with a damp cloth once unplugged.

ADAPT FAVORITE RECIPES

Adjusting recipes to or from the slow cooker usually involves adjusting one or more of the following: the liquid, oil, spices, beans, or cooking time. Read the manual that came with your model for more hints, but here are some basic guidelines:

LIQUIDS: Usually, liquid quantity is less in slow cooking, about half the recommended amount for conventional cooking methods. Use this "rule of half" as a starting point, although the conversion will vary depending on the water content of your ingredients.

OIL: Many conventional recipes start with a sauté of the onion and garlic (or other aromatics) in oil. Personally, I haven't found this necessary for most of my slow cooker recipes, as I find the longer time in the slow cooker draws out the flavors in these quite nicely.

HERBS AND SPICES: Ground herbs and spices need to be increased to at least 1½ times the amount called for in conventional recipes when converted to slow cooking. You should taste and adjust seasonings, if necessary, just prior to serving. Remember, it's much easier to add spices and herbs than to take them out.

BEANS: Use precooked beans (canned, or soaked and boiled at home) when converting a slow cooker recipe to the stovetop.

COOKING TIMES: A very rough rule of thumb is to multiply your conventional recipe time by 8 and start with that as the slow cooker time on LOW heat (or by 4 if you want to cook on HIGH heat), checking doneness and adding more time as required.

Equipment

Let's look in more detail at the slow cooker itself and the other equipment you'll need to make the recipes.

SLOW COOKER

Whether it be old-fashioned or up to date with more features than you know how to use, your slow cooker will be perfect for the recipes in this book. Because of their construction, slow cookers, even the really old ones, are generally safe to use while you are away from home or sleeping. They use many small electrical coils, each emitting very little heat, and use very little energy to do so, making them a very low fire risk. Most models cook at a temperature of 200°F on the LOW setting and 300°F on the HIGH setting. They provide a long, slow, moist cooking environment that essentially braises the ingredients, infusing them with flavor. Slow cookers' snug-fitting lids and the thick walls of their ceramic inserts maintain moisture by locking in steam, so they need less liquid to cook the food.

All the recipes in this book were developed and tested with medium-sized (roughly four- to six-quart) slow cookers. Because all brands, makes, and models are of slightly different dimensions and even shapes, you may need to make slight tweaks and adjustments to the recipes to suit your specific slow cooker. I also found that all slow cookers (even ones of similar ages) cook at slightly different rates, so please bear in mind that the recipes were created using a modern, relatively rapid-cooking model, which the times noted will reflect. You may need to make minor timing adjustments to suit your model.

If your slow cooker is new to you, please carefully read its instruction booklet to familiarize yourself with specifics on operation, safety, timing, and special features.

TIMER

If you plan to use your slow cooker while you are away from home or asleep (and who doesn't?), I really recommend you purchase a timer switch for the outlet you'll use in your kitchen. Timers are small devices that plug into the wall outlet into which you plug your slow cooker. They all work in a similar way: Set the current time and the time to start (and in some cases stop) the power flow. Turn the slow cooker to the setting specified in the recipe; when the timer reaches the start time you have set, the power will flow and the slow cooker will start the cooking process. I bought mine from the electrical items aisle (with the surge protectors) at a department store, but they are also available from hardware stores and are inexpensive.

A few things to remember when using these switches:

Make sure you turn on your slow cooker to the desired heat setting *prior to* plugging into the timer switch. If you haven't turned on the slow cooker, the power will come through the switch but the slow cooker will not cook. (Yes, I'm speaking from experience.)

If you set an off time for the switch, remember to ensure there is enough time to cook your items as the slow cooker will stop cooking at the off time set on the timer switch regardless of how cooked the food is (again speaking from experience, unfortunately).

These switches do not work with all models of slow cookers,

such as those with electronic control pads and settings. Check your model and the instruction booklet it comes with.

Other items that I use often include:

IMMERSION BLENDER

For blending super-smooth soups in the slow cooker. If you don't have an immersion blender (also known as a stick blender or a handheld blender), you'll have to blend in batches in your blender, very carefully.

FOOD PROCESSOR

Used for making nut meal, blending tofu and liquids, and, if you wish, chopping vegetables.

SPICE GRINDER

Not only for grinding spices! I also use mine to grind small quantities of nuts and seeds. If you don't have one, use a mini food processor, coffee grinder, or blender. A pastry brush makes it easy to get out the last few bits of ground spice.

SKILLET AND SAUCEPAN

Used for stovetop sautéing and ingredient preparation if your slow cooker insert is not stovetop safe. If you buy only one, make it a 10-inch skillet, which should serve all your needs. If you'd rather use a saucepan (which is also used in several recipes), use a medium-size one.

KNIVES

A good quality 8- to 10-inch chef's knife is really all you need, but a smaller paring knife (for fine fruit and vegetable work) and a serrated knife (for bread and acidic items) are handy, too. For some recipes a mandoline is handy for making perfectly even vegetable slices.

MICROPLANE GRATER

Very handy if you'd rather not mince garlic and ginger by hand. This rasp-shape tool is also great for zesting citrus. If you don't have one, a box grater does the trick.

BOWLS AND MEASURING EQUIPMENT

Have a variety of different-size bowls for different mixing uses. Always choose a bowl to use that is one size larger than the one you think you'll need; it'll make mixing much easier. You'll also need standard measuring equipment—spoons and cups.

WOODEN SPOONS, WHISKS, AND SPATULAS

You'll need these, or something similar, to mix items together. Note that flexible silicon spatulas are better than wooden spoons for removing the last traces of mixes from bowls.

STEAMER BASKET

Where required I use a small, metal, collapsible vegetable steamer basket insert, found in many supermarkets or department stores (and even dollar stores) at minimal cost.

Additional items are required for making some of the dishes in To Serve With: baking sheets and pans, roasting pans, and muffin or mini loaf tins, all easily found in supermarkets, department stores, and kitchenware stores.

Ingredients

In this section we're going to look at the common and not-so-common ingredients I use in the recipes, including substitutes for hard-to-find (or disliked) items.

Produce

Unless otherwise stated all produce used is of medium size. I don't specify that the produce should be organic and as local as possible, but as you most likely know from newspapers, magazines, and television, these have the best flavor and a low carbon footprint. Do what you can.

GARLIC

Peeling garlic is easy. If you are planning on making Poached Garlic (page 54) anytime soon, you'll want to know how.

First remove the papery outer skin from the head of garlic and separate the cloves from each other and from the hard base. If you are strong enough (and have large enough hands), you can push down on the whole head and rock back and forth to both break up the head and loosen the skins.

Place the garlic clove to be peeled on a hard board. Place the flat of your chef's knife on top of the clove, hold your knife still, and press down with the heel of your other hand. The goal is to crack the garlic just slightly, which lets its skin slip off easily. At first you may end up with squished garlic or need to press harder, but you'll get better at judging the pressure the more you do it.

If you are peeling a lot of garlic in one go, slightly damp hands are great for peeling off the skin; otherwise, the garlic juice will make the garlic skin stick to your hands.

MINCING GARLIC

I MINCE THE garlic, even if it's going straight into the slow cooker for a blended soup; it allows the flavor to be drawn out more, to mingle with the flavors from the rest of the ingredients. Here's how to mince (unless you're cheating and using a Microplane grater or garlic press).

Peel the clove, cut off its base, and slice in half lengthwise, giving you a flat surface to place downward on the cutting board. Cut the garlic lengthwise into very thin strips (as thin as you can), then turn the slices and cut into tiny pieces. From here use your knife in a rocking motion, holding the top edge of the tip of your knife in your nondominant hand for support, and grind the garlic into a pastelike consistency, moving the handle end back and forth as you chop.

If you prefer a mellow garlic taste, try using some Poached Garlic (page 54) in place of some, or all, of the raw garlic called for in any recipe. Also feel free to use larger, or smaller, cloves as your tastes dictate.

ONIONS

Chopping onions is something many people complain about, but there is really no need for goggles, water, or whatever the latest no-cry fad is. This is the method I was taught in basic chef's training and the one I have used ever since. I rarely cry and then only if it is a super juicy onion.

1. Slice the onion in half through the root base. **2.** Cut the straggly top bits off and discard or use for stock, leaving the root end intact on each piece, which is what keeps the tears at bay. Peel back the outer layers; they should come right off. Lay the peeled halves cut side down on your chopping board. **3.** Taking each onion half in turn, apply gentle pressure with your non-dominant hand to the top of the onion and use a chef's knife in your dominant hand to make a series of horizontal cuts parallel to the cutting board surface, from the stalk end toward the root. The pressure of your hand will stop the onion from moving and give more control over the knife. **4.** Holding the onion half by the root end, make a series of vertical cuts down through the onion to your cutting board with your knife pointing toward the root. **5.** Slice the onion parallel to the initial cut you made and the finely chopped onion will fall all over your cutting board.

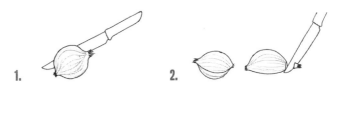

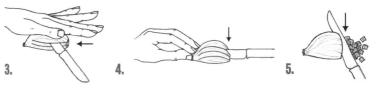

I also use spring onions in some recipes. Although scallions (also known as green onions) aren't exactly the same thing, use whichever you have on hand.

GINGER

Fresh ginger is used either minced (see Mincing Garlic, page 13) or in larger pieces that are removed at the end of cooking. I always peel ginger and crush larger pieces to release both oils and flavor, but this is up to you. However, I would definitely recommend peeling it before mincing. If you would rather not mince by hand or prefer smaller pieces of ginger, use a Microplane (or box) grater to get the ginger really fine. Ginger stores well in the fridge and can even be minced and frozen in ice cube trays for handy one-tablespoon amounts. Add to the slow cooker while still frozen.

LEMONGRASS

Lemongrass is found in many supermarkets and fruit and vegetable stores. It is a hard, wiry grass and smells faintly of lemon. When mincing, use only the very center of the stalks, the parts that are tender and soft. You need to bruise the stalks with the side of your chef's knife (like you do when peeling garlic) to crack open the stems and to peel off the hard outside parts. Be a little aggressive; a bit of force is beneficial to tenderize the insides and to release the flavor oils. The softer inside layers are then minced and measured. If using the whole stalk, it is usually trimmed for length, crushed as described, then removed from the dish just prior to serving.

GREENS

Some recipes call for shredding greens such as kale, chard, or cabbage, or herbs such as basil.

To shred greens, remove the hard stem from the center of each leaf, then pile the leaves on top of one another. Roll into a cylinder, then using a sharp chef's knife make thin cuts off the end of the roll so the greens are left in long thin strands.

For cabbage, cut in half through the stalk. Cut around the hard stalk in the center with a paring knife, lift it out, and discard. Place the half cabbage cut side down on the chopping board, press it flat, and use the chef's knife to cut thin strands.

For basil and other small-leaf items, there's no need to remove the center stem. Place the leaves on top of one another, roll, and cut as you would kale.

Fresh spinach may be substituted for frozen where noted. For a 14-ounce box of frozen spinach, use 4 cups of fresh spinach, packed and roughly chopped.

Arugula (also known as rocket) is slightly sharp and bitter, and if not to your taste may be replaced with spinach for a milder result.

LEEKS

Leeks love dirt. They hide it among their leaves (mainly the outer ones) and stubbornly hold onto it when you try to wash it off. The best way I've found to clean leeks is Jamie Oliver's: Cut the very dark green leaves from the leek. The lighter green parts are perfectly fine and will become tender when cooked. Leave the base or root end intact. Slice the leek in half lengthwise. Holding each half in turn, with the base (white) end uppermost, rinse under cold running water. Separate all the layers and force the water to run down through them toward the green end. Because most of the dirt accumulates toward the green end of the leek, the water washes toward that end and takes the dirt straight out without depositing it on other parts of the leek. Leaving the base end on to hold everything together, slice the leeks into half or quarter moons.

ROOT VEGETABLES AND WINTER SQUASH

Root vegetables such as potatoes, beets, turnips, parsnips, and rutabaga take a very long time to cook in the slow cooker, so they must be cut into small pieces for best results. Because they are rarely perfectly round, they may not be easy to cut, but try this method: Once peeled, cut a side off the vegetable to form a flat surface, then place flat side down on the chopping board to hold the rest of the vegetable stable while cutting. To peel or not to peel is up to you if not specified (though do ensure they are thoroughly washed if you don't peel them).

Winter squashes, such as butternut, are peeled. The easiest way to peel a hard-skinned squash is to halve it lengthwise and remove the seeds with a spoon. Cut it into manageable chunks and cut a flat surface on each chunk. Use a chef's knife to run down the length of each chunk to remove the skin. Where I have used canned pumpkin, you can make a puree of the flesh of roasted or steamed pumpkin, if desired. If buying canned pumpkin, ensure the label does not say "pie filling" and that the only ingredient is pumpkin.

If you buy beets with the greens attached and intend to use them, for best results remove the greens, wrap in damp kitchen towels, and store in the crisper of your fridge. If you store the beets and greens attached, the beets will remove all the moisture from the greens and they won't be as nice when cooked.

If your parsnips are older and larger, the centers may be hard and woody. If so, cut out the center sections and discard, using only the outer sections of the root.

EGGPLANT AND SUMMER SQUASH

To salt or not to salt? I don't, although if the eggplant or zucchini is large and old with tough-looking flesh and skin, I might consider it. If you feel salting decreases bitterness, you may do so this way: First cut as required by the recipe. Sprinkle the pieces generously with salt, toss to distribute evenly, and let them sit in a colander for an hour or so. Rinse the eggplant in plenty of water to remove the salt; pat dry with paper towels.

I apply the same rule to deciding whether or not to peel and remove the seeds. If it is large and looks older with a thick skin, I peel and remove any large seeds. If tender and young, I use it without peeling and seeding.

MUSHROOMS

I use a range of mushrooms, from white button, cremini, and portobello (all actually the same mushroom at different ages!) to shiitake, oyster, and even dried. In many recipes I use a combination, and you can adjust the mushrooms to taste. To a certain extent they are interchangeable—use what you have, even if it's all white button. In some recipes I do note that substitution is not recommended, usually because I want a specific texture. However, you can always interchange different varieties of dried mushrooms. When preparing mushrooms use the caps and stems if you wish, except for shiitakes—the stems are far too tough and stringy to ever become tender. Then again, they are great for making Mushroom Stock (page 44).

I wipe the mushroom caps with a damp cloth to remove any dirt and proceed from there. You may briefly soak and dry mush-

rooms if you like. I do not remove the gills from portobello mushrooms because I like the deeper earthy flavor and color they bring. If you prefer to remove them, scoop them out with a small spoon.

TOMATOES

When I use fresh tomatoes, I use mainly Roma (also known as plum or Italian), which are less juicy and less acidic than mainstream tomatoes. The slow cooker does tend to bring out the acidity in the tomato, which is why some recipes using fresh tomatoes have a little sweetener added for balance.

I frequently use canned diced, stewed, or crushed tomatoes; tomato sauce; and tomato paste. If you have access to reasonably priced organic canned tomatoes, use them, and try fire-roasted varieties for a nice flavor variation.

When I use sun-dried tomatoes they are not oil packed; if this is the only type you can get, remove them from the oil and use as directed. You will not need to soak to reconstitute.

The easiest and most efficient way to cut sun-dried tomatoes is to use kitchen shears and snip them into little pieces. If you'd rather use a knife, use a serrated one for easiest cutting.

If you have a garden with lots of tomatoes, you can dry your own in a dehydrator or the oven. If using a dehydrator, follow the directions that come with your model, but for oven drying here is a quick how-to:

OVEN-DRYING TOMATOES

AFTER WASHING THE tomatoes, quarter them, remove the seeds, and spread in a single layer on a large baking sheet. Pack them together as you lay them out because they will contract. Sprinkle with a little salt and pepper, then bake in a cool oven (250°F) for *hours* until they shrivel up and become firm. Times are flexible because the moisture content of the tomatoes will affect how long it takes, but start with 5 hours and adjust from there. Presto, homemade sun-dried tomatoes, without the sun part.

ASPARAGUS

I use green asparagus (as opposed to white) that has not been peeled prior to use. Fresh asparagus will snap at the correct break point if the bottom end of the stalk is bent with light pressure. Breaking does, however, leave a raggedy end you might like to neaten up. I generally don't bother. The tops are used in the recipes, the bottom ends for Asparagus Stock (page 44).

FENNEL

Fennel is a peculiarly shaped vegetable. The fronds and stalks (if yours has any) are cut off and discarded, composted, or made into stock, or you can keep the fronds and use as a garnish or as a fresh herb. Cut the bulb in half and remove the hard center stem before cutting up further as specified in the recipe.

Fennel seeds are purchased dried and usually whole, though I use them ground. If you can't find ground fennel seeds, grind them in a spice grinder or small food processor. Try looking in Asian spice stores or health food stores for fennel seeds. If you can't find them with the spices, look with the teas for a fennel seed tea, which is usually only fennel seeds, either ground or whole. There is about 1 teaspoon of seeds in each teabag.

PEAS

As frozen green peas are more commonly available (and available year-round) this is what I use. If you have access to fresh peas in season, please use them in place of the frozen. If you are not a fan of green peas, substitute finely chopped green beans or any other finely chopped vegetable, or leave them out entirely.

CORN

One ear of corn, stripped, usually provides the same amount of kernels as ¾ cup of either drained canned or frozen corn. These may be used interchangeably, and when corn is in season I do recommend using fresh.

If you want to make your own creamed corn you can do so easily in your blender. Use ¾ cup of cooked corn kernels and partially blend, with a little water if necessary to ease the blending, until thick and still a little chunky.

PEPPERS

I use peppers, both fresh and roasted, in many recipes. You can buy jarred roasted peppers or roast your own (see Roasting Peppers, below). If I call for a red, yellow, or green pepper, I am referring to bell peppers. I do call for jalapeño and serrano peppers by name. Green peppers tend to get bitter after cooking in the slow cooker, so I use them sparingly and pair them with ingredients to counteract the effect.

ROASTING PEPPERS

SLICE THE PEPPER in half and remove the seeds and membranes. Heat the broiler and place the pepper cut side down on a foil-lined baking sheet. Place under the broiler until the skin becomes blackened in places. Remove from the heat. Using the foil, wrap the pepper completely and leave for 5 minutes or so, which will make the skin easier to remove. When you can handle the pepper without burning your hands, peel off and discard the skin and slice pepper as required.

Canned chipotle chile peppers in adobo, usually found in the ethnic aisle of most supermarkets, are dried jalapeño peppers (the chipotle) in a rich, tangy, tomato-based sauce. Seed the peppers prior to using (unless you like them really hot) and use a little of the sauce with each pepper when called for.

Ground dried ancho and chipotle chile peppers are used in many recipes. They are available in the spice aisle of many supermarkets. If you do not have access to either of them, use a blended chile powder that suits your taste and level of heat.

FRUIT

I use apples and pears in savory dishes to add bursts of sweetness and depth of flavor. I also use dried fruit on occasion for the same reason. You'll find dried cranberries, raisins, apricots, prunes, and golden raisins in some recipes. These are all easily found in supermarkets, often in the bulk food aisle. The easiest way to cut these if necessary is to use kitchen shears or a serrated knife.

I use citrus fruit in the form of juice and zest. Remember to remove the zest from the fruit prior to juicing for easiest results. Freshly squeezed is best if you have a juicer; otherwise, canned is fine too.

HERBS AND SPICES

I specify if herbs are required to be dried or fresh. Sometimes both forms are used in the same recipe, one to cook with the main ingredients and the other to provide dazzle and lift at the end of cooking. You can substitute dried herbs for fresh, using 1 teaspoon of the dried herb for every 1 tablespoon of fresh. Add the dried herbs with the other seasonings in the recipe.

I use both regular (curly) and flat-leaf (Italian) parsley in recipes, sometimes interchangeably when the parsley is providing an accent, but not when the parsley flavor desired is the main focus. The recipe will guide you, though substitute if you don't have access to the one specified.

With dried sage I use both powdered and rubbed leaves. Both are readily available in most supermarkets and provide a different level and slightly different taste of sage.

I use both white and black pepper, the black freshly ground, and the white pre-ground. I find there is a difference in heat level and flavor, but it is subtle. They are interchangeable depending on what you have available, but you will need to be aware of heat levels and adjust amounts to taste.

I use both paprika and smoked paprika, sometimes in the same recipe. The peppers for smoked paprika have been smoked before drying and grinding, adding an intense background depth of smoky flavor. It is available in the spice aisle of supermarkets. If you do not have smoked paprika you may use paprika in its place, though the results will not be quite as intended.

GRAINS

I use both gluten- and non-gluten-containing grains. Grains include rice (many varieties), wild rice, barley, oats (steel-cut and rolled), millet, bulgur, amaranth (a small South American grain available at health food stores), and quinoa; flours include all-purpose, wheat, spelt, rice, and chickpea. Please don't taste any uncooked mixture containing chickpea flour; prior to cooking it tastes really awful! If your supermarket doesn't stock all the grains or flours, try a health food store.

I am firmly in the quinoa-rinsing camp, even though modern quinoa is prerinsed. I have had a batch of less than perfectly rinsed quinoa, and it was not nice!

I don't usually soak grains for slow cooking (I do usually soak brown rice for stovetop cooking to shorten the cooking time), although sometimes I soak barley; soaking, draining, and rinsing well will remove some of the starch that causes the sliminess after barley is cooked.

I use bread (any sturdy store-bought or homemade bread is fine), dry bread crumbs, and panko in some recipes. Panko is a crispy Japanese-style bread crumb, available from most supermarkets in the bread aisle or bakery section.

NUTS

I use a selection of nuts, including cashews, almonds, pecans, walnuts, pine nuts, pistachios, and peanuts, though often you can substitute any nuts you like. I know pine nuts can be expensive, so instead of mortgaging your house, substitute almonds, cashews, or even hazelnuts if you can't get pine nuts at a reasonable price. Keep in mind that the flavor of the finished dish will subtly change.

TOASTING NUTS

OCCASIONALLY YOU NEED to quickly toast nuts prior to using.

EASY SKILLET METHOD

Place the nuts in a small skillet over medium low heat. Stir frequently as they heat and keep a close eye on them; they can go from bland to burnt very quickly. After about 5 minutes, the nuts should start to color and you should get a lovely, toasty aroma filling your kitchen. Remove from the heat as they become a golden color but continue stirring off the heat in the hot skillet for a few more minutes. Remove from the skillet, and you're done.

EASY MICROWAVE METHOD

Spread the nuts to be toasted on a large plate in a single layer. Microwave on high for 1 minute, check and carefully toss with a fork. Heat for a further minute and check again. Repeat in 10-second increments until the nuts obtain the level of toast required. Take care removing from the plate as they will be hot. Watch carefully to avoid burning, and keep in mind that you may need to adjust the timing depending on your microwave.

In some recipes you will be asked to soak raw nuts prior to blending or processing to a paste. This is just a simple matter of submerging the nuts in water—three times as much water as there are nuts—covering, and placing in the fridge overnight. The nuts will absorb some of the water, making them softer and easier to process. You can also quick soak your nuts using the quick method for soaking beans (see page 24).

Nut meal and ground nuts can sometimes be found in well-stocked supermarkets. If you can't find a nut meal already ground, use a quantity of nuts or seeds equal to the meal required (toasted or untoasted). Chop roughly and place them into your trusty spice grinder or high-powered blender. Pulse in short bursts until the desired flourlike consistency is achieved. Keep a close eye on the process and only do a few pulses at a time—the nuts can quickly become nut butter! A spice grinder works best for small amounts, a powerful blender or food processor for larger quantities.

BEANS

Oh, beans, how the slow cooker loves you! Except kidney beans that is. Raw kidney beans (and fava beans, which I don't use) contain a toxin, a lectin (*phytohaemagglutinin,* if you're interested) that is destroyed by boiling for at least 10 minutes but not by the lower temperatures of a slow cooker. Dry kidney and cannellini beans *must be boiled* prior to slow cooking to avoid poisoning. For this reason I use only fully precooked (usually canned) kidney beans in these recipes. Most other beans are started from dry after a good long soak.

To soak beans, first pick them over and remove anything that is not a bean (stones, for example) or any that are completely shriveled up and hard; they will never cook to tender. Place the beans in a large container, cover with at least three times as much water as beans, cover, and allow to soak overnight. If the weather and your kitchen are cool, leave on the counter; otherwise, place in the fridge overnight to ensure the beans do not germinate. When ready to add to the slow cooker, drain and rinse well under running cold water, moving the beans around to ensure all get a rinse, then use as directed. If you need to soak beans for more than one day, please change the soaking water daily to prevent the beans from starting to decay.

A quick soak method can be used as well, handy for when you forgot to put the beans to soak the night before. Place the picked-over beans in a large bowl. Pour three times the amount of boiling water as beans over the beans, cover, and let stand for as long as possible, but for at least 1 hour. The beans will absorb some of the water, soften, and then can be drained and well rinsed prior to adding to the recipe. (This method also works fine for nuts.)

I specify an overnight soak of at least 8 hours, but as you get to know your slow cooker (and beans), you may find that an even longer soak works better for you. Remember that all slow cookers have their individual quirks!

When I call for a quantity for dry beans, it is a *presoaked* quantity. You can use cooked beans instead with some changes to the recipe: reduce the cooking time to 4 to 6 hours and reduce the liquid, also. As a rule of thumb remove 1 cup; you can always add more back in if required later. When substituting cooked beans, use three times the amount of dry called for. Remember also that cans of beans are different sizes, but a 15-ounce can is about 1½ cups. And also keep in mind that canned beans won't absorb as much flavor as dry ones.

You can skip the bean presoak if the (ahem) gaseous side effects of beans don't affect you in a negative way, but otherwise, always soak as I recommend in all recipes calling for dry beans. The choice is yours. If this is a nonissue for you, then feel free to add the picked-over dried beans to the longer-cooking (more than 8-hour-long) recipes without soaking.

Several items can be added to beans as they cook to stop the flatulence, such as bay leaves, fresh ginger, kombu (seaweed), or asafoetida (herb). I use bay leaves in some recipes and ginger in others to complement the flavors of the finished dish. If you know which addition works best for you, please continue to use it. To further reduce the incidence of gas, cook your own dry beans instead of using canned and ensure your beans are always completely tender before eating.

Some ingredients retard the softening of the beans, so I usually add them later in the cooking process or cook the whole dish longer. These are generally items that are salty, acidic, or sweet, like tomatoes, lime juice, or sugar.

Some legumes, especially hard, dense ones such as chickpeas, in some slow cookers take a very long time to cook, sometimes 12 hours or even longer. Bean cooking time does depend to a degree on the age of the beans, which, unless you have dried them yourself, you will not know. Be prepared to increase cooking time as required.

To determine whether your beans are cooked properly, use the squish test (yes, that's the technical term!). Between your finger and thumb or using a fork on the counter if the beans are too hot, press the bean lightly; it should break apart without too much pressure. If you'd like a second opinion, place a (cooled) bean in your mouth and press against the roof of your mouth with your tongue. If cooked, the bean will squish against your hard palate with no resistance. Sometimes in the same batch you'll find some beans are more tender than others, so using this test on a few beans from different areas of the slow cooker is a good way to gauge if all the beans are done.

Soy Foods

I use soy foods as a main ingredient in the form of tofu (regular water-packed Chinese-style extra firm, vacuum-packed Japanese-style firm silken, and smoked), tempeh, soy curls, and TVP (textured vegetable protein, also known as TSP or textured soy protein) granules or chunks. I also use soy sauce and miso paste as condiments and flavor enhancers. Sometimes I use commercial soy dairy substitutes such as milk, creamer, yogurt, sour cream, and mayonnaise, although the final two highly processed items I use only sparingly or as garnish.

REGULAR (WATER-PACKED, CHINESE-STYLE) TOFU
I often require firm or extra-firm tofu (the ones used most) to be drained and pressed prior to using, which removes most of the water, enabling the tofu to absorb flavors from the other ingredients as it cooks and giving it a firmer texture. To drain, remove from the packaging, let the water run off, and squeeze gently with your hands. Once drained, either slice as instructed and then press, or press as a block. To press, place a clean dish towel on the counter, place the tofu on top, cover with another clean dish towel, and place a chopping board on top. Weigh down the board with thick, heavy, hardcover books, large cans, or that huge bag of rice you have—anything heavy but not so heavy it would squish the tofu completely. Leave for 30 minutes and check. If you feel the tofu is pressed enough, continue with

the recipe. If you would like more pressing time, change the dish towels so the tofu is sitting on the drier one and replace the pressing items. If you have that magical device called a ToufuXpress, use it for perfectly pressed tofu. I don't own this item but I sometimes wish I did!

SILKEN (VACUUM-PACKED, JAPANESE-STYLE) TOFU

No pressing needed. This smooth-textured tofu is perfect for blending and using when creaminess is required. In those recipes I often use silken tofu in conjunction with a firmer regular tofu to provide shape to the finished dish because silken tofu doesn't really provide shape. Although you'll most likely find this tofu sold in the refrigerator section with the other tofu, it doesn't need refrigeration until opened.

SMOKED TOFU

I like to buy ready-smoked tofu because I love the texture that doesn't change too much as it cooks. Alternatively, if you can't find smoked tofu, use an equal quantity of pressed water-packed Chinese-style super-firm or extra-firm tofu instead, or use this simple recipe to create your own:

SMOKED TOFU

2 tablespoons maple syrup

¼ cup soy sauce

2 tablespoons liquid smoke

½ cup water

1 pound extra- or super-firm regular water-
packed (Chinese-style) tofu

Combine the syrup, soy sauce, liquid smoke, and water in a bowl. Cut the tofu into ½-inch or smaller pieces and marinate for at least 1 hour.

Sauté the tofu in a dry pan to form a slight crust and use as directed for the smoked tofu in the recipe.

PROTEIN SUBSTITUTIONS

ALTHOUGH THE RECIPES mostly use one main protein, be it beans, tofu, tempeh, TVP chunks (or soy curls), or seitan, there is no reason why you cannot mix and match to taste or for reasons of intolerance or allergy. All the protein sources will become tender in the same length of time, which is generally about 6 hours. Please don't write off a recipe as being "not for you" just because you don't like tempeh or are cooking for Auntie Jean who is gluten free. When you substitute, ensure the protein you are using is cut as specified in the recipe, and if you are substituting for soy curls (or TVP chunks), cut the protein into ½-inch pieces. At the end of the cooking time, you may need to thicken (or thin) the sauce since different absorption may have occurred.

TEMPEH

All the recipes were developed using soybean-only tempeh. You can use whatever you have on hand or prefer. Because the cooking time is already long, I do not presteam the tempeh, even though I'm usually firmly in the tempeh steaming camp. I find the extended cooking time rids it of any bitterness. If you want your tempeh to have a browned exterior in the finished dish, prior to adding to the slow cooker you can sear the pieces in a little oil in a skillet on the stovetop. Browning does not affect final cooking time.

SOY CURLS

I know not everyone has access to soy curls, but they are available online so try to get them if you can. They cook so wonderfully tender and absorb flavor so well. They do not need to be reconstituted prior to use because of the long cooking time. If you don't have access to soy curls, my first preference for a substitute is TVP chunks, then extra-firm tofu or seitan cut into ½-inch cubes.

SOY SAUCE

I use regular soy sauce containing wheat, but if you are wheat sensitive or eat gluten free, please use a wheat-free soy sauce or even Bragg Liquid Aminos instead.

MISO PASTE

I use a mild white miso because that is my preference. If you have a favorite miso, use it. Miso paste is available in Asian supermarkets.

SOY CREAMER

Although I specify soy, you can use any nondairy creamer or even make your own using my recipe (page 56), which works just as well with nonsoy nondairy milks.

Other Ingredients

The following are used in a few recipes and are items you may not be completely familiar with depending on where you live and what you are used to cooking.

SEITAN AND VITAL WHEAT GLUTEN

In Basic Recipes, you will find recipes for slow-cooker-made seitan pieces and sausages. I use either homemade seitan or its store-bought counterpart with great success. As always, use whichever you prefer.

Seitan is made from vital wheat gluten, which is sometimes sold under the name of gluten flour (but not usually *high* gluten flour, which is used in bread and pasta). Confused? I recommend sticking with a brand you can trust, such as Bob's Red Mill, until you are comfortable with what you are buying.

STOCK

I don't always make my own, but see page 43 for how to do so in the slow cooker. It is really very simple. If you are using a commercially made stock (or broth—both terms are used commercially and the products are pretty much interchangeable), choose one you like that isn't too salty. You may, however, have to adjust salt to taste in the recipe. I use mushroom and onion stocks as well as a generic vegetable one (either light or dark) and like the flexibility of commercially made cubes, powders, and pastes. Use ready-made stock if that is what you prefer.

MARMITE

Marmite is a thick, dark yeast spread that adds a savory *umami-ness* to recipes. Popular in parts of the world with a strong British tradition, in the United States Marmite is often found in specialty British stores, from online retailers, and in well-stocked supermarkets in the peanut butter aisle. To avoid sticking, spray the measuring spoon with nonstick spray before measuring. If you don't have or don't like Marmite, make a simple substitution: For every teaspoon of Marmite, use 1 teaspoon soy sauce and $\frac{1}{8}$ teaspoon liquid smoke. Depending on the origin of the Marmite you use, it may or may not be gluten free.

LIQUID SMOKE

The smoke from burning aromatic woods is captured and distilled in liquid smoke. It adds a wonderful aromatic smokiness to dishes, a little like barbecuing over hot coals. This product is available in most supermarkets in the aisle with the barbeque sauces.

TAMARIND PASTE

From the fruit of the tamarind tree, this concentrated paste is at once sour and sweet. It adds an authentic depth of flavor to some curries and a background hint of "I can't put my finger on what that is" to others. If you don't have tamarind paste you can leave it out, but when you taste for seasoning, you may need to add a teaspoon or so of lime juice for the little sour kick the paste would provide. You want the type that is a smooth paste, with no lumps or seeds. It's available in many health food stores, Middle Eastern markets, or Asian spice shops.

POMEGRANATE MOLASSES

Thick and sour-sweet, this concentrated pomegranate juice adds a wonderful background to other flavors, like tamarind paste does. You need only a little so a bottle lasts a long time. Like tamarind paste, it is found in health food stores, Middle Eastern grocers, or Asian spice shops. You can even make your own by reducing a mixture of 4 cups pomegranate juice, ½ cup granulated sugar, and 1 tablespoon lemon juice until thick and syrupy and at a volume of about 1 cup.

THAI CURRY PASTE

These pastes are ready made, containing all the ingredients to make your dishes taste authentic. However, be sure to read the labels, because some brands contain fish sauce. I use both red and green paste, generally available in supermarkets in the ethnic foods aisle.

NUTRITIONAL YEAST

This yellow flakey powder adds a hint of cheesy *umami*-ness to recipes. Although strong, it is really good in small amounts. It's available online and from most health food stores, sometimes in bulk bins.

CHIA SEEDS

Commonly sold under the brand name Salba in health food stores and larger supermarkets, these small seeds become gelatinous when mixed with water and make a great binder. These are readily available ground, which is how I use them and recommend you buy them.

ALCOHOL

Red and white wine, beer, and vodka are all used as liquids in some of the recipes. Please check out www.barnivore.com to check the vegan-ness of your chosen alcoholic ingredient. Some beverages are filtered though animal parts or otherwise use animal products in their production. To avoid alcohol, use an equal amount of vegetable stock (page 43) for the beverage specified.

SWEETENERS

I use very few sweeteners—this book is about savory meals, after all—but sometimes a touch of sweetness elevates the dish. I use cane sugar (such as Sucanat), brown rice syrup, maple syrup, agave syrup (or nectar), and molasses, both regular and blackstrap, at times. They aren't really interchangeable because they each bring a different flavor profile and flavor accent to the dish. All are available in most supermarkets.

THICKENERS

Not flour, though they look like flour. Cornstarch is the ground endosperm (the bran- and germ-stripped starchy part) of a grain. Tapioca flour or starch, and arrowroot powder are from the roots of tropical plants. All are used for thickening sauces and binding ingredients. These thickeners are pretty much interchangeable, so if you do not have my specified thickener, use the one you have. When making sauces, however, arrowroot is the best option for clear, thick results.

COCONUT MILK AND CREAM

I use canned coconut milk, not boxed milk for drinking. I usually use the full-fat version, but if you prefer low-fat, use it. The dish may not be as creamy.

Coconut cream can be purchased canned in the beverage aisle in many supermarkets, or just remove the cream from the top of a can of coconut milk (don't shake the can prior to opening).

SALT

I don't use a lot of salt because I tend to use commercially made stocks that I find salty enough and because I am quite salt sensitive—you'll need to salt to taste.

Black salt is actually pink in color and has a strong, sulfurous odor remarkably like eggs or strong cheese. Available from spice stores, specialty markets, and online, it is worth obtaining for the depth of flavor it adds. If you don't have this ingredient it is fine to omit but be aware your dish may not be quite as flavorful as intended.

Techniques

The following section is intended to provide the basic techniques, knowledge, and kitchen confidence you will need to make the recipes in this book.

BLANCHING   Submerging items, usually vegetables, in boiling water and allowing to remain in the water for the length of time it takes for the water to return to the boil, so they are very lightly cooked and become brightly colored. Blanching is usually followed by immersion in cold water to stop the cooking process.

CRUSHING   Using the side of the knife and applying pressure downward to lightly crush an item, bruising it so flavors are released.

CUTTING IN   Mixing fat (usually chilled) into flour so it is evenly distributed. Work the fat into the flour until the mixture resembles pebbly sand, using either a pastry cutter (available from kitchen supply and department stores) or two butter knives. Hold the knives side by side in the fist of your dominant hand, the extra width of the handles leaving a space between the blades, and mimic the action of the pastry cutter.

DEGLAZING   Using a liquid to loosen and remove any items and flavor left in a pan after sautéing or roasting. The liquid is added and moved around the pan so any cooked-on bits are scraped off and incorporated into the liquid, which is then added to the slow cooker to add flavor.

DRY SAUTÉING   Sautéing but with no oil or any other liquid in the skillet. Done in a nonstick or well-seasoned cast-iron skillet.

FINELY CHOPPING   Cutting the item into equal pieces smaller than ¼ inch so they cook evenly and quickly.

MAKING A SLURRY   Mixing a little cornstarch (or arrowroot, or tapioca starch), usually 1 or 2 tablespoons, in a small container with 2 to 3 tablespoons of water to form a paste, which is then added to the hot slow cooker and stirred to thicken.

MINCING   Cutting items very, very fine until almost a paste. See the instructions under Garlic in the Ingredients section (page 13).

MAKING A ROUX   Mixing fat (usually but not always a solid fat that has been melted) and flour and cooking to a light brown (although sometimes darker), then adding liquid (often milk or stock) a little at a time and stirring as it cooks and thickens. A roux forms the base for sauces and is also a thickener for stews.

SAUTÉING   Stovetop cooking when the items being cooked are moved around in the skillet as they cook, preventing sticking and burning. Essentially the items are "jumped" (sauté is French for jump) around as they are heated.

SHREDDING   Cutting long, very fine thin pieces of an item, usually a leafy green vegetable. See the instructions in the Ingredients section (page 15).

Basic Knife Skills

Hold a chef's knife where the handle meets the blade and pinch the top of the blade, where it is widest, between your thumb and the first knuckle (up from the palm) of your first finger—this gives stability and control. Keep your knife as sharp as possible; if you do cut yourself accidentally, a clean cut from a sharp blade bleeds less and heals faster than a cut from a dull blade. When using your chef's knife make sure you have an appropriate cutting board. Place a folded cloth under the board to stop the board from slipping.

Hold the items to be cut in your nondominant hand (holding the knife as described above in your dominant one), with your thumb tucked out of the way and your fingers forming a vertical wall, with no gaps, and the fingernail joint tucked slightly inwards so as not to be caught by the knife. Use this "finger wall" as a guide when cutting. Work slowly at first, and cut by sliding the arm holding the knife smoothly down and forward rather than pushing straight down with force.

> **HERE'S ANOTHER HANDY** hint for you: Measure your fingers. If you measure on your own index (or any other) finger how much an inch, half an inch, and quarter of an inch is from the tip down you are more likely to be able to easily visualize these measurements than you would if you tried to look at something you've cut against an imaginary ruler. This helps with cutting things to even sizes. Though, of course, there is no need to mark these measurements on your finger!

Slow Cooking Throughout the Year

You'd be forgiven for thinking that your slow cooker is for use only during the cooler months since most of the dishes you make are warming, comfort foods. But that isn't the entire story. Using your slow cooker in the warmer months is a godsend, as slow cookers use very little energy and emit very little heat. Let's take a spin through the seasons and the recipes and look at how you can use your slow cooker all through the year.

(Apologies to my family members and readers in the southern hemisphere. For the purposes of this stroll through the seasons, I use northern hemisphere time—so Easter is in spring, where it really belongs.)

Spring

The days are getting longer, the weather warmer, and spring produce is finally starting to hit the stores. Using spring produce in recipes such as Spicy Beets and Beans (page 134) and Spinach and Parsley Soup (page 64) is a wonderful way to use nature's bounty.

In spring there are theme days, and using your slow cooker to create a theme meal is a neat tie-in. I'm thinking of St. Patrick's Day (March 17) and making the St. Patrick's Day Irish Stew (page 99) to serve alongside a decidedly nontraditional Savoy Cabbage with Raisins and Pecans (page 226).

Following closely behind St. Patrick's Day is Easter. No roast spring lamb for me, thanks very much, but I will take a slow cooker roast such as Stuffed and Rolled Seitan Roast (page 166).

Mother's Day is also in spring. Choose a recipe you know your mother will like, set the slow cooker, and let it do the hard work of dinner while you do something else for (or with) your mom. Impressive, full of love, yet so simple. (Use the same theory to spoil your dad on Father's Day!)

Summer

Does the idea of cooking during summer make you want to melt? Me too, and not in a good way. Now, using a slow cooker in the heat of summer may seem like a strange idea, but it's not really, considering that it frees you up to enjoy the swimming pool or the beach while it cooks your dinner. It also doesn't make your house any hotter than it is already.

In To Serve With (page 211) you'll find several salads that would be excellent as sides, such as Bean and Olive Salad (page 227) or Chickpea Slaw (page 231). Fancy a chili dog at your barbecue? Make the chili in your slow cooker. A summer-friendly option is the Pepper and Cherry Chili (page 132), which uses fresh summer stone fruit as a main ingredient, and tastes divine.

Other excellent choices for summer are those that make use of the bounty of nature. Gardens, community supported agriculture (CSA) boxes, and farmers' markets everywhere are bursting with fresh fruits and vegetables. I've used some of these in hot evening–friendly chilled soups like Roast Tomato and Pepper Gazpacho (page 61) and Chilled Corn Soup (page 62), and in dishes for the cooler evenings such as Mediterranean Vegetable and Bean Stew (page 95) and Ratatouille (page 92).

Use your slow cooker to make batches of Simple Tomato Sauce (page 55) using fresh tomatoes, and store in your freezer for those midwinter months when a little summery tomato goodness is a huge mood lift.

If you're celebrating the 4th of July with a picnic or barbecue, use your slow cooker to produce some regionally inspired items such as No-Crust Southwestern Onion Quiche (page 158), Spicy

Carrot Soup (page 69), or Baked Beans (page 145) to enhance your cookout. For other barbeques (like Canada Day, for my Canadian readers), make the Maple-Infused Sausage Chili (page 139) and serve it as the filling for a Sloppy Joe–type sandwich, in a hot dog, or even over a veggie burger in a bun.

I know this is thinking a little outside the box, but please be assured that summer and slow cookers are not mutually exclusive. There's always room for quick and easy meals that virtually make themselves, whatever the weather.

Autumn

"Now we're getting somewhere," you're thinking. "This is when the slow cooker really comes into its own." Of course, you're right. Although the slow cooker is great to use all year long, when the weather turns cooler with days getting shorter and darker, the ability to have a warm, nutritious, and tasty dinner ready when you are is such a huge draw.

Autumn is a very busy time in many households, with people getting back into the routine of school, extracurricular activities, and classes. Time is at a premium, and using a slow cooker so meals are ready when you and your family are is a lifesaver. Leftovers make perfect additions to school (or work) lunches, especially soup in a Thermos or items such as No-Crust Roast Fennel and Red Pepper Quiche (page 160), which are just as good cold for lunch as they were hot for dinner the night before.

Autumn months bring the fall harvest and all the wonderful produce it entails. Vegetables galore grace the stores and farmers' markets and are well suited not only for winter storage but also for braising in the slow cooker, as recipes such as Peasant Vegetable and Sausage Stew (page 97) attest.

Now, no discussion of autumn would be complete without reference to Thanksgiving. Whether you celebrate in November (US) or October (Canada), it can be a stressful time with extended family, meals with many courses, and out-of-town friends. If you are hosting Thanksgiving dinner, make it less stressful by using your slow cooker to cook a Nut Roast (page 164), a side such as Squash and Cranberry Bake (page 209), or

just a starter course of a seasonal soup such as Sour and Spiced Sweet Potato (page 72), freeing up space in your oven or on your stovetop for other dishes. It's one less thing to worry about, and it allows you more time to focus on hosting your dinner. If you're not the Thanksgiving host this year (big sigh of thanks), contribute a dish to the meal that you've cooked, transported, and served in your slow cooker.

Winter

If autumn is when the slow cooker starts to come into its own, then winter is when it excels. Winter produce really suits the long, slow, moist cooking inherent to slow cooking and gives tender, succulent results that fill you up and warm you through. Winter and stored produce is used to great effect in recipes such as Parsnip and Chickpea Soup (page 82) and Winter Vegetables with Quinoa (page 202). Don't think of winter vegetables as boring ever again!

Celebrations in winter are often focused around warming, filling food (as well as friends and family, laughter and love), and the slow cooker really can elevate them to another level. Celebrating Christmas is another stressful time, just like Thanksgiving, but you can make the cooking easier by using the slow cooker for a festive soup like Magnificent Mushroom (page 74), a side dish like Bread Crust Stuffing (page 208), or even a main course like Not-Meat Loaf (page 162). This leaves you with more time to spend with your loved ones, and more time with the presents!

On New Year's Day you may not be able to face cooking, but you'll still want to have some traditional black-eyed peas. Prepare everything the night before, prior to seeing in the new year, and you'll have Chipotle'd Black-Eyed Pea Stew (page 147) ready for dinner with little effort, bringing you luck—and extra time— for the year ahead.

If you live in a cold climate, winter seems to last forever, so it is nice to have the odd nonholiday to look forward to. I am, of course, talking about Super Bowl Sunday. Plan to use your slow cooker to make a chili before the game, keep it warm until halftime, and then bring out the tortilla chips, vegan cheese or cheesy sauce, and Classic Guacamole (page 236), and assemble your halftime lunch as you watch the commercials.

Although this trip through the slow cooker year has been a little simplistic, I hope it has given you ideas and greater insight into how your slow cooker can best be used whatever the season, weather, or day of the year.

ALLERGEN AWARENESS SYMBOLS

I USE SYMBOLS to point out three common allergens in the recipes, but please check recipes carefully if you are allergic to anything else. Allergens can hide everywhere, so be especially careful with products that are new to you. Read ingredient labels very carefully every time, even on products purchased previously, in case producers have changed the ingredients.

GLUTEN FREE GF

Any recipe with this icon doesn't include the following ingredients, or any others with gluten: seitan, vital wheat gluten, all-purpose flour, spelt flour, barley, beer, bulgur wheat, couscous, panko and regular bread crumbs, bread, and pasta.

Depending on the brand, some products that I use as ingredients may or may not be gluten free. If you are avoiding gluten, please be sure to choose gluten-free versions of the below, as well as any other processed ingredient I call for. Better safe than sorry!

A PARTIAL LIST OF INGREDIENTS TO CHECK:

Asian hot sauce, black bean sauce,
    and other bottled sauces
brown rice syrup
chocolate chips

(continued)

curry paste

curry powder, garam masala, and other spice blends

liquid smoke

Marmite

miso paste

oats

prepared mustard

soy sauce

vegetable stock (my recipe, on page 43, is gluten-free)

SOY FREE SF

Any recipe with this icon doesn't include the following ingredients, or any others with soy: tofu, tempeh, soy milk, miso paste, soy sauce, TVP granules and chunks, soy curls, soybeans, black bean paste, soy creamer, margarine, vegan mayonnaise, or garnishes like vegan sour cream, vegan cream cheese, and vegan cheese.

CONTAINS NUTS N

When I use the icon I don't specify which nut is contained in the recipe, so please check carefully. If there is an allergy to the specific nut, please substitute a safe nut so you can still enjoy the recipe. Nuts I use include almonds, cashews, peanuts, hazelnuts, pine nuts, pistachios, pecans, and walnuts.

INSERT ALERT!

Any recipe marked with the 📷 icon is pictured in the photo insert.

Basic Recipes

I N THIS CHAPTER you'll find recipes that will be used as ingredients in other recipes. These items all last a long time in the pantry, the fridge, or even the freezer (some for months), so it makes sense to start making them so you have the supplies for in the future. Included you will find seasoning mixes, soy creamer, and seitan cooked in several methods such as seitan sausages. If you find a recipe for one of the seitan variations you like, use it in recipes from other books or those of your own devising. Conversely, if you have a favorite (slow cooker or conventional) seitan recipe from elsewhere, or prefer store-bought seitan, feel free to use it even when I suggest recipes from this section.

BEANS

LET'S START WITH a basic method of cooking beans in the slow cooker so you can freeze them in 1- or 1½-cup portions for recipes that require cooked beans. Again the caveat: Do *not* cook kidney beans (white or red) in the slow cooker (see page 24).

Soak beans overnight, drain, and rinse, then place in the slow cooker along with a bay leaf, a piece of ginger, or a strip of kombu, if so desired. Cover the beans with three times the volume of water as there are beans, cover, turn heat to LOW, and cook until the beans are tender, roughly 6 to 8 hours, though denser beans such as chickpeas will often take longer. Drain, rinse, cool, and store in the fridge or freezer until required.

Vegetable Stock

AKING YOUR OWN stock is more simple than you may expect. Not as quick and easy as using bouillon cubes or powder (which are perfectly acceptable), but doing it yourself means you can control the ingredients, and use whatever you have on hand. I often have a resealable plastic bag in my freezer for stock, and to this I add the ends of onions, carrot and potato peelings, celery tops, and the like, ready for when I have enough to make stock. The other thing I like about making my own stock is that I can make it as salty (or otherwise) as I like and also enhance whichever flavor I want to be dominant. See the variations below for ideas. When making your own stock, do not use cabbage and other members of the brassica family such as cauliflower, broccoli, Brussels sprouts, turnips, or rutabagas; their flavors are too strong and will overpower the stock, unless you plan to use it in a recipe that also uses these vegetables.

MAKES 6 CUPS

PREPARATION TIME:
25 MINUTES

1½ to 2 pounds roughly
    chopped vegetables
    such as carrots, onions,
    potatoes, celery, sweet
    potato, including skins
    and peelings if using
    organic vegetables
Pinch each salt and black
    pepper
6 cups water

1. Place the vegetables in the slow cooker. Season with a little salt and pepper (you can always adjust to taste later) and cover with the water. Your slow cooker will be quite full.
2. Cover, set heat to LOW, and cook for 6 to 8 hours, or longer if you wish. Taste the stock and adjust cooking times and seasoning as required.

VARIATIONS:

ROASTED VEGETABLE STOCK

Roast vegetables in the oven at 425°F for 30 minutes; deglaze the roasting pan with stock or white wine prior to continuing with the steps above.

REDUCED VEGETABLE STOCK

After straining, return the stock to the slow cooker and cook uncovered on HIGH for 1 hour to reduce the volume slightly and intensify the flavor.

ONION STOCK

Use only onions, leeks, and shallots, roughly chopped and including the skin. If you wish you can caramelize the onions with a tablespoon of oil and a pinch of salt in the slow cooker for 4 hours on LOW until very soft, or roast them in the oven at 425°F for 20 minutes first.

MUSHROOM STOCK

Use a selection of dried and fresh mushrooms, especially the stalks, as the main ingredients, supported by onions, celery, and carrots.

ASPARAGUS STOCK

Roast the seasoned hard stalk ends of asparagus in a hot (425°F) oven until soft, about 25 minutes. Deglaze the roasting pan with white wine prior to continuing with the steps above, using additional vegetables as desired.

Basic Slow Cooker Seitan, Darker and Lighter

WHILE SEITAN CAN be purchased ready-made from the refrigerator section of health food stores and well-stocked supermarkets, it is rewarding to make your own when time permits. The texture of this seitan, if simmered, is both moist and firm. Cooking in the broth and turning helps to maintain moisture, so it's perfect for all your seitan needs. For best texture and taste, make it the day prior to using. If you are steaming or dry cooking, it will be firmer and less moist.

There is a "beef-y" darker-style seitan and, to provide balance, a "chicken-y" lighter-style seitan. I felt there was the need for both and have used them in recipes to suit the finished product. Of course, if you have a clear preference for either, please mix and match to suit; the recipes will work just fine. Also, you can use chopped seitan as a substitute in any of the recipes that call for soy curls, TVP chunks, tempeh, or even tofu, though the results will differ slightly.

WHAT TO DO WITH LEFTOVER SEITAN BROTH?

SOME RECIPES, FOR example Seitan in Onion Gravy (page 98), use the broth as an ingredient. You could also use it whenever a dark vegetable stock is called for. Save the stock, even freeze it, and use to make future batches of seitan. Use as a base for your own recipes for soups, stews, and gravies. Strain and use a broth to drink (if you like that sort of thing). Use to cook lentils for an instantly flavored dish.

MAKES 4 GENEROUS
SERVINGS, ROUGHLY
1 POUND, OR ABOUT 4
CUPS CHOPPED

PREPARATION TIME:
10 MINUTES

SEITAN
¾ cup mushroom stock, at
room temperature
1 tablespoon soy sauce
1 tablespoon tomato paste
1½ teaspoons blackstrap
molasses
1½ teaspoons liquid
smoke
1 teaspoon Marmite

⅓ cup nutritional yeast
1 teaspoon onion powder
1 teaspoon garlic powder
½ teaspoon paprika
¼ teaspoon white pepper

1 cup vital wheat gluten

BROTH
4½ cups mushroom stock,
at room temperature
¼ cup red wine or
vegetable stock, store-
bought or homemade
(page 43)
1 tablespoon soy sauce
1 tablespoon tomato paste
1 teaspoon garlic powder
1 teaspoon Marmite
1 teaspoon onion powder
½ teaspoon black pepper
½ teaspoon dried oregano
½ teaspoon dried thyme
1 bay leaf
1 whole clove

Darker Seitan

IF YOU DON'T have mushroom stock, using plain vegetable stock is just fine, though I do prefer the depth of flavor you get from mushroom stock.

1. In a large bowl whisk together the stock through the Marmite.
2. Whisk in the nutritional yeast through the pepper, then add the gluten and mix well with a fork.
3. When well mixed knead in the bowl for 3 to 4 minutes to develop the gluten.
4. Divide into 4 pieces, shape each into a ½-inch-thick disc, and allow to rest for 5 minutes.
5. To prepare the broth, whisk all ingredients, except the bay leaf and clove, together in the slow cooker insert. Add the bay leaf and clove.
6. Add the seitan pieces to the cold broth, cover, turn heat to LOW, and cook for 4 hours, turning after 2 hours if possible.
7. After the full time has elapsed, turn off the heat, uncover, and allow the seitan to cool in the broth for at least 1 hour. Remove the bay leaf and clove.
8. When cool, store the seitan pieces in the broth in the fridge or freezer until needed.

Lighter Seitan

CHOOSE A LIGHT vegetable stock (or broth) that is not too darkly colored. Dilute with some water if all you have is dark stock. Crushing the garlic and celery with the side of a chef's knife will break them up and allow the flavors out.

1. In a medium bowl combine the yeast through the gluten.
2. Add the stock and mix to combine well.
3. Knead for 3 to 4 minutes either in the bowl or on a clean counter to activate the gluten, then flatten to a 1-inch-high circle and cut into 4 equal pieces.
4. To prepare the broth, mix the stock through the celery in the slow cooker.
5. Add the seitan pieces to the cold broth, cover, turn heat to LOW, and cook for 4 hours, turning after 2 hours if possible.
6. After the full time has elapsed, turn off the heat, uncover, and allow the seitan to cool in the broth for at least 1 hour. Remove the bay leaf, garlic, and celery.
7. When cool, store the seitan pieces in the broth in the fridge or freezer until needed.

VARIATIONS

Dry cooking or steaming the seitan gives a firmer, less moist result than simmering, which may suit you better. Use the following alternate cooking methods for both seitan recipes. Try each method and see which you prefer.

DRY COOKING INSTRUCTIONS

1. Have ready four 6-inch-long pieces of foil.
2. Make and shape the seitan as in the above recipes and wrap in the prepared foil pieces.
3. Place in the slow cooker, cover, turn heat to LOW, and cook for 4 hours until the foil has filled out and the seitan is firm.
4. Allow to cool 15 minutes in the foil, then either unwrap

MAKES 4 GENEROUS SERVINGS, ROUGHLY 1 POUND, OR ABOUT 4 CUPS CHOPPED

PREPARATION TIME: 15 MINUTES

SEITAN
¼ cup nutritional yeast
1½ teaspoons poultry seasoning mix, store-bought or homemade (page 52)
1 cup plus 2 tablespoons vital wheat gluten
1 cup cold light vegetable stock, store-bought or homemade (page 43)

BROTH
5 cups cold light vegetable stock
½ cup white wine or vegetable stock
1 tablespoon soy sauce
1 teaspoon onion powder
1 teaspoon dried rubbed sage
½ teaspoon dried thyme
½ teaspoon dried oregano
1 bay leaf
2 garlic cloves, crushed and peeled
1 celery stalk, chopped into 3-inch lengths and crushed

and allow the seitan to cool prior to using or place in fridge to complete cooling and to store for future use.

STEAMING INSTRUCTIONS

1. Place a collapsible steamer basket in the slow cooker. Add water to reach the bottom of the basket. Have ready four 6-inch-long pieces of tinfoil.
2. Make and shape the seitan as in the above recipes and wrap each piece, firmly but not too tightly, in tinfoil.
3. Place in the steamer basket. Cover slow cooker, turn heat to LOW, and cook for 4 hours, or until firm.

Chipotle Lentil Sausages

MAKES 4 SAUSAGES

PREPARATION TIME:
15 MINUTES

THIS IS AN inspired variation on the basic steamed seitan sausage recipe (created for the stovetop by cookbook author Julie Hasson) that took the vegan world by storm a few years back. These are good anywhere you'd use sausages but especially anywhere you'd like a little spice. As with seitan, vegan sausages are becoming more widely available in grocery stores, if you would prefer not to make your own.

½ recipe (¾ cup) Chipotle Lentil Pâté (page 50)
½ cup plus 2 tablespoons vegetable stock, store-bought or homemade (page 43)
3 tablespoons olive oil
½ teaspoon salt
½ teaspoon smoked paprika
¼ teaspoon black pepper
¼ or ½ teaspoon chipotle chile powder (see Note)

¼ cup nutritional yeast

1 cup vital wheat gluten

1. Place a collapsible steamer basket in the slow cooker insert. Add water to reach the bottom of the basket. Prepare four 8-inch lengths of foil.
2. In a large bowl, with a fork, mix the pâté through the chipotle powder.
3. Add the nutritional yeast, mix, then add the gluten and mix well with the fork. With your hands knead in the bowl for 3 to 4 minutes to activate the gluten.
4. Divide into 4 equal pieces and shape into logs about 5 inches long, roughly 1 inch in diameter. Wrap each piece firmly in the foil, twisting the ends to seal, and place in the steamer basket. Cover the slow cooker, turn heat to LOW, and cook for 4 hours, checking the water level periodically, if possible, until the sausage is firm.
5. Remove from the heat and allow the sausages to cool until you can handle them; unwrap and serve. If not using immediately, allow to cool fully prior to storing in the fridge.

NOTE: I love the smoky heat of the chipotle powder but not everyone does; use the level of spice you are most comfortable with.

Chipotle Lentil Pâté

MAKES ABOUT 1½ CUPS

PREPARATION TIME:
10 MINUTES

2 cups cooked brown
　　lentils or one 19-ounce
　　can, drained and rinsed
1 shallot, chopped
1 celery stalk, chopped
1 tablespoon olive oil
1 chipotle in adobo,
　　seeded and chopped

1 teaspoon garlic powder
1 teaspoon onion powder
½ teaspoon salt
¼ teaspoon white pepper

¼ cup dry bread crumbs

Salt and black pepper

KEEP THIS SMOKY, spicy, thick spread low in fat, with only
a little oil. It is firm and spreadable and perfect for crackers or
triangles of brown toast, or even as a dip for sturdy vegetables
such as carrots and celery, if you're looking for ways to use the
leftovers after you make the sausages. This pâté is also used to
make the "Not-Meat" Balls and Spaghetti (page 180), so you can
use half the recipe in the sausages and half in that recipe if you'd
like. Cook the lentils in the slow cooker or on the stovetop
instead of using canned lentils if you'd prefer. You'll need to start
with ⅔ to 1 cup of dry brown lentils if cooking them yourself.

1.　Place the lentils through the chipotle in a food processor.
　　Pulse until finely chopped, and well mixed.
2.　Add the garlic powder through the white pepper and blend
　　until smooth. Stop and scrape down the sides as required.
3.　Add the bread crumbs and pulse until well combined. The
　　texture should be thick and smooth, yet moist to the touch.
4.　Taste and season with the salt and pepper as required.
5.　Chill for at least 1 hour prior to serving or making the sau-
　　sages, or make the pâté up to 5 days before making the
　　sausage and store in the fridge.

Dry Chees-y Mix

INITIALLY INSPIRED MANY years and changes ago by the recipe for Dragonfly's Bulk Dry Uncheese Mix (VegWeb.com), this is handy to have on hand. Use it for whipping up a tasty chees-y sauce or salad dressing in a flash, or sprinkle onto dishes as a Parmesan substitute. I use this mix as an ingredient in a few recipes, so make this one first! It lasts a couple of months in a sealed container in the fridge or in the freezer (using straight from the freezer is okay).

To replace this mix in any recipe where you would prefer to have a nut-free result, for each tablespoon of the Dry Chees-y Mix use instead 2 teaspoons of nutritional yeast and 1 teaspoon of cornstarch. This substitution only works well for small amounts (less than ¼ cup) of the Dry Chees-y Mix; any more will impair results.

1. In a food processor, pulse together the cashews, oats, hemp seeds, and pine nuts until a smooth and lump-free powder forms. Scrape the sides as required.
2. Add the remaining ingredients and pulse to combine.
3. Store in a covered container in the fridge for up to 2 months until needed.

TO MAKE INTO A SIMPLE CHEES-Y SAUCE:
MAKES 1 CUP

1. Combine ½ cup of the Dry Chees-y Mix with ½ cup soy (or other) milk and ½ cup water in a small pot. Heat over medium heat, stirring frequently until thickened, 8 to 10 minutes.
2. Taste and season with the salt and pepper as required.

TO MAKE INTO A SIMPLE CHEES-Y SALAD DRESSING:
MAKES ¼ CUP

1. Combine ¼ cup of your favorite vegan mayonnaise and 1 tablespoon of the Dry Chees-y Mix and whisk to combine.
2. Taste and season with salt and black pepper if required.

MAKES ABOUT 2½ CUPS

PREPARATION TIME:
10 MINUTES

GF *

SF powder only

N

½ cup raw cashews
½ cup quick-cooking rolled oats
¼ cup hemp seeds
2 tablespoons raw pine nuts
1 cup nutritional yeast
¼ cup arrowroot powder or cornstarch

1 tablespoon garlic powder
1 tablespoon onion powder
½ teaspoon salt
½ teaspoon mustard powder
¼ teaspoon cumin
¼ teaspoon turmeric

Salt and black pepper

*Please check all packaged ingredients, as noted on page 39.

Faux Poultry Seasoning Mix

MAKES JUST OVER
¼ CUP

PREPARATION TIME:
5 MINUTES

4 teaspoons powdered
   dried sage
2 teaspoons dried thyme
2 teaspoons dried
   rosemary, crumbled
1 teaspoon dried
   marjoram (see Notes)
1 teaspoon dried oregano
1 teaspoon onion powder
1 teaspoon garlic powder
¼ teaspoon nutmeg
¼ teaspoon white pepper
¼ teaspoon celery salt or
   sea salt

1 bay leaf (see Notes)

SURE, YOU CAN buy a commercial blend of poultry season-ing mix from the store. As with steak sauce, there is noth-ing animal derived in the mix—the name comes from where it is most commonly used—but this is super easy to whip up at home, and if you have flavor preferences you can customize. Whenever I've called for this ingredient, you can use a commer-cial blend instead. No big deal.

1. Mix the sage through the celery salt in a small sealable container.
2. Add the bay leaf, seal, and store until ready to use.
3. The mix will keep as long as regular dried herbs keep, about 6 months.

NOTES:
If you don't have marjoram, use more oregano.

Don't add the bay leaf to recipes along with the mix; it is just meant to infuse the mix with a little flavor the same way a cinnamon stick or vanilla bean flavors sugar.

Tandoori Spice Mix

MAKES ABOUT ¼ CUP

PREPARATION TIME:
5 MINUTES

NOT ENTIRELY AUTHENTIC tandoori, as I have only used spices widely available in North America, but with the same warmth and depth of flavor as the original. The mix is used for several recipes, like Tandoori Baked Tofu (page 118) and Tandoori Spiced Potatoes with Spinach (page 112). Prepare a batch to have in your cupboard at all times, making these recipes (and more) much easier. Where I have used this in recipes, you may use a mild to medium curry powder if you don't have the mix prepared. The flavor profile of the finished dish will be different but close to the intended result.

1½ tablespoons cumin
2 teaspoons smoked
  paprika
1 teaspoon turmeric
1 teaspoon white pepper
1 teaspoon coriander
1 teaspoon cardamom
1 teaspoon ginger
½ teaspoon cloves
½ teaspoon cinnamon
¼ teaspoon chile flakes, or
  more to taste

Mix the cumin through the chile flakes in an airtight container. Store until required.

VARIATION:

It's less quick and easy, but you can try using whole versions of the spices listed above and grinding them yourself in place of the purchased ones if you prefer spices freshly ground.

Poached Garlic and Garlic Infused Oil

**MAKES 2 CUPS OIL
AND ABOUT 70 CLOVES
POACHED GARLIC**

**PREPARATION TIME:
20 MINUTES**

6 heads (about 70 cloves)
   garlic, separated into
   cloves, bases removed,
   and peeled
2 cups canola or
   grapeseed oil, or other
   neutral oil (see Note)

NOT ONLY A recipe, but two recipes in one—wonderful! The component parts can be used in myriad ways. Use the poached garlic whenever you would use roasted garlic and in recipes such as Poached Garlic and Roast Cauliflower Soup (page 76). Use the Garlic Infused Oil to replace the oil in any recipe you feel could use a little more mellow garlic flavor or as a drizzled highlight over the top of a plated meal or salad. This recipe makes a lot, but it keeps for months in the fridge. The oil gets more garlic flavor the longer it sits, so plan to make ahead for the best taste. It will always be a mellow garlic, nothing too over the top.

1. Combine the garlic and oil in the slow cooker. The garlic should be covered by the oil.
2. Cover, set heat to LOW, and cook for 2 hours and 15 minutes.
3. Leave in the slow cooker insert with the power off until cooled to room temperature.
4. Transfer to a sealed container and store in the fridge together; remove individual cloves when you need them for recipes.

NOTE: You want to use a neutral-flavored oil so it will really pick up the flavor from the garlic. A lower quality olive oil would also work, but not an extra virgin "bursting with olive flavors" oil; save that for when you want the olive flavors to come through.

VARIATION

HERBED POACHED GARLIC

Add fresh woody herbs of your choice (rosemary or thyme, for example) and simmer along with the garlic.

Simple Tomato Sauce

THIS IS AN easy, basic, and very tasty tomato sauce, perfect as a sauce over pasta or wherever a recipe calls for canned tomato sauce. If you want to incorporate more vegetables into your sauce, you can add other longer-cooking veggies with the onion and garlic—mushrooms, for example—or quick-cooking ones such as spinach at the end just before blending. This sauce also makes a great dipping sauce for appetizer "meat" balls or smeared onto a pizza base.

1. Combine the tomatoes with the boiling water in a small bowl; cover and let stand for 15 minutes. Drain the liquid into the slow cooker; roughly chop the tomatoes and add to the slow cooker.

2. Add the onion through the stock to the slow cooker; stir to combine.

3. Cover, set heat to LOW, and cook for 6 hours, or until reduced and thickened.

4. Using an immersion blender, blend until the mixture is as smooth as you'd like, adding more stock if required. I like to blend roughly half smooth and leave the rest to add texture.

5. Taste and season with the salt and pepper as required.

VARIATION
FRESH TOMATO SAUCE

Instead of using the canned diced tomatoes when your garden is producing more tomatoes than you can eat, use 5 cups of seeded, diced fresh tomatoes. Cook for at least 12 hours on LOW, then for 2 hours, uncovered, on HIGH (check and increase the time if needed) to reduce the tomatoes sufficiently.

MAKES ABOUT 4½ CUPS

PREPARATION TIME:
15 MINUTES

¼ cup sun-dried tomatoes
½ cup boiling water

½ medium onion, finely chopped
2 garlic cloves, minced
½ medium red pepper, finely chopped (about ½ cup)
¼ cup red wine or vegetable stock, store-bought or homemade (page 43)
2 tablespoons tomato paste
1 teaspoon dried oregano
1 teaspoon dried basil
½ teaspoon salt
¼ teaspoon black pepper
One 19-ounce can diced tomatoes
1½ cups vegetable stock

Additional stock, if required

Salt and black pepper

*Please check all packaged ingredients, as noted on page 39.

Homemade Soy Creamer

MAKES 1¼ CUPS

PREPARATION TIME:
5 MINUTES

GF

¼ cup plain soymilk (see
   Note)
¼ cup canola oil

¾ cup plain soymilk
1 to 2 teaspoons agave, to
   taste, optional
½ teaspoon vanilla extract,
   optional

SOMETIMES YOU DON'T have soy creamer in the fridge but need some and don't want to go to the store—not to worry, make some yourself! This recipe was originally published in *Quick and Easy Vegan Bake Sale* and is always a handy one to have. How much sweetener you'll need will depend on how sweet you like your creamer and how sweet your soymilk was initially. Because in this book it is used in savory applications, if you wish to omit the agave and vanilla completely, that is fine.

1. Place ¼ cup of the soymilk and the canola oil in a blender and blend on high until really smooth and creamy.
2. Add the remaining soymilk through the vanilla, if using, and blend until super smooth and frothy.
3. Use as you would commercial soy creamer and store in a tightly covered container in the fridge. I use leftover agave bottles!

NOTE: If you want to use almond, oat, or drinking-style coconut milk instead of the soy milk to make this recipe, feel free.

Soups

AH, SOUP. YOU warm me up from the tips of my toes to the top of my head and keep me in your snug embrace for hours. I love soup. I could eat soup every day, as long as it was a different soup every day! There are loads of soups in this chapter, from the lightweight and purely vegetable to the dense and heavy, loaded with grains and beans. There really is something to suit every season and every taste.

A few things need to be pointed out about soups before you get started:

I give instructions for blending (or not blending) the soups to my desired consistency, how I serve the soup and think it works best. It may not be your desired consistency, though. I know some people who prefer chunky soups and can't stand the texture of smooth ones; I know other people who are the exact opposite. Blend to your desired texture, and take my instructions as a suggestion or guideline if you really have no clear preference.

You may need to add more liquid to reach your desired consistency. Please do so, using the main liquid used in the recipe (be it vegetable stock, mushroom stock, tomato juice, or whatever) and heat through thoroughly.

I always list "Salt and black pepper to taste" (sometimes hot sauce, too) because I aimed for a midrange of seasoning that will suit all taste buds. You may feel I've erred on the side of not enough if you are a salt fiend, or even too much if you aren't a spice or chile fanatic. Please taste the soup prior to adding more seasoning, especially if you made it with a commercially prepared broth; they can be salty.

I often suggest garnishes to make your final soup look pretty. These are just suggestions; feel free to present your soup however you wish!

I like to serve soups with savory baked goods. I give suggestions in many soup recipes, but for general ideas check To Serve With (page 211). I also love Croutons (page 239) tossed on top, or a sandwich, preferably loaded with vegetables, on the side.

If you serve the soup as a starter, you will get more servings than stated in the recipes; I assume the soup is being served as a meal in itself, with sides.

If you have leftover soup, allow it to come to room temperature, then refrigerate or freeze in a sealable container. Store cooled soup for 5 days in the fridge or up to 3 months in the freezer unless otherwise specified.

Always reheat soup until bubbling and piping hot for both safety and best taste. Do so slowly over medium heat on the stovetop or in the microwave, stirring frequently. Some soups, mainly those with beans, lentils, or grains, thicken as they sit; be prepared to add a little liquid when reheating.

If I know I will have a chunky soup left over, I serve it the first time as is, then puree it smooth for the second serving. It's like having two different soups!

Roast Tomato and Pepper Gazpacho

THIS IS A perfect summertime soup: cooling, refreshing, and bursting with flavor when all the vegetables are in season, at their ripest and sweetest. Using the slow cooker means you don't have to turn on the oven during the hottest part of the summer, but for best results do plan ahead and start this the day before you plan to serve it. Add the chopped raw vegetables just prior to serving, so they stay crisp. The base soup mix can be held in the fridge for up to three days, so it is a great make-ahead option.

1. Toss together the tomatoes, peppers, onion, and oil in the slow cooker. Season with the salt and pepper.
2. Cover, set heat to HIGH, and cook for 4 hours, or until the vegetables have released their liquid and are reduced to about half the original volume. Uncover, add the stock, and cook on HIGH for 2 hours, or until enough of the liquid has cooked off that the mixture is further reduced by a quarter.
3. Turn off the slow cooker and allow to cool until you can easily transfer all the contents to a blender.
4. Blend until smooth and creamy.
5. Transfer the blender jar to the fridge and chill for at least 2 hours, or overnight.
6. Just prior to serving, reblend if desired; add the finely chopped raw vegetables to the chilled soup mix and stir well. Taste and season with the salt and pepper as required.
7. Serve cold drizzled with a little olive oil to garnish.

VARIATION

For an additional hint of smokiness, roast the red pepper under the broiler (see page 20) prior to placing in the slow cooker.

SERVES 4

PREPARATION TIME:
20 MINUTES, DIVIDED

 GF * SF

2 pounds Roma tomatoes, quartered
1 red pepper, seeded and cut into 1-inch pieces
½ red onion, roughly chopped into 1-inch pieces
2 tablespoons olive oil
Salt and black pepper

1 cup vegetable stock, store-bought or homemade (page 43)

2 Roma tomatoes, finely chopped and seeded
½ medium red pepper, finely chopped
¼ cup finely chopped, peeled, and seeded English cucumber
2 tablespoons finely chopped red onion
Salt and black pepper

Olive oil

*Please check all packaged ingredients, as noted on page 39.

Chilled Corn Soup

6 medium ears corn,
    husked, cut in half if
    too long to fit in your
    slow cooker
2 tablespoons olive oil
Salt and black pepper

5 cups vegetable stock,
    store-bought or
    homemade (page 43)
1 shallot, finely chopped
1 teaspoon lime zest
1 teaspoon coriander
2 tablespoons cilantro
    stalks and leaves, finely
    chopped
½ to 1 jalapeño pepper,
    finely chopped, to taste

2 tablespoons fresh lime
    juice
2 tablespoons finely
    chopped red pepper
Salt and black pepper
Cilantro leaves, optional

*Please check all packaged
ingredients, as noted on
page 39.

WHEN SUMMER PRODUCE is here and corn is ridicu-lously cheap, super fresh, and deliciously sweet, I like to use it in many ways. Although I like to serve this soup chilled, it also tastes good warm and freshly made, especially if served alongside Cornbread Scones (page 243) for a total corn overload experience. If you want to serve it chilled, this becomes a make-ahead soup. You can cook the corn and strip the cobs in advance, then hold and complete the remaining steps on another day, if desired. Steps 1 and 2 are also a great method for cooking corn on the cob, if you aren't in a hurry!

1. Place the husked corn into the slow cooker. Drizzle with the oil and sprinkle with the salt and pepper; turn to coat.
2. Set heat to HIGH and cook for 3 hours, or until the corn is tender and very aromatic.
3. Remove the corn from the slow cooker and allow to cool on a cooling rack. Turn off the slow cooker.
4. With a sharp knife slice the cooked kernels from the cobs. Set aside the kernels.
5. Place the stripped cobs in the slow cooker with the stock through jalapeño.
6. Cover, set heat to LOW, and cook for 6 hours. With this step you are making a rich, corn-flavored stock.
7. Remove the cobs with tongs and use the back of a knife to scrape out any remaining pieces of corn or liquid on the cobs. Add these scrapings to the slow cooker.
8. Put the reserved kernels in the slow cooker. Cover, set heat to LOW, and cook 1 hour to meld flavors.
9. Blend until smooth using an immersion blender. If you would like a super smooth soup, strain through a sieve to remove any remaining pieces of corn.
10. If serving warm, stir in the red pepper. Add the lime juice 1 tablespoon at a time, and taste after each addition. Taste and season with the salt and pepper as required, unless planning to serve chilled.

11. If serving chilled, transfer to a storage container, allow to cool to room temperature, and refrigerate overnight. Just prior to serving, stir in the red pepper and the lime juice 1 tablespoon at a time; taste and season with the salt and pepper as required.

12. Serve garnished with cilantro leaves, if desired.

Spinach and Parsley Soup

SERVES 4

PREPARATION TIME:
20 MINUTES

GF *

1 tablespoon olive oil
¼ cup finely chopped
    (flat-leaf or curly) fresh
    parsley stalks
2 shallots, finely chopped
1 medium onion, finely
    chopped
1 celery stalk, finely
    chopped

¼ cup white wine or
    vegetable stock, store-
    bought or homemade
    (page 43)

3 cups vegetable stock
1 large potato, peeled
    and finely chopped to
    no more than ¼-inch
    pieces
½ cup fresh flat-leaf
    (Italian) parsley leaves,
    packed (see Note)
½ cup fresh curly (plain)
    parsley leaves, packed

4 cups fresh spinach,
    packed

½ cup soy creamer or
    nondairy milk
Salt and black pepper

*Please check all packaged
ingredients, as noted on
page 39.

WHAT TO DO with that half-bunch of parsley you have left after making tabbouleh or when your garden seems overrun with the stuff mid-summer? Make this soup, of course! It is a bright, fresh flavored, vibrant green soup that doesn't taste overpoweringly of parsley; you may find yourself buying parsley for this, never mind for the tabbouleh! Remember—the spinach goes in at the end. If you put it in with everything else the color won't be as vibrant and the spinach will be cooked just a touch too much.

1. Heat the oil in a skillet over medium heat and sauté the parsley stalks, shallots, onion, and celery until the onion is soft and translucent, about 5 minutes.
2. Deglaze the pan with the wine and transfer the contents to the slow cooker.
3. Add the stock through the curly parsley; stir to combine.
4. Cover, set the heat to LOW, and cook for 5½ hours, or until the potato is extremely tender.
5. Add the spinach, stir into the soup to wilt, cover, and cook for 30 minutes to meld the flavors.
6. Using an immersion blender, blend the soup until silky smooth.
7. Add the soy creamer, taste, and season with the salt and pepper as required.

NOTE: If you have only curly parsley, you can use it instead, but the soup will be noticeably more parsley flavored.

Black Bean, Red Pepper, and Arugula Soup

FOR A BEAN soup I find this one quite light and almost refreshing, and I like to serve it in late spring or early summer when the evenings can still be cool. It is still satisfying and warming, but I think that with all the vegetables and the different flavors, this soup remains interesting to the last mouthful. You can blend the soup as little or as much as you like prior to adding the arugula and pepper. If you're unsure of the soy sauce amount or are salt sensitive, add it 1 tablespoon at a time, tasting after each addition. If you are making the soup ahead, add the lime juice after reheating and just prior to serving.

1. Combine the onion through the stock in the slow cooker.
2. Cover, set heat to LOW, and cook for 8 hours, or until the beans are tender.
3. Using an immersion blender, blend half the soup until it is mainly smooth with some chunks, adding additional stock as required to reach your desired consistency.
4. Add the arugula and remaining red pepper pieces. Cook for 20 minutes to completely wilt the arugula.
5. Add the lime juice and soy sauce, and season to taste. Garnish with arugula leaves, if desired.

SERVES 4

PREPARATION TIME:
20 MINUTES, DIVIDED

1 medium onion, finely
  chopped
1 celery stalk, finely
  chopped
½ red pepper, finely
  chopped
2 garlic cloves, minced
⅓ medium sweet potato,
  grated (1 cup)
½ teaspoon liquid smoke
1 teaspoon prepared
  yellow mustard
½ cup dry black beans,
  soaked overnight,
  drained, and rinsed
3½ cups vegetable stock,
  store-bought or
  homemade (page 43)

Additional stock

2 cups baby arugula
½ red pepper, finely
  chopped

1 tablespoon lime juice
2 tablespoons soy sauce
Salt and black pepper

Arugula leaves, optional

*Please check all packaged
ingredients, as noted on
page 39.

Triple Tomato Soup

SERVES 4

PREPARATION TIME:
30 MINUTES

3 cups cherry tomatoes,
   stems removed but
   tomatoes left whole
   (about 18 ounces)
1 tablespoon olive oil
1 tablespoon balsamic
   vinegar
½ teaspoon salt
¼ teaspoon chile flakes,
   optional
Black pepper

¼ cup red wine or
   vegetable stock, store-
   bought or homemade
   (page 43)

2 garlic cloves, minced
2 shallots, finely chopped
2 tablespoons tomato
   paste
1 tablespoon agave
1 teaspoon dried basil
½ teaspoon dried oregano
1 cup vegetable stock
One 15-ounce can diced
   tomatoes in juice,
   undrained
1½ cups tomato juice
2 tablespoons finely
   chopped sun-dried
   tomatoes

Salt and black pepper

Sliced cherry tomatoes,
   optional

*Please check all packaged
ingredients, as noted on
page 39.

THERE ARE ACTUALLY five forms of tomato in this soup, but the alliteration works better this way, in case you count and wonder what I am going on about! A childhood friend's mother used to make the best tomato soup, and I have recreated it. I later learned that the secret recipe was just a can of Campbell's Cream of Tomato and a can of diced tomatoes mixed together! But with no cream or help from Campbell's, I matched the soup in my memory. This is rich, heavy, and very intensely tomato flavored, so only a small amount is enough. If you find the finished soup a little acidic (depends on your tomatoes), add an extra teaspoon of agave to balance it out. Drizzle with a little homemade or store-bought pesto for a luscious touch of summer.

1. Preheat the oven to 425°F.
2. Toss the cherry tomatoes through the black pepper in a 7 by 11-inch baking pan, and roast, uncovered, for 20 minutes, or until the tomatoes split and release their juice.
3. Deglaze with the wine and transfer to the slow cooker.
4. Add the garlic through the sun-dried tomatoes; stir to combine.
5. Cover, set heat to LOW, and cook for 5 hours, or until everything is completely melded.
6. Blend with an immersion blender until smooth. If you don't want the few seeds and skin that will be left, strain to remove. Taste and season with the salt and pepper as required.
7. Serve hot garnished with sliced cherry tomatoes, if desired.

Crème of Broccoli Soup

SO THICK, RICH, creamy, and velvety smooth, I would forgive you for thinking this soup is loaded with a cream substitute and lashings of margarine. You'd be wrong, though.

Actually, the wonderful texture comes from the potato and lentils, both cooked until really tender and then blended to add their special smoothness to the soup. All the powerful flavor comes from the broccoli. It's really good! Unfortunately, this soup doesn't freeze well because of the potato.

1. Combine the onion through the bay leaf in the slow cooker.
2. Set heat to LOW and cook for 6 hours, or until the potatoes and lentils are tender.
3. Add the broccoli, salt, and pepper; stir well and cook for 2 hours, or until the broccoli is soft.
4. Remove the bay leaf, then use an immersion blender to blend until smooth.
5. Taste and season with the salt and pepper as required. Add stock to adjust the texture of the soup to reach your preferred consistency.

SERVES 4

PREPARATION TIME:
10 MINUTES

½ medium onion, finely
    chopped
2 garlic cloves, minced
3½ cups light vegetable
    stock, store-bought or
    homemade (page 43)
1 large white potato,
    peeled and cut in
    ¼-inch pieces
½ cup red lentils
1 bay leaf

1 head broccoli, stalk and
    top chopped
1 teaspoon salt
½ teaspoon black pepper

Salt and black pepper
Additional stock

*Please check all packaged
ingredients, as noted on
page 39.

Butternut Squash and Pear Soup

½ large or 1 small
    butternut squash,
    peeled, seeded, and
    cut into ½-inch cubes
    (about 4 cups)
2 medium ripe pears,
    peeled, cored, and cut
    into 1-inch cubes
4 garlic cloves, minced
1 medium onion, finely
    chopped
1 teaspoon coriander
1 teaspoon cumin
½ teaspoon cardamom
½ teaspoon salt
¼ teaspoon black pepper
¼ teaspoon allspice
½ cup pear juice or
    vegetable stock, store-
    bought or homemade
    (page 43)
3 cups vegetable stock

Additional stock
Salt and black pepper

Toasted pumpkin seeds to
    garnish, optional

*Please check all packaged
ingredients, as noted on
page 39.

THIS SOUP ISN'T excessively sweet, just fragrant, and light for such a filling soup. You need the pears to be ripe but not overly so, with a nice sweetness. They should not be too soft or they'll just turn to mush when you try to peel them. If you can't find reasonably priced pear juice, do what I did once and buy a can of pear halves in juice. Drain the juice, use it in this recipe, then blend the pears to use in place of applesauce. You can also use canned pears in place of fresh for this recipe. Use the rest of your butternut squash in a stew such as Curried Sausages with Apricots, Squash, and Pistachios (page 127).

1. Combine the squash through the stock in the slow cooker.
2. Cover, set heat to LOW, and cook for 6 hours, or until the squash is tender enough to mash using the back of a wooden spoon.
3. Blend with an immersion blender until silky smooth, adding stock to reach your preferred consistency.
4. Taste and season with the salt and pepper as required.
5. Serve garnished with pumpkin seeds if desired.

Spicy Carrot Soup

SORT OF ASIAN-SOUTHWESTERN fusion vibe is going on in this *extremely spicy* soup. The heat is tempered somewhat by the natural sweetness of the carrots, coaxed out even more with the long cooking time, the creaminess of the coconut milk, and the lifting addition of lime. You may be expecting a vibrant orange soup, but the final color will be more yellow than orange. To save time washing dishes, use a handheld box grater and grate the carrot directly into the slow cooker. It may take longer, but there will be less to clean. If you'd rather use your food processor for speedy grating, go right ahead.

1. Combine the carrots through the coconut milk in the slow cooker.
2. Cover, set heat to LOW, and cook for 8 hours, or until the carrots are very soft and flavors are completely melded.
3. Blend until smooth using an immersion blender.
4. Add the lime juice, taste, and season with the salt and pepper as required.
5. Garnish with the sliced pepper, if using.

NOTE: Remember that the level and intensity of heat is up to you. If you like less heat use jalapeño, and maybe even only half of one if you are super heat phobic, and choose ancho chile powder, which is more aromatic and smoky than hot. If you feel hotter is always better, use the serrano peppers (at least two) and the chipotle chile powder, or even try the super spicy variation. Remember: It is better to start off not spicy enough and add more heat later. Err on the side of caution.

VARIATION:

SUPER SPICY CARROT SOUP

In addition to choosing the hotter options, add 1 teaspoon chile flakes with the chile powder and serve with your choice of hot sauce on the side.

SERVES 6 TO 8

PREPARATION TIME:
25 MINUTES

GF * SF

2½ pounds carrots, grated
½ medium onion, finely chopped
2 garlic cloves, minced
1 shallot, finely chopped
1 celery stalk, finely chopped
1 tablespoon minced fresh ginger
1 or 2 jalapeño or serrano peppers, minced (see Note)
1 teaspoon ancho or chipotle chile powder (see Note)
½ teaspoon salt
¼ teaspoon black pepper
3 cups vegetable stock, store-bought or homemade (page 43)
1½ cups canned coconut milk

1 tablespoon lime juice
Salt and black pepper

Sliced jalapeño pepper or lime, optional

*Please check all packaged ingredients, as noted on page 39.

Sweet Potato with Lime Soup

SERVES 4 TO 6

PREPARATION TIME:
40 MINUTES, INCLUDING
ROASTING THE SWEET
POTATOES

2 large sweet potatoes,
    peeled and cut into
    1-inch chunks
1 tablespoon canola oil
Salt and black pepper

½ cup vegetable stock,
    store-bought or
    homemade (page 43)

½ medium onion, finely
    chopped
2 garlic cloves, minced
1 celery stalk, finely
    chopped
1½ tablespoons lime zest
    from 2 medium limes
½ cup vegetable stock
1½ cups canned coconut
    milk

Additional stock
1 to 3 tablespoons lime
    juice from 2 medium
    limes, to taste

Salt and black pepper

Lime wedges or zest
    spirals, optional

*Please check all packaged
ingredients, as noted on
page 39.

THIS IS A rich and creamy smooth soup that goes down very easily. The richness is lifted and lightened by the touch of lime. Perfect for a rainy autumn (or spring) day when you need a belly full of warmth. If, on another day, you are using the oven for something else, you can roast the sweet potatoes ahead of time and hold in the fridge until required for this recipe. Use low-fat canned coconut milk if this is a consideration for you, or substitute half the coconut milk with vegetable stock. The soup will be less rich but still very yummy.

1. Preheat the oven to 425°F. In a 9 by 13-inch baking pan, toss the sweet potato in the oil, season with the salt and pepper, and roast for 30 minutes, until soft and lightly caramelized.

2. Add the ½ cup vegetable stock to deglaze the baking pan, collecting all the stuck pieces of sweet potato. Transfer to the slow cooker and add the onion through the coconut milk; stir to combine.

3. Cover, set heat to LOW, and cook for 5 hours, or until the flavors are well melded and the sweet potato is very soft.

4. Using an immersion blender, blend the soup until smooth. Add stock as required to make to desired consistency.

5. Just prior to serving add the lime juice 1 tablespoon at a time, tasting after each addition until it is to your taste, stirring well to make sure well mixed. Season with the salt and pepper as required.

6. Garnish with a wedge of lime, or a spiral of lime zest, if desired.

VARIATION
SQUASH SOUP WITH LIME
Also very good made with butternut (or other winter) squash, prepared the same as you would the sweet potatoes.

Leek and Potato Soup with Fennel

RICH, SILKY SMOOTH, creamy, and oh so absolutely divine. I run out of superlatives when I describe this soup because it is one I just adore! The ingredients are really simple and the method just as simple, but the depth of flavor and the balance is perfect. The leeks and fennel work hand in hand instead of one being dominant. If you prefer a chunkier soup, don't blend at the final step. Use a potato masher to mash the vegetables so they are partially broken up but not smooth. Serve cold as a modern vichyssoise for a perfect summertime soup, for a change.

1. Heat the oil in a large skillet over high heat. Add the leek, fennel, potato, and garlic; sauté, stirring only occasionally not obsessively, until vegetables are starting to caramelize, 6 to 7 minutes.
2. Deglaze with the wine.
3. Transfer to the slow cooker. Add the bay leaf through the stock.
4. Cover, set heat to LOW, and cook for 6 hours, or until the fennel is easily crushed against the side of the slow cooker and the potato is tender.
5. Remove the bay leaf and blend with an immersion blender until silky smooth.
6. Taste and season with the salt and pepper to taste.
7. Serve garnished with a tiny drizzle of the oil and a sprinkling of fennel fronds or seeds, if desired.

SERVES 4 TO 6

PREPARATION TIME:
20 MINUTES

GF * SF

3 tablespoons olive oil

3 medium leeks, trimmed, rinsed, halved lengthwise, and cut into ½-inch-thick slices

1 small bulb fennel, trimmed, cut into ½-inch slices, fronds reserved for optional garnish

3 medium white potatoes, peeled and cut into ¼-inch cubes

3 garlic cloves, crushed with the flat of a knife and peeled

½ cup white wine or vegetable stock, store-bought or homemade (page 43)

1 bay leaf
½ teaspoon salt
¼ teaspoon black pepper
2 cups light vegetable stock

Salt and black pepper

Olive oil and fennel seeds, optional

*Please check all packaged ingredients, as noted on page 39.

Sour and Spiced Sweet Potato Soup

SERVES 4 TO 6

PREPARATION TIME:
15 MINUTES

 GF *

SF without vegan sour
cream

½ medium onion, finely
chopped
1 celery stalk, finely
chopped
1 jalapeño pepper, minced
3 garlic cloves, minced
1 tablespoon minced fresh
ginger
1 tablespoon Tandoori
Spice Mix, or other
mild or medium curry
powder
1 bay leaf
¾ cup chopped rhubarb
(1 stalk), quartered
lengthwise and cut into
¼-inch lengths (see
Note)
1 medium potato (any
kind), peeled and cut
into ¼-inch dice
1 medium sweet potato,
peeled and cut into
¼-inch dice
½ cup red lentils
6 cups vegetable stock,
store-bought or
homemade (page 43)

Salt and black pepper
Vegan sour cream,
optional

*Please check all packaged
ingredients, as noted on
page 39.

THIS CREAMY SOUP is hiding a little surprise. It looks like your run-of-the-mill sweet potato soup, but when you taste it you're hit with a sour and spicy kick that contrasts so nicely with the smoothness of the sweet potatoes. It's not overly hot or overly sour, just interesting and different, and it's perfect for using up all that rhubarb your garden may be producing, if you don't have a sweet tooth! If you are serving rhubarb haters, however, don't tell them it's there; no one need know when it's all blended together. The longer-than-usual cooking time for red lentils is due to the sourness of the rhubarb.

1. Combine the onion through the stock in the slow cooker.
2. Cover, set heat to LOW, and cook for 8 hours, or until the lentils and potatoes are tender and the rhubarb is incorporated into the soup.
3. Remove the bay leaf and blend the soup with an immersion blender until smooth.
4. Taste and season with the salt and pepper as required. To serve, top with the sour cream, if desired.

NOTE: You may think rhubarb is a funny ingredient to include in a book of savory recipes, but try it and see! Be sure to remove all leaves and leaf bases from the rhubarb stalks; they are poisonous.

Sort-of Borscht Beet Soup

NONTRADITIONAL BUT STILL really yummy, incorporating elements of the original, this beet soup is a beautiful orange-y red color with darker red highlights from the raw beet shreds and is loaded with earthy goodness. A perfect hearty filler on a cold day. I like to puree about half the soup, leaving chunks of both beet and potato to produce an interesting texture. If you'd like to puree it smooth, or not at all, go right ahead. This soup reheats well, though it does get thicker as it stands and may need additional water or stock to adjust the texture.

1. Combine the onion through the carrot in the slow cooker. In a measuring cup or small bowl, whisk together the stock through the black pepper; add to the slow cooker and stir to combine.

2. Cover, set heat to LOW, and cook 6 hours, or until the beets and potato are tender.

3. Remove the bay leaf, taste, and season with the salt and pepper as required. Using an immersion blender, blend until as smooth as desired, adding extra stock to reach your desired consistency.

4. Add the grated raw beet and stir though for color.

5. Serve garnished with a little sour cream, if desired.

VARIATION:

Use half a medium sweet potato in place of the baking potato for a more earthy soup.

SERVES 4

PREPARATION TIME:
20 MINUTES

GF *

SF   without vegan sour
      cream

1 medium onion, finely
    chopped
2 garlic cloves, minced
1 celery stalk, finely
    chopped
1 bay leaf
1 medium baking potato,
    peeled and cut to
    ¼-inch pieces
2 large beets, peeled and
    cut to ¼-inch pieces
2 medium carrots, peeled
    and cut to ¼-inch
    pieces

4 cups vegetable stock,
    store-bought or
    homemade (page 43)
1 tablespoon tomato paste
1½ teaspoons smoked
    paprika
1 teaspoon ground
    caraway seeds
1 teaspoon salt
¼ teaspoon black pepper

Salt and black pepper
Additional stock

1 small beet, peeled and
    finely grated (about 4
    ounces)

Vegan sour cream,
    optional

*Please check all packaged
ingredients, as noted on
page 39.

Magnificent Mushroom Soup

SERVES 4 TO 6

PREPARATION TIME:
35 MINUTES, INCLUDING
GARNISH

2 portobello mushrooms,
about 8 ounces
2 ounces shiitake
mushrooms
6 ounces cremini
mushrooms
12 ounces white button
mushrooms
3 ounces other
mushrooms as desired,
or more of one of the
above (see Variations)
1 tablespoon canola oil

¼ cup all-purpose flour
4 cups mushroom stock,
or vegetable stock, at
room temperature,
store-bought or
homemade (page 43)
1 tablespoon soy sauce

2 shallots, minced
2 garlic cloves, minced
1 teaspoon dried thyme

1½ cups soy milk

Additional stock

2 tablespoons nutritional
yeast

Salt and black pepper

WAY BACK WHEN I was still working toward my hotel and catering diploma, I worked part-time for a restaurant as a general kitchen hand, dishwasher, and prep cook. One of the many things I remember was a wonderful mushroom soup, recreated here. I've changed several things over the years, but I always make this soup; it is so thick, creamy, earthy, rich, and mushroom-y! If you're a mushroom hater, please, turn to another page. The soup is quite thick, especially after standing, so thin with a little stock as required.

1. Finely dice 1 portobello cap, 3 shiitake, 2 cremini, and 3 white button mushrooms into no more than ¼-inch pieces. Sauté in a large skillet in the oil over high heat until brown, about 10 minutes. Take care that the mushrooms do not overbrown. Set aside. (If desired, you can do this step at the end of the main soup cooking time.)

2. Chop the remaining mushrooms into ½-inch pieces and place in the slow cooker.

3. Combine the flour, stock, and soy sauce in a measuring cup or bowl and whisk until the flour is completely dissolved. Transfer the mixture to the slow cooker.

4. Add the shallots through the thyme to the slow cooker; stir well.

5. Cover, set heat to LOW, and cook for 6 hours, or until the mushrooms are very soft and the soup has thickened.

6. Add the soy milk and blend with an immersion blender until smooth. Add additional stock to reach your preferred consistency.

7. Mix in the nutritional yeast and about ¾ cup of the reserved sautéed mushrooms. Taste and season with the salt and pepper as required.

8. Garnish with the remaining sautéed mushrooms and serve hot.

VARIATIONS:

SMOOTH MUSHROOM SOUP

Omit the garnish step and incorporate those mushrooms into the soup.

DRIED MUSHROOM-INFUSED MUSHROOM SOUP

For the 3 ounces "other" mushrooms, use ½ cup dried porcini or shiitake mushrooms. Submerge in boiling water in a large bowl, cover for 20 minutes, drain, and add to the recipe as indicated. Use the soaking liquid (well strained) as part of the measure of mushroom stock.

CREAMIER MUSHROOM SOUP

Replace ¼ cup of soy milk with soy creamer; be warned: this variation is heavy and rich.

MEGA MUSHROOM SOUP

Add an extra portobello cap for an immensely mushroom-y soup (my husband's preference).

Poached Garlic and Roast Cauliflower Soup

SERVES 6 TO 8

PREPARATION TIME:
30 MINUTES, INCLUDING
ROASTING THE
CAULIFLOWER BUT NOT
MAKING THE POACHED
GARLIC

1 head cauliflower,
    roughly chopped into
    large florets
2 tablespoons Garlic
    Infused Oil (page 54) or
    olive oil
Salt and black pepper

1 onion, finely chopped
22 cloves Poached Garlic
    (page 54) (see Note)
1 bay leaf
2 teaspoons dried rubbed
    sage
1 teaspoon dried thyme
½ teaspoon salt
¼ teaspoon black pepper
¼ teaspoon caraway seeds
5 cups vegetable stock,
    store-bought or
    homemade (page 43)

Additional stock
Salt and black pepper

*Please check all packaged
ingredients, as noted on
page 39.

THE EXTRA STEP of roasting adds such a depth of flavor and sweetness to the final soup that it is so worthwhile. You can do it in advance and add the cold roasted veggies to the soup if you find that easier. The soup itself is smooth, thick, and creamy with a mild garlic and rich cauliflower taste, lifted by hints of the caraway and sage. It is wonderful served with Spelt Crackers (page 241) if you're a cracker dunker.

1. Preheat oven to 425°F. In a 9 by 13-inch baking pan toss the cauliflower in the oil to coat. Sprinkle with a little salt and pepper and roast until golden and soft, about 25 minutes.

2. Combine the onion through the stock in the slow cooker, add the roasted cauliflower, scraping out the baking pan to remove all traces. Stir well.

3. Cover, set heat to LOW, and cook for 4 hours, or until the cauliflower is very soft and essentially falling apart and the flavors are well combined.

4. Remove the bay leaf and blend the soup using an immersion blender until completely smooth, adding stock if required to reach your ideal consistency.

5. Taste and season with the salt and pepper as required.

NOTE: Yes, I do mean 22 cloves of poached garlic; it's not a typo! This is about 2 heads' worth.

Roasted Carrot and Sweet Potato Soup

THICK, EARTHY, AND just a little sweet, this soup bursts with orange goodness. The flavors of the carrots and the sweet potato are enhanced by the quick blast of high heat in the oven, which gives a little light carmelization, then simmering for hours develops those flavors even more. Perfect for a day when you need warming from the inside out, any time of the year. If your produce is organic, there is no need to peel it. Leftovers will thicken as they stand, so add more stock as required when you reheat.

1. Preheat the oven to 425°F. Toss the sweet potato, carrot, and oil in a roasting pan, season with the salt and pepper, and roast for 25 minutes, or until aromatic and starting to caramelize on the bottom. Remove from the pan and transfer to the slow cooker.

2. Deglaze the roasting pan with the red wine and transfer to the slow cooker.

3. Add the onion through the stock to the slow cooker; stir to combine.

4. Cover, set heat to LOW, and cook for 6½ hours, or until the vegetables are completely soft.

5. Blend until smooth using an immersion blender; add stock if desired. Taste and season with the salt and pepper as required.

SERVES 4 TO 6

PREPARATION TIME:
35 MINUTES, INCLUDING
ROASTING THE
VEGETABLES

1 medium sweet potato, peeled and cut into ½-inch pieces
3 medium carrots, peeled and cut into ½-inch pieces
2 tablespoons Garlic Infused Oil (page 54) or canola oil
Salt and black pepper

2 tablespoons red wine or vegetable stock, store-bought or homemade (page 43)

1 medium onion, finely chopped
8 cloves Poached Garlic (page 54)
1 celery stalk, finely chopped 1 teaspoon minced fresh ginger
½ teaspoon cardamom
½ teaspoon coriander
1 teaspoon tomato paste
1 teaspoon blackstrap molasses
3 cups vegetable stock

Additional stock
Salt and black pepper

*Please check all packaged ingredients, as noted on page 39.

Green Curry Lentil Soup

2 garlic cloves, minced
½ medium onion, finely
    chopped
1 celery stalk, finely
    chopped
¼ cup finely chopped
    cilantro stems and
    leaves
2½ teaspoons Thai green
    curry paste
1 teaspoon coriander
1 teaspoon cumin
1 cup red lentils
3½ cups vegetable stock,
    store-bought or
    homemade (page 43)

½ head broccoli, florets
    and stalk finely
    chopped
One 14½-ounce package
    frozen spinach (see
    Note)
½ teaspoon salt
½ teaspoon black pepper

Additional stock, as
    required

1 cup fresh or frozen green
    peas

Salt and black pepper

*Please check all packaged
ingredients, as noted on
page 39.

GREEN IS GOOD. Green is power. Green is healthy. Go green! Wonderful in springtime, especially if you can use fresh peas instead of frozen, this soup is infused with the subtle heat of Thai curry paste. The vibrantly colored finished soup has a smooth feel, which is enhanced by the bright pops of flavor and texture from the peas. You'll never look at green the same way again.

1. Combine the garlic through the stock in the slow cooker. Cover, set heat to LOW, and cook for 4 hours, or until tender.
2. Add the broccoli through the pepper in the order given *without stirring*. Cover and cook 2 hours, or until the lentils are tender and the spinach is broken up. Stir well.
3. Using an immersion blender, blend the mix until smooth and creamy. Add stock as required to reach your preferred consistency.
4. Add the peas, cover, and cook 30 minutes or until tender.
5. Add the salt and pepper to taste.

NOTE: If you prefer to use fresh spinach instead of frozen, add 4 cups roughly chopped about 30 minutes before the end of the cooking time.

Lentil, Cauliflower, and Potato Soup

THESE INGREDIENTS ARE old friends in Indian cuisine, but this is not an Indian-inspired soup. The flavors that shine are the main ones—the cauliflower especially—and these are lifted and enhanced by the herbs and spices, with a twist of caraway at the end. This is a soup that lends itself very well to being served either chunky or smooth. Chop the potato and cauliflower as finely as the celery and onion so that everything will cook as stated. Use the rest of your cauliflower to make a side dish, such as Ginger and Garlic Cauliflower (page 219), for another night.

1. In a medium skillet over medium heat, sauté the garlic through the celery in the oil until soft, about 5 minutes.

2. Add the wine to deglaze, then transfer the contents to the slow cooker.

3. Add the potato through the stock; stir to combine.

4. Cover, set heat to LOW, and cook for 8 hours, or until the lentils, cauliflower, and potatoes are tender.

5. Remove the bay leaf and partially blend using an immersion blender.

6. Season with the salt and pepper to taste.

SERVES 4

PREPARATION TIME:
20 MINUTES

8 cloves Poached Garlic
  (page 54)
½ medium onion, finely
  chopped
1 shallot, finely chopped
1 celery stalk, finely
  chopped
1 tablespoon Garlic
  Infused Oil (page 54) or
  canola oil

⅓ cup white wine or
  vegetable stock, store-
  bought or homemade
  (page 43)

1 medium white potato
  peeled and finely
  chopped
¾ cup red lentils
½ medium head
  cauliflower, finely
  chopped
2 teaspoons poultry
  seasoning mix, store-
  bought or homemade
  (page 52)
½ teaspoon dried rubbed
  sage
⅛ teaspoon caraway seeds
1 bay leaf
4 cups vegetable stock

Salt and black pepper

*Please check all packaged
ingredients, as noted on
page 39.

Roasted Carrot and Lentil Soup

SERVES 4

PREPARATION TIME:
45 MINUTES, INCLUDING
ROASTING THE CARROTS

1 tablespoon olive oil
6 medium carrots, peeled
    and chopped into
    ½-inch lengths
½ teaspoon dried thyme
½ teaspoon dried rubbed
    sage
½ teaspoon dried oregano
Salt and black pepper

¼ cup white wine or
    vegetable stock, store-
    bought or homemade
    (page 43)

1 medium onion, finely
    chopped
3 garlic cloves, minced
½ teaspoon dried rubbed
    sage
½ teaspoon dried oregano
½ teaspoon dried
    marjoram
¼ teaspoon black pepper
1 teaspoon regular
    molasses
1 teaspoon maple syrup
1 cup red lentils
4 cups vegetable stock

Additional stock
Salt and black pepper

*Please check all packaged
ingredients, as noted on
page 39.

THICK AND ALMOST reminiscent of dal, this soup has the natural sweetness of carrots enhanced by the roasting as well as by the spices and sweet additions in the main body of the soup. Not *too* sweet, and definitely a savory taste delight. You can even roast the carrots in advance and hold until required.

1. Preheat the oven to 425°F. In an 8-inch by 12-inch roasting pan, toss together the oil through the salt and pepper. Roast for 30 minutes, or until tender and lightly caramelized.
2. Deglaze the roasting pan with the wine.
3. Transfer the contents to the slow cooker, add the onion through the stock, and stir to combine.
4. Cover, set heat to LOW, and cook for 8 hours, or until the carrots are perfectly tender and the lentils are almost falling apart.
5. Using an immersion blender, blend until the carrots are broken up but not completely smooth; add stock if desired.
6. Taste and season with the salt and pepper as required.

QUICK AND EASY VEGAN SLOW COOKING

"Ham" and Pea Soup

GREEN AND TASTY pea soup, just like Grandma would make if Grandma were vegan. The original nonvegan version got an infusion of flavor from a ham bone. This take on the quintessential favorite gets all its ham-like flavor from the addition of the tofu marinade toward the end of the cooking time. The smoky taste of the sautéed tofu adds a touch more authenticity, as well as texture. The tofu and peas can be marinated— soaked for up to 3 days in advance. Just change the soaking water daily. The soup is wonderful the next day, but will most likely need thinning as it will thicken as it stands.

1. Combine the split peas through the stock in the slow cooker.
2. Cover, set heat to LOW, and cook for 6 hours, or until the peas are completely tender and almost falling apart.
3. While the peas are cooking, mix the maple syrup through the water in a bowl. Add the smoked tofu and marinate in the fridge the entire time the peas cook.
4. Drain the tofu, add the marinade to the slow cooker, and cook 2 hours.
5. In a large nonstick skillet over medium-high heat, dry sauté the tofu cubes, turning frequently until brown and crispy, 3 to 4 minutes. Set aside.
6. When the soup is finished, remove the bay leaf and blend with an immersion blender until silky smooth, adding stock to reach your preferred consistency.
7. Add ¾ of the reserved tofu cubes to the soup and stir in; taste and season with the salt and pepper as required. Thin with extra stock if it's too thick for your tastes.
8. Use the remaining tofu as a garnish.

SERVES 4

PREPARATION TIME:
10 MINUTES

 *

1 cup green split peas, soaked overnight, drained and rinsed
3 garlic cloves, minced
3 shallots, finely chopped
1 bay leaf
½ teaspoon dried rubbed sage
½ teaspoon cumin
1 teaspoon dried thyme
1 teaspoon dried oregano
3¼ cups vegetable stock, store-bought or homemade (page 43)

1 tablespoon maple syrup
2 tablespoons soy sauce
1 tablespoon liquid smoke
4 tablespoons water

4 ounces smoked tofu, cut into ¼-inch cubes, store-bought or homemade (page 27)

Additional stock
Salt and black pepper

*Please check all packaged ingredients, as noted on page 39.

Parsnip and Chickpea Soup

SERVES 4 TO 6

PREPARATION TIME:
25 MINUTES

½ medium onion, finely
  chopped
2 garlic cloves, minced
1 shallot, finely chopped
½ cup finely chopped
  fresh flat-leaf (Italian)
  parsley
1 tablespoon minced fresh
  ginger
1 teaspoon cumin
1 teaspoon coriander
¼ teaspoon allspice
¼ teaspoon cinnamon
1 bay leaf
4 medium parsnips,
  peeled and cut into
  ¼-inch pieces
¼ medium rutabaga,
  peeled and cut into
  ¼-inch pieces
½ cup dry chickpeas,
  soaked overnight,
  drained, and rinsed
4 cups vegetable stock,
  store-bought or
  homemade (page 43)

Salt and pepper
Additional stock

*Please check all packaged
ingredients, as noted on
page 39.

MY KIDS STILL laugh about the one year when Santa brought me chickpeas for Christmas—but he was right to, as I do love them! I also love parsnips, a root vegetable I feel is often underappreciated and underloved. I've combined these sweet and earthy flavors with some equally sweet and earthy spices to really bring out the best of all the ingredients. The finished soup is definitely rustic in appearance but grounding and warming all the same. Because this is a long-cooking soup, it works well cooking overnight to be ready at lunchtime. Use the remainder of your rutabaga in Winter Vegetables and Quinoa (page 202).

1. Combine the onion through the stock in the slow cooker.
2. Cover, set heat to LOW, and cook for about 12 hours, or until chickpeas and vegetables are very tender.
3. Remove the bay leaf.
4. Puree half the soup with an immersion blender, leaving the other half textured for interest.

Minestrone-Inspired
Chunky Fennel and White Bean Soup

I WAS GIVEN SOME rice beans, which are an heirloom variety shaped like large grains of rice and tasting similar to navy beans. In playing around with them, I came up with this minestrone-like soup. It is less tomato-y than a true minestrone and more anise-flavored because of the lovely fennel and celery. If you like a more tomato-based soup, replace up to half a cup of the stock with tomato juice. Drizzle this soup with a little homemade or store-bought pesto for an extra touch of summer.

1. Drain and rinse the soaked beans, combine with the water and bay leaves in the slow cooker, set heat to LOW, and cook for 8 hours, or until the beans are tender. Drain and rinse under running warm water. Remove the bay leaves.

2. Return the beans to the slow cooker and add the onion through the black pepper.

3. Mix the stock and tomato paste in a measuring cup or small bowl; add to the slow cooker. The vegetables will not be covered by the stock.

4. Stir, cover, and set heat to LOW. Cook for 2 hours, or until the vegetables are tender.

5. Stir in the fresh basil and pasta, if using. Let stand, covered, for 10 minutes prior to serving.

6. Taste and season with the salt and pepper as required, adjusting the consistency with extra stock if desired.

VARIATION:

Use 3 cups of cooked white beans (either canned, drained and rinsed, or home-cooked) and add with the vegetables. Cook for 2 hours as directed.

SERVES 4 TO 6

PREPARATION TIME:
20 MINUTES, DIVIDED

GF* without optional pasta

SF

1½ cups dry small white beans, such as rice or navy, soaked overnight or up to 8 hours
6 cups water
2 bay leaves

½ medium onion, finely chopped
2 celery stalks, cut into ½-inch pieces
1 small fennel bulb, cut into ½-inch pieces
½ red pepper, cut into ½-inch pieces
½ yellow pepper, cut into ½-inch pieces
4 Roma tomatoes, cut into ½-inch chunks
1 teaspoon salt
1 teaspoon dried basil
½ teaspoon dried oregano
½ teaspoon black pepper

1½ cups vegetable stock, store-bought or homemade (page 43)
1 teaspoon tomato paste

3 tablespoons finely chopped fresh basil
2 cups cooked small or soup pasta, optional

Salt and black pepper
Additional stock

*Please check all packaged ingredients, as noted on page 39.

Mock-a-Leekie ("Chicken" and Leek) Soup 📷

SERVES 6 TO 8

PREPARATION TIME:
20 MINUTES, NOT
INCLUDING MAKING THE
SEITAN

½ pound (2 cups) seitan,
    preferably light,
    either store-bought or
    homemade (page 47, ½
    recipe), randomly cut
    into very small pieces
4 medium leeks, rinsed,
    trimmed, halved
    lengthwise, and thinly
    sliced
2 cups seitan cooking
    broth, or vegetable
    stock, store-bought or
    homemade (page 43)
4 cups vegetable stock
⅓ cup pearl barley, soaked
    overnight, drained and
    rinsed
⅓ cup finely chopped
    prunes
2 tablespoons finely
    chopped fresh parsley
2 teaspoons poultry
    seasoning mix, store-
    bought or homemade
    (page 52)
½ teaspoon salt
½ teaspoon black pepper
1 bay leaf

2 tablespoons sliced
    prunes

Salt and black pepper

L ET ME SET the scene for you. Imagine October in Glasgow, Scotland, with a cold wind that is more winter than fall blowing. My friend and I had been out all morning and were freezing cold. We popped into a little corner pub in the hope of getting something warm to eat (expecting only French fries!). My friend asked the waitress what they had that was vegetarian and was told, "The soup of the day is always vegetarian." At this point I was getting excited—soup would be perfect. "What is it?" she asked. "Cock-a-Leekie," the waitress replied, totally clueless that a chicken-based soup might not qualify as vegetarian! That day I had French fries, but the incident became a running gag, and I swore one day I would make a Cock-a-Leekie soup *without* the chicken. Well, here it is!

1. Combine the seitan through the bay leaf in the slow cooker.
2. Cover, set heat to LOW, and cook for 6 hours, or until the barley is tender and the leeks are very soft.
3. Remove the bay leaf; garnish with the sliced prunes. Season to taste with the salt and black pepper.

NOTE: You may need to increase the herbs at the end of the cooking time if not using the seitan recipe I reference. Reduce the salt if you are using a store-bought seitan; it tends to be on the salty side.

Sausage, Rice, and Salsa Soup

SOUPS WITH MEATBALLS (or sausages) pop up all over the world. This one is Mexican inspired, using up that half-jar of leftover salsa you have from nachos or from making Tomato Salsa Pasta Bake (page 173), but with chopped seitan sausages instead of meatballs. I like this dish served as is because it is quite a substantial soup, but a dollop of Classic Guacamole (page 236) on top is never amiss. You can make the soup in advance, but you will need to add more stock when you reheat because the rice and sausages will absorb liquid while it sits. For best results cook the rice just before adding it to the soup.

1. Combine the onion through the cilantro in the slow cooker.
2. Cover, set heat to LOW, and cook for 4 hours, or until the sausages are very tender and flavors are melded.
3. Stir in the rice. Cook for 30 minutes to combine but not so long that the rice becomes mushy.
4. Taste and season with the salt and pepper as required. Remove the bay leaf and add stock to reach the desired consistency.
5. Garnish with the pepper slices and chopped cilantro.

SERVES 4 TO 6

PREPARATION TIME:
10 MINUTES

 if using soy-free sausages

½ medium onion, finely chopped
2 garlic cloves, minced
½ medium red pepper, finely chopped
3½ cups vegetable stock, store-bought or homemade (page 43)
One 15-ounce can diced tomatoes
1 cup prepared chunky tomato salsa, your preferred heat
1 bay leaf
2 vegan sausages, store-bought or homemade (page 49, ½ recipe), chopped into ¼-inch pieces
¼ cup finely chopped cilantro, packed

1 cup hot cooked long-grain white rice

Salt and black pepper
Additional vegetable stock

Sliced red pepper strips and finely chopped cilantro

Stews

I N THIS CHAPTER you will find a selection of mainly European-influenced stews, some in a meat-and-potatoes style, and some enlivened further with tasty vegetables and warming spices. A few hail from as far as North Africa and beyond, but most should be familiar to you. I use beans, seitan, tempeh, tofu, soy curls, and TVP in these stews, so you are bound to find one that suits your fancy.

Serve with what you feel suits the dish best, be it plain steamed rice, Garlic and Onion Mashed Potatoes (page 215), a vegetable side such as Savoy Cabbage with Raisins and Pecans (page 226), or even Herbed Caramelized Onion Mini Loaves (page 247). Recipes will have suggestions, but feel free to browse To Serve With (page 211) for ideas.

Some of these may be too thick for your taste, especially if they spend any time in the fridge. If so, please add stock just by the quarter cup until you reach your desired consistency. If the stew is too liquid-y, either scoop a little out and discard or make a slurry (see page 33) and stir this in over low heat until the liquid thickens, usually 5 minutes. I find that the thickness I desire in a stew is influenced by what I am planning to serve with it, so adjust according to your tastes.

If you have leftover stew, a good way to use it is to make it into the filling of a pot pie: Place in a casserole dish and cover with homemade or store-bought pastry. Bake at 400°F until the pastry is golden and the filling piping hot, about 25 minutes.

You can also use the stew as the base for a shepherd's pie–style dish—place it in a casserole dish and cover with a layer of mashed (white or sweet) potato. Bake at 400°F until the potato is golden and the filling piping hot, about 30 minutes.

Thick and substantial stews are often great when reheated (you may need to add more liquid) and served on toast for break-fast! It may sound strange, but just try it!

Store any thoroughly cooled stew leftovers in the fridge for up to 5 days, or in the freezer for up to 3 months. The stews which contain soy creamer do not freeze well. Ensure any leftovers are thawed fully then completely reheated prior to serving.

You can turn some stews into soup by adding more liquid and blending all or part of them.

French White Bean Asparagus Stew

WHY DO I call this stew "French"? Well, because of the tarragon, thyme, marjoram, and bay leaf! It looks decidedly rustic, but it is a bean stew after all. Because hours of cooking would not be good for asparagus, it's added toward the end to preserve its color and flavor. Keep the hard ends for stock (page 44), and enjoy the stew with rice or potatoes.

1. Combine the garlic through the stock in the slow cooker.
2. Cover, set heat to LOW, and cook for 8 hours, or until the beans are tender.
3. Remove the bay leaf. Using an immersion blender, partially blend the beans so some are still whole but the stew is thick and creamy.
4. Add the peas and asparagus and cook for 1 hour, or until the vegetables are tender but still vibrantly colored.
5. Make a slurry of the lemon juice and arrowroot; add to the stew. Stir as it thickens, for about 3 minutes.
6. Taste and season with the salt and pepper as required just prior to serving.

SERVES 4

PREPARATION TIME:
15 MINUTES, DIVIDED

2 garlic cloves, minced
½ medium onion, finely chopped
1½ teaspoons dried tarragon
1 teaspoon dried marjoram
½ teaspoon dried thyme
1 bay leaf
Ground black pepper
½ cup dry navy or other small white beans, soaked overnight, drained and rinsed
2½ cups Asparagus Stock (page 44), vegetable stock, or combination

1 cup frozen green peas
½ pound asparagus, hard ends removed, cut into ¼-inch lengths

1 tablespoon lemon juice
1 teaspoon arrowroot powder or cornstarch

Salt and black pepper

*Please check all packaged ingredients, as noted on page 39.

Lima Bean and Shiitake Stew

SERVES 4

PREPARATION TIME:
20 MINUTES, DIVIDED

GF * **SF**

1 cup large, dry lima
    beans, soaked
    overnight, drained and
    rinsed (see Notes)
1 celery stalk, finely
    chopped
½ medium onion, finely
    chopped
2 garlic cloves, minced
2 tablespoons dried
    shiitake mushroom
    (or other mushroom)
    pieces
1 bay leaf
4 fresh thyme sprigs about
    5 inches long (see
    Notes)
3¼ cups mushroom or
    dark vegetable stock,
    store-bought or
    homemade (page 43)

1 celery stalk, cut into thin
    slices
½ medium red pepper,
    cut into ½-inch-wide,
    1-inch-long pieces
6 large fresh shiitake
    mushrooms, halved
    and thinly sliced

2 Roma tomatoes,
    quartered, seeded, and
    sliced ½-inch wide
1 teaspoon finely chopped
    fresh thyme leaves

Salt and black pepper

*Please check all packaged
ingredients, as noted on
page 39.

IN THIS RICHLY hued stew, the lima beans are so very creamy and contrast with the just-cooked vegetables, chewy mushrooms, and fresh tomato. It's like a lima bean party right here in the bowl.

1. Combine the lima beans through the stock in the slow cooker; stir well.
2. Cover, set heat to LOW, and cook 4½ to 5 hours, until the beans are very tender.
3. Add the sliced vegetables, recover, and cook 30 minutes, or until the vegetables are tender but still bright.
4. Remove the thyme sprigs and bay leaf. Add the tomatoes and thyme leaves.
5. Taste and season with the salt and pepper as required.

NOTES:

Dried lima beans are often sold in two sizes: baby and large. For this recipe use the big ones, also known as butter beans.

If you're not a thyme fan, reduce the fresh sprigs to only 2 (or less, if you're *really* not a fan) and replace the leaves with finely chopped parsley.

Ethiopian Fusion Squash Stew

THE BEST ETHIOPIAN food I've ever had was in a restaurant in Dar-es-Salaam, Tanzania. This delight brings back memories for me and will be a winner for you, loaded with vegetables, some protein, and just the right touch of spice without being too hot. As a bonus it is warming, comforting, and satisfying. It is by no means authentic but is loosely based on the vegetable wats of Ethiopian cooking, in a fusion sort of way. If you have store-bought or homemade *injera,* serve it with the stew for a touch more authenticity; if not, serve over millet or rice.

1. Combine the chickpeas through the stock in the slow cooker. The liquid will just about cover the contents.
2. Cover, set heat to medium, and cook for 9½ to 10 hours, until the chickpeas are tender and the vegetables are very soft.
3. Taste and season with the salt and pepper as required; cover and let stand 5 minutes prior to serving.
4. Garnish with the pumpkin seeds, if desired.

SERVES 4

PREPARATION TIME:
30 MINUTES

½ cup dry chickpeas, soaked overnight, drained, and rinsed
1½ pounds butternut squash, peeled, seeded and cut into ½-inch cubes
1 medium leek, trimmed and rinsed, halved lengthwise and thinly sliced
½ medium onion, finely chopped
3 garlic cloves, minced
1 tablespoon minced fresh ginger
¼ cup finely chopped red pepper
¼ cup finely chopped green pepper
½ teaspoon cardamom
½ teaspoon cinnamon
½ teaspoon turmeric
¼ teaspoon cloves
¼ teaspoon nutmeg
¼ teaspoon fenugreek
¼ teaspoon cayenne, or more to taste
3 cups vegetable stock, store-bought or homemade (page 43)

Salt and black pepper

Toasted pumpkin seeds, optional

*Please check all packaged ingredients, as noted on page 39.

Ratatouille

SERVES 4 TO 6

PREPARATION TIME:
30 MINUTES

1 tablespoon Garlic
   Infused Oil (page 54) or
   olive oil
1 medium onion, finely
   chopped
2 garlic cloves, minced
2 cloves Poached Garlic
   (page 54)
1 small carrot, finely
   chopped
1 celery stalk, finely
   chopped

1 medium eggplant cut
   into ½-inch pieces,
   salted if desired (see
   page 17)
2 medium zucchini cut into
   ½-inch pieces
4 Roma tomatoes, seeded
   and roughly chopped
1 medium red pepper,
   roughly chopped
1 bay leaf
1 teaspoon dried
   marjoram
1 teaspoon dried basil
1 teaspoon dried thyme
1 teaspoon salt
½ teaspoon black pepper
¼ cup finely chopped
   green olives, optional
One 15-ounce can tomato
   juice (see Note)

Salt and black pepper

I WENT FOR THE rustic, "throw everything in the pot" version as opposed to the fancy pants "layered by the rat in the movie" version. It might not look as delicate but it sure tastes just as good thanks to all the flavorful produce, especially in the summer when these items are at their ripest and best. Not much liquid is added to this dish; the vegetables release a lot as they cook. Serve simply with Garlic Bread (page 235) for a nice lunch, or vegetable-rich dinner. If you are not an eggplant lover, replace with an additional 4 cups of zucchini for a summery zucchini stew.

1. Heat the oil in a skillet over medium heat and sauté the onion through the celery until they are softened, aromatic, and starting to brown, 8 to 10 minutes. Transfer to the slow cooker.
2. Add the eggplant through the juice and stir to combine. The mixture will look damp but not overly liquid.
3. Cover, set heat to LOW, and cook for 5 hours, or until the vegetables are tender. Stir after 4 hours, if you wish.
4. Taste and season with the salt and pepper as required.

NOTE: If you don't have tomato juice, use 1 cup vegetable stock and 1 tablespoon tomato paste instead.

Moroccan Spiced Vegetable Stew with Couscous

I'M FASCINATED BY the Moroccan tagine—not the food itself but the volcano-shaped cooking pot it is made in. I started looking into the spices used in Moroccan cooking and thought that instead of the tagine I don't have, I would use the slow cooker I do have to recreate a Moroccan-inspired dish. I think it works really well, with warming spices and not too much heat, luscious plump raisins, and tender chickpeas. I have no idea if it tastes like anything you'd get in Morocco or cooked in a tagine, but it is very satisfying. You'll need to pull the aromatics out of the stew at the end of cooking, so poke the whole cloves into the pieces of ginger to make them easier to find when the time comes to remove them. Alternatively, make a cheesecloth bag with all the whole flavorings inside so they will be easier to take out. If you don't have enough liquid after draining, use water or stock to make up the 1½ cups. If you don't want to serve with the couscous as written, discard the liquid drained (or save it for something else) and make the Israeli Couscous with Almonds and Parsley (page 218) as your side dish.

1. Combine the onion through the whole cloves in the slow cooker; stir well.
2. Cover, set heat to LOW, and cook for 8 hours, or until the chickpeas are tender.
3. Drain, reserving 1½ cups of the liquid, and return the vegetables, chickpeas, and additional liquid to the slow cooker.
4. Remove the bay leaves, garlic cloves, ginger pieces, jalapeño pieces, cinnamon stick, and whole cloves. Taste and season with the salt and pepper as required. Stir in the parsley and tomatoes, cover, and let stand while preparing the couscous.
5. Heat the reserved 1½ cups of liquid to boiling in the microwave or in a saucepan on the stovetop. Combine with the couscous, cover, and stand for 10 minutes. Fluff with a fork just prior to serving alongside the stew.

SERVES 4 TO 6

PREPARATION TIME:
30 MINUTES, DIVIDED

* if not using couscous

1 onion, finely chopped
2 stalks celery chopped into ½-inch pieces
2 medium carrots cut into ½-inch pieces
1 cup dry chickpeas, soaked 8 hours or overnight, drained, and rinsed
⅓ cup golden raisins
6 cups vegetable stock, store-bought or homemade (page 43)
1 teaspoon coriander
1 teaspoon cumin
½ teaspoon cardamom
½ teaspoon turmeric
¼ teaspoon black pepper
⅛ teaspoon cayenne, optional
2 bay leaves
3 whole peeled garlic cloves
One 2-inch piece fresh ginger, peeled and sliced ½-inch thick
1 jalapeño pepper, halved and seeded
One 3-inch cinnamon stick
1 teaspoon whole cloves

Salt and black pepper
⅓ cup fresh flat-leaf (Italian) parsley, finely chopped
4 Roma tomatoes, seeded and roughly chopped

1½ cups couscous

*Please check all packaged ingredients, as noted on page 39.

Tomato, Barley, and Lentil Stew

SERVES 4 TO 6

PREPARATION TIME:
15 MINUTES

½ large onion, finely
    chopped
1 celery stalk, finely
    chopped
1 medium carrot, finely
    chopped
2 garlic cloves, minced
½ teaspoon paprika
½ teaspoon ground fennel
    seeds
1 teaspoon cumin
½ cup pearl barley
½ cup brown lentils
One 15-ounce can diced
    tomatoes in juice,
    undrained
4 cups vegetable stock,
    store-bought or
    homemade (page 43)

Salt and black pepper

THIS IS SIMPLE, hearty, warming, and filling. You could add more stock if you prefer and make it into a soup, but I like it as a stew. Serve alongside hearty homemade or good-quality store-bought bread, with potatoes, or by itself. If you reheat leftovers, you may need to add stock; the lentils and barley will absorb the liquid over time.

1. Combine the onion through the stock in the slow cooker.
2. Cover, set heat to LOW, and cook for 7 hours, or until the lentils and barley are tender and most of the liquid is absorbed.
3. Taste and season with the salt and pepper as required.

Mediterranean Vegetable and Bean Stew

BURSTING WITH PRODUCE and tasting of summer, yet warm, comforting, and substantial enough to stand up to any chill in the air, this stew is perfect when served with a loaf of crusty bread or even Spelt Crackers (page 241) for dunking. It's easy to assemble; you can forget it as it cooks. I like the visual appeal of varied bean sizes and shapes. Use whatever beans you have; you want a variety of them totaling 1 cup dry. Soak the beans separately or the black beans will turn everything purple! This is extra nice if you drizzle with a little homemade or store-bought pesto for a true Mediterranean touch.

1. Combine the onion through stock in the slow cooker; stir well.
2. Cover, set heat to LOW, and cook for 7 hours, or until the beans are just tender. Drain, return the beans and vegetables to the slow cooker.
3. Add the zucchini through the tomato paste; stir to combine.
4. Cook for 2 hours, or until the vegetables are tender yet still firm.
5. Stir in the basil and parsley. Remove the bay leaf.
6. Taste and season with the salt and pepper as required.

VARIATION
MEDITERRANEAN STEW WITH OLIVES

Add ⅓ cup roughly chopped black olives with the basil and parsley.

SERVES 4 TO 6

PREPARATION TIME:
25 MINUTES, DIVIDED

GF * **SF**

½ onion, finely chopped
3 garlic cloves, minced
1 celery stalk, finely chopped
1¼ teaspoons dried oregano
1 teaspoon dried basil
¼ teaspoon black pepper
1 bay leaf
¼ cup dry pinto beans, soaked overnight, drained, and rinsed
¼ cup dry black beans, soaked overnight, drained, and rinsed
¼ cup dry chickpeas, soaked overnight, drained, and rinsed
¼ cup dry navy beans, soaked overnight, drained, and rinsed
4½ cups vegetable stock, store-bought or homemade (page 43) or water

3 medium zucchini, diced
2 stalks celery, diced
½ red onion, diced
1 red pepper, diced
½ teaspoon salt
One 15-ounce can whole stewed tomatoes in juice
¼ cup sun-dried tomatoes, finely chopped
½ cup tomato juice
1 tablespoon tomato paste

½ cup chopped fresh basil
½ cup chopped fresh flat-leaf (Italian) parsley

Salt and pepper

*Please check all packaged ingredients, as noted on page 39.

Smoky Mushroom and Tofu Stroganoff

SERVES 4

PREPARATION TIME:
25 MINUTES

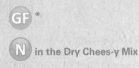

in the Dry Chees-y Mix

1 medium onion, finely
    chopped
2 garlic cloves, minced
1 pound cremini
    mushrooms, halved
    and sliced thinly
4 ounces shiitake
    mushroom caps, cut
    into ¼-inch pieces
8 ounces smoked tofu, cut
    into ¼-inch dice, store-
    bought or homemade
    (page 27)
2 teaspoons dried thyme
1 teaspoon smoked
    paprika (page 22)
1 teaspoon paprika
¼ teaspoon ground fennel
    seeds
2 teaspoons liquid smoke
2 tablespoons soy sauce
3 tablespoons coconut
    cream
½ cup soy creamer, store-
    bought or homemade
    (page 56)
1 cup mushroom or
    vegetable stock, store-
    bought or homemade
    (page 43)

2 tablespoons Dry Chees-y
    Mix (page 51)

Vegan sour cream,
    optional (but good)

*Please check all packaged
ingredients, as noted on
page 39.

RICH, EARTHY, HEARTY, with a smoky undertone that really accentuates the flavors of the mushrooms, this stroganoff is a meal in a bowl. Great served with a slice of dense rye bread or over mashed potatoes, as well as with the more traditional long, thick noodles. This is a dish that will satisfy you completely. If you prefer, white button mushrooms are a perfectly acceptable variation on the cremini specified.

1. Combine the onion through the stock in the slow cooker. The mushrooms won't be covered, but this is okay because they will release liquid as they cook.
2. Cover, turn heat to LOW, and cook for 5 hours, or until the mushrooms are very soft and their liquid has reduced.
3. Uncover and stir in the Chees-y Mix. Cook for 30 minutes uncovered on HIGH.
4. Serve warm garnished, with a dollop of vegan sour cream if desired.

Peasant Vegetable and Sausage Stew

RUSTIC, HEARTY, AND warming—a true "one dish meal"—this stew is the sort of thing you can imagine peasants in the "olden days" sitting down to enjoy, minus the vegan sausage, of course! It is great served with some crusty bread. You will have half a head of cabbage left after this recipe; use it to make a side dish for another meal, such as the Savoy Cabbage with Raisins and Pecans (page 226).

1. Place the beans through the stock in the slow cooker; stir to combine.
2. Cover, set heat to LOW, and cook for 5½ hours, or until the beans and potato are tender.
3. Add the cabbage through the sausages, stir to combine, cover, and cook for 1½ hours, or until the cabbage is tender.
4. Add the spinach, if using, and cook for 15 minutes, or until completely wilted.
5. Add the lemon juice, cover, and let stand for 5 minutes. Just prior to serving, taste and season with the salt, pepper, and hot sauce as required.

SERVES 4

PREPARATION TIME:
15 MINUTES

½ cup dry large lima beans, soaked overnight, drained, and rinsed
1 medium red pepper, finely chopped
1 medium onion, finely chopped
2 garlic cloves, minced
1 teaspoon smoked paprika
1 teaspoon paprika
1 teaspoon salt
½ teaspoon black pepper
½ teaspoon marjoram
½ teaspoon chili flakes, optional, to taste
½ cup finely chopped fresh parsley, packed
3 to 4 small white potatoes, peeled and cut into ¼-inch dice
2½ cups vegetable stock, store-bought or homemade (page 43)

½ large head savoy cabbage, shredded
One 14-ounce can diced tomatoes in juice, undrained
2 links vegan sausage, store-bought or homemade (page 49, ½ recipe), cut into ½-inch pieces (about 2 cups)

2 cups roughly chopped fresh spinach, optional

1 tablespoon lemon juice
Salt, black pepper, and hot sauce

Seitan in Onion Gravy

SERVES 4

PREPARATION TIME:
30 MINUTES

2 tablespoons olive oil
1 medium onion, finely
    chopped

1 garlic clove, minced
2 large Vidalia or other
    sweet onions,
    quartered and thinly
    sliced
½ teaspoon salt

½ pound (2 cups) seitan,
    preferably darker,
    store-bought or
    homemade (page 46,
    ½ recipe), cut into
    cubes no larger than
    ½ inch
1½ cups leftover seitan
    cooking broth, or 1½
    cups mushroom stock
    plus 1 teaspoon soy
    sauce
1 teaspoon Marmite
½ teaspoon dried thyme

2 tablespoons cornstarch

Salt and black pepper

SEMI-REGULARLY POST ON an online vegan forum and notice that about every six months there is a new "What do I do with leftover seitan broth?" thread. I discuss seitan broth in Basic Recipes (see page 45) but thought it would be nice to give a couple of recipes, too. This warming comfort food, with a depth of onion flavor you may not have thought possible, is also good made with seitan sausages, store-bought or homemade, such as the Chipotle Lentil Sausages (page 49), instead of seitan. Serve with Garlic and Onion Mashed Potatoes (page 215) for a super dose of onion love!

1. Heat the oil in a large skillet over medium-high heat and sauté the onion until quite browned, roughly 7 minutes.
2. Reduce the heat to medium, add the garlic through the salt, stir, cover, and cook, stirring occasionally, until lightly golden and soft with all the liquid released and reduced to half the original volume, about 12 minutes. Transfer to the slow cooker.
3. Add the seitan through the thyme; stir to combine.
4. Cover, set heat to LOW, and cook for 4 hours, or until the onions are very soft and broken down, the seitan is very tender, and the flavors have melded.
5. Combine the cornstarch with a little water in a small cup to make a slurry. Stir into the gravy until thick, about 2 minutes.
6. Taste and season with the salt and pepper as required.

VARIATIONS:

Cook the gravy without the seitan for a gluten-free meal, served over French lentils and mashed potatoes, or turn the seitanless gravy into a French onion soup by thinning it with faux beef stock (to preferred thickness).

St. Patrick's Day Irish Stew

THIS THICK, SAVORY, gravy-rich stew is great for any day, not just for March 17th or even just for the spring. It is traditionally made with mutton or lamb. I used seitan but kept in the other traditional ingredients: potatoes, carrots, onions, and—according to some—oats. In the slow cooker root vegetables take longest to cook so they need to go on the bottom and be cooked without stirring (until directed). If time permits, make the seitan in advance and use the cooking broth for best results. I know vegan stout is hard to find; if you can't, the darkest vegan beer you can get your hands on is perfect.

1. Place the potatoes through the seitan in the slow cooker in the order listed, stacking on top of each other in layers. *Do not stir.*

2. In a measuring cup or small bowl, whisk together the cooking broth through the Marmite. Pour into the slow cooker over the other ingredients.

3. Cover, set heat to LOW, and cook for 8 hours, or until the vegetables are tender. Hold on the warm setting or turn off the slow cooker, leaving the insert in place.

4. Remove 1 cup of the cooking liquid and reserve.

5. Melt the margarine in a small pan on the stovetop; add the flour and cook to form a light roux. Add the reserved cooking liquid ¼ cup at a time and cook to thicken, stirring constantly after each addition. When all the cooking liquid is added, add the water ¼ cup at a time.

6. When the sauce is thick, add it to the slow cooker and stir to combine and thicken the remaining liquid. Let stand covered for 10 minutes on WARM.

7. Sprinkle with the parsley and serve.

SERVES 4

PREPARATION TIME: 20 MINUTES

3 medium white potatoes, peeled and cut into 1-inch chunks

3 medium carrots, peeled and cut into 1-inch chunks

1 medium onion, peeled and cut into 1-inch chunks

2 tablespoons steel-cut oats

½ pound (2 cups) seitan, preferably darker, store-bought or homemade (page 46, ½ recipe), cut into 1-inch chunks

¾ cup seitan cooking broth or dark vegetable stock, store-bought or homemade (page 43)

2 cups dark beer (1 large can), vegan stout if you can find it, or dark vegetable stock

1 tablespoon fresh thyme, leaves only

1½ teaspoons tomato paste

1 teaspoon Marmite

3 tablespoons margarine

3 tablespoons plain flour

½ cup water

2 tablespoons finely chopped fresh parsley

Beer Stew with Sweet Potato and Celery

SERVES 4

PREPARATION TIME:
10 MINUTES

½ medium onion, finely
  chopped
2 stalks celery, 1 finely
  chopped, 1 cut into
  ¼-inch pieces
1 medium sweet potato,
  peeled and cut into
  ¼-inch pieces
1 bay leaf
3 whole sprigs fresh
  thyme
½ teaspoon salt
½ teaspoon cumin
¼ teaspoon black pepper
¼ teaspoon dried oregano
½ cup TVP chunks
½ cup TVP granules
1 tablespoon agave
1½ cups (1 can) vegan
  lager or other pale
  beer, or vegetable
  stock, store-bought or
  homemade (page 43)
1½ cups vegetable stock

2 teaspoons lime juice
Salt and black pepper

THE IDEA FOR this came from a Food Network show. The host was stewing a tough cut of meat in copious amounts of beer and some spices with sweet potato. It looked like something worth replicating for vegans—so I did. In this recipe I used soy protein instead and reduced the amount of beer—I found that using more made the finished stew taste too "beery" and yeasty, a bit unbalanced. The servings are not huge; it does end up being quite rich as the sweet potato cooks down. It's nice served with rice, Baked Garlic Potatoes (page 214), or a baked sweet potato (just in case you need more), and some green vegetables.

1. Combine the onion through stock in the slow cooker.
2. Cover, set heat to LOW, and cook for 6½ hours, or until the TVP and sweet potato are very tender and the liquid is reduced and thickened.
3. Remove the bay leaf and thyme sprigs.
4. Stir in the lime juice; taste and season with the salt and pepper as required.

White Stew

BASED ON A stew traditionally made with chicken, and called simply white stew, this is true comfort food. I like it served with boring old boiled peas and carrots. Leftover stew would make a great filling for a pot pie—if you have any leftover stew, that is! You may find the creamy, herbed gravy too hard to resist. Note that the soy curls don't need presoaking when cooked for this long because they become wonderfully tender while cooking.

1. Combine the stock through the black pepper in the slow cooker.
2. Cover, set heat to LOW, and cook for 6 hours, or until the potato is tender and the liquid is mostly absorbed.
3. In a small measuring cup or bowl, combine the creamer and the cornstarch, whisking with a fork until smooth. Add to the stew and stir for 5 minutes to thicken.
4. Remove bay leaf. Taste and season with the salt and pepper as required.

SERVES 4

PREPARATION TIME:
10 MINUTES

 *

2½ cups vegetable stock, store-bought or homemade (page 43)
2 teaspoons poultry seasoning mix, store-bought or homemade (page 52)
2 cups (about 6 ounces) soy curls or TVP chunks
2 garlic cloves, minced
8 cloves Poached Garlic (page 54)
2 shallots, minced
½ cup white wine or vegetable stock
4 small peeled white potatoes, cut into ¼-inch pieces
1 bay leaf
1 teaspoon salt
½ teaspoon black pepper

1 cup soy creamer, store-bought or homemade (page 56)
2 tablespoons cornstarch

Salt and black pepper

*Please check all packaged ingredients, as noted on page 39.

Cannellini Mustard Tempeh

SERVES 4 TO 6

PREPARATION TIME:
10 MINUTES

 *

8 ounces tempeh, cut into
  ½-inch cubes
1½ cups cooked cannellini
  or white kidney beans
2¼ cups vegetable stock,
  store-bought or
  homemade (page 43)
2 tablespoons agave (see
  Note)
2 tablespoons lemon juice
2 tablespoons soy sauce
2 tablespoons white
  balsamic vinegar
2 tablespoons prepared
  Dijon mustard
2 teaspoons mustard
  seeds, lightly crushed
2 teaspoons garlic powder
2 teaspoons dried
  marjoram
1 teaspoon dried tarragon

¼ cup white wine or
  vegetable stock
2 tablespoons cornstarch

Salt and black pepper

*Please check all packaged
ingredients, as noted on
page 39.

IT LOOKS LIKE there is a lot of mustard going into the slow cooker, and you might be a little scared or think I have lost my mind. Let me reassure you that all is okay. The flavor of the mustard is tempered by the long cooking (and the combination of other ingredients) so the dish comes out creamy, mild, and rich, though still mustard-y. There is no bitterness or sourness in the finished sauce, which is luscious. Serve with a perfectly cooked plain grain and a lovely simple salad for an elegant dinner.

1. Combine the tempeh through the tarragon in the slow cooker and stir to combine.
2. Cover, set heat to LOW, and cook for 6 hours, or until the tempeh is tender.
3. Mix the wine and cornstarch in a small container to make a slurry.
4. Add the slurry to the slow cooker and stir to thicken for 5 minutes.
5. Taste and season with the salt and pepper as required.

NOTE: If you are a mustard lover, reduce the agave by ½ tablespoon to reduce the sweetness in the finished sauce.

Tempeh à la King

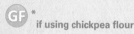

IF YOU CAN find a way to present this dish that isn't completely unstructured, please let me know! It is such a tasty dish with tender tempeh smothered in a thick, rich vegetable-laden sauce, which is very more-ish! I kept the portions small because it is so rich and loaded with creaminess. Serve with rice, pasta, potatoes, Asian noodles, or toast, whatever you have on hand. The green pepper is cooked separately and added at the end because it tends to cause a bitter taste after a long cooking time. If the stew isn't thick enough for your tastes after it's cooked, make a slurry and stir into the stew to thicken. If you'd like more sauce, stir in a little more soy creamer or soy milk.

1. Combine the tempeh through the white pepper in the slow cooker.
2. In a measuring cup or small bowl, whisk together the flour through the agave until smooth. Pour the flour mixture into the slow cooker and stir to combine.
3. Cover, set heat to LOW, and cook for 6 hours, or until the tempeh is tender and the sauce has reduced a little.
4. Heat the oil in a medium skillet over medium-high heat; sauté the garlic and green pepper for 5 minutes, or until soft and aromatic. Stir into the stew.
5. Taste and season with the salt and black pepper as required. Serve garnished with the parsley.

SERVES 4

PREPARATION TIME:
10 MINUTES

GF *
if using chickpea flour

8-ounces tempeh, cut into
    ½-inch cubes
5 large white mushroom
    caps, finely chopped
½ medium red pepper,
    finely chopped
1 celery stalk, finely
    chopped
1 shallot, finely chopped
2 tablespoons finely
    chopped fresh parsley
1 tablespoon finely
    chopped fresh thyme
½ teaspoon salt
¼ teaspoon white pepper

3 tablespoons chickpea
    flour or all-purpose
    flour, sifted if lumpy
¾ cup soy creamer, store-
    bought or homemade
    (page 56)
½ cup vegetable stock,
    store-bought or
    homemade (page 43)
1 teaspoon agave

1 tablespoon olive oil
2 garlic cloves, minced
½ medium green pepper,
    finely chopped

Salt and black pepper
1 tablespoon finely
    chopped fresh parsley

*Please check all packaged
ingredients, as noted on
page 39.

Curries and Asian-Inspired Dishes

A S YOU CAN see from the recipe list, the dishes in this chapter run the gamut of Asian cuisines—from Indian-influenced curries to Chinese-influenced meals to Southeast Asian–style dishes, all the way to a nonauthentic British curry house favorite! These are all made with my own unique twist, influenced by meals eaten in pre-vegan days.

These dishes are best served with long-grain rice, be it brown, white, jasmine, basmati, or even my Coconut Rice (page 216)—or in a pinch, other grains. Indian-influenced curries are also wonderful served with an Indian-style bread on the side: naan, chapatti, paratha, roti, or *papadum*. I have even had curries in the UK served with chips (fat French fries)! If you're having an English curry house–style curry, such as Cauliflower and Cashew Korma (page 116), try it with French fries at least once. It is much tastier than you may think. Specific serving suggestions are given on individual recipes where warranted.

If you have leftovers, try them warmed up with Baked Garlic Potatoes (page 214), or cold as a filling in a wrap (with or without salad vegetables). You could also blend the dish until smooth, add a little liquid, and reheat as a "soup" (if the ingredients are suitable).

Peas, Potatoes, and Broccoli

SERVES 4

**PREPARATION TIME:
20 MINUTES**

2 tablespoons olive oil
1 teaspoon cumin
1 teaspoon coriander
½ teaspoon salt
½ teaspoon garlic powder
½ teaspoon onion powder
½ teaspoon ancho chile
　　powder
¼ teaspoon black pepper
¼ teaspoon chipotle chile
　　powder, or cayenne
¼ teaspoon cinnamon

One 19-ounce can
　　chickpeas, drained and
　　rinsed (2 cups)
½ medium sweet potato,
　　peeled and cut into
　　¼-inch dice
1 medium potato, peeled
　　and cut into ¼-inch dice
2 tablespoons vegetable
　　stock, store-bought or
　　homemade (page 43),
　　or water

½ large head broccoli, cut
　　into small florets
½ cup frozen peas,
　　optional

*Please check all packaged
ingredients, as noted on
page 39.

THIS IS A good illustration of how a recipe sometimes comes to be. My friend gave me a recipe for spiced chickpeas baked *en papillote* (in parchment) because she knows I am a chickpea lover. I couldn't be bothered to make it *en papillote*, so I roasted them in a foil-covered pan after changing the spices to suit my taste. I then thought the dish needed more, so I added broccoli—which I loved, but I still felt it could use something else and decided to add a potato the next time to make it a more balanced meal. When the next time came, I didn't have as much white potato as I wanted so I added some sweet potato. Finally, I felt I really should try it in the slow cooker, so I did, adding the green peas too. After all that, the result is super yummy with lots going on, filling enough to eat as is, and flavorful enough to serve over a grain, with bread, or in a wrap. This is a little bit like a "dry fusion curry." If time is not an issue, cook previously soaked chickpeas in the slow cooker on the LOW setting for 8 hours or until tender, drain, rinse, and use in this recipe.

1. Mix together the oil though the cinnamon in the slow cooker.
2. Add the chickpeas through the stock; toss well to coat everything with the spices and oil, rubbing in as necessary.
3. Cover, set heat to LOW, and cook for 3 hours, or until the potato is tender.
4. Add the broccoli and peas. Stir well to combine. Cover, turn heat to HIGH, and cook for 30 minutes, or until the broccoli and peas are tender.

VARIATIONS:

PEAS, POTATOES, AND BRUSSELS SPROUTS

If you are all out of broccoli, try using quartered Brussels sprouts instead.

PIGEON PEAS, POTATOES, AND BROCCOLI

Replace the chickpeas with cooked pigeon peas.

QUICK AND EASY VEGAN SLOW COOKING

Spiced Spinach and Pea Lentils

THIS DISH WAS inspired in part by a wonderful meal I had on my trip to Tanzania more than a decade ago. As a vegetarian in Tanzania, I ate a great deal of spinach! On one occasion my cousin, who was living there at the time, arranged for us to eat in the home of an East Indian family. The food was fabulous, and this dish, with its aromatic spice notes, flavor pops from the peas, and earthy spinach, reminds me of that meal.

1. Combine the onion through the stock in the slow cooker.
2. Cover, set heat to LOW, and cook for 6 hours, or until the lentils are just tender.
3. Add the spinach and peas; cook for 1 hour, or until tender.
4. Taste and season with the salt and pepper as required.
5. Let stand for 10 minutes prior to serving.

SERVES 4 TO 6

PREPARATION TIME:
10 MINUTES

1 medium onion, finely chopped
2 garlic cloves, minced
1 tablespoon minced fresh ginger
1 celery stalk, finely chopped
½ cup red lentils
½ cup green or brown lentils
1 teaspoon cumin
1 teaspoon cardamom
1 teaspoon paprika
¼ teaspoon allspice
¼ teaspoon black pepper
⅛ teaspoon ground fenugreek
⅛ teaspoon cloves
⅛ teaspoon nutmeg
⅛ teaspoon turmeric
⅛ to ¼ teaspoon cayenne, or to taste
2½ cups vegetable stock, store-bought or homemade (page 43)

1 cup thawed and squeezed frozen spinach (measured after squeezing), or 4 cups fresh, tightly packed
1 cup frozen green peas

Salt and black pepper

*Please check all packaged ingredients, as noted on page 39.

Pumpkin and Tomato Dal

SERVES 4

PREPARATION TIME:
10 MINUTES

½ onion, finely chopped
2 garlic cloves, minced
1 stalk celery, finely
    chopped
1 tablespoon Tandoori
    Spice Mix (page 53), or
    other mild or medium
    curry powder
½ cup brown or green
    lentils
½ cup dry chickpeas,
    soaked overnight,
    drained, and rinsed
2 tablespoons tomato
    paste
One 15-ounce can diced
    tomatoes
1 cup canned pumpkin
    puree
2¼ cups vegetable stock,
    store-bought or
    homemade (page 43)

Salt and black pepper

1 medium tomato, seeded
    and finely chopped,
    optional
Toasted pumpkin seeds,
    optional

*Please check all packaged
ingredients, as noted on
page 39.

PERFECT SERVED ALONGSIDE naan, over rice, or even in a wrap, this warming, filling mild curry, with a smooth pumpkin flavor and tender chickpeas for textural variation, is a "set and forget" dish. It does take the full 8 hours (if not longer) to make the beans tender because they are working against the acid in the tomatoes. The dish is really thick; if you prefer a thinner, soupier dal, add stock after cooking until it reaches your desired consistency.

1. Combine the onion through the stock in the slow cooker.
2. Cover, set heat to LOW, and cook for 8 hours, or until the chickpeas are tender, stirring every now and then if possible.
3. Taste and season with the salt and pepper as required.
4. Garnish with the tomato and pumpkin seeds, if desired.

Roasted Cauliflower and Carrot Dal

ROASTED VEGGIES AND lentils cooked until thick and delicious. Mmmm. With rice, with naan, or by itself, this is the perfect foil to winter weather. The vegetables get double exposure to the spices, so they act as bursts of flavor in the dal. You can double the amount of cauliflower, carrots, oil, and spice mix for the roasting portion and roast a day in advance, use half the vegetables as a side dish, and reserve the rest for this recipe the next day. If you prefer, make the remaining cauliflower into soup such as the Lentil, Cauliflower, and Potato Soup (page 79).

1. Preheat the oven to 400°F. In a rimmed baking pan, toss the cauliflower, carrots, and garlic in the oil and 1 tablespoon spice mix. Roast uncovered for 35 minutes, or until tender.

2. Remove the vegetables, squeeze out the garlic, discard the garlic skins, and deglaze the pan with the ½ cup of stock. Transfer the stock and vegetables to the slow cooker.

3. Add the onion through the stock; stir to combine.

4. Cover, set heat to LOW, and cook for 6 hours, or until the lentils are very tender and falling apart. The dal will be quite thick. Adjust the thickness with additional stock as desired.

5. Season to taste with the salt and pepper just prior to serving.

VARIATION:

ROASTED CAULIFLOWER, CARROT, AND PEA DAL

Add ½ cup frozen peas ½ hour prior to the end of cooking.

SERVES 4 TO 6

PREPARATION TIME:
45 MINUTES, INCLUDING
ROASTING THE
VEGETABLES

½ head cauliflower, cut into large florets
2 large carrots, peeled and cut into 1-inch lengths
1 head garlic, outer skin peeled and top trimmed just to expose cloves
1 tablespoon canola oil
1 tablespoon Tandoori Spice Mix (page 53), or other mild or medium curry powder

½ cup vegetable stock, store-bought or homemade (page 43)

1 small onion or large shallot, finely chopped
1 celery stalk, finely chopped
1½ teaspoons Tandoori Spice Mix (page 53), or other mild or medium curry powder
1 cup red lentils
2½ cups vegetable stock

Additional stock
Salt and black pepper

*Please check all packaged ingredients, as noted on page 39.

Tandoori Spiced Potatoes with Spinach

SERVES 4

PREPARATION TIME:
15 MINUTES

½ medium onion, finely
  chopped
2 garlic cloves, minced
1 tablespoon minced fresh
  ginger
1 tablespoon Tandoori
  Spice Mix (page 53), or
  other mild or medium
  curry powder
½ teaspoon salt
4 medium firm yellow-
  fleshed potatoes like
  Yukon gold, peeling
  optional, cut into
  ¼-inch pieces
¾ cup vegetable stock,
  store-bought or
  homemade (page 43)
½ cup coconut cream or
  full-fat canned coconut
  milk

4 cups fresh spinach,
  packed, roughly
  chopped

Salt, black pepper, and
  chile flakes

*Please check all packaged
ingredients, as noted on
page 39.

NOT QUITE A traditional Saag Aloo, although that name does translate to potatoes and spinach. This creamy, warmly spiced dish is good served as a quick and hearty dinner with a crusty bread roll (or even better, naan or roti) or as part of an Indian-themed dinner. It also goes well with Coconut Rice (page 216). To bulk it into more of a main-course curry, add 1½ cups (one 15-ounce can) cooked chickpeas with the spinach.

1. Combine the onions through the coconut cream in the slow cooker. Stir well; don't worry if the vegetables are not completely covered.
2. Cover, set heat to LOW, and cook for 6 hours, or until the potatoes are very tender.
3. Add the spinach 1 cup at a time, stirring to wilt after each addition. Cover and cook on LOW for 10 to 15 minutes.
4. Taste and season with the salt, pepper, and chile flakes as required.

Spiced Sweet Potato Satay

THIS RECIPE CAPTURES both the spiciness and the peanut-enhanced taste of satay, although this isn't a traditional satay serving style. The end result is hearty and autumnal fare for any peanut butter lover. Make sure you don't chop the sweet potato too small; small pieces will disappear into the dish as it cooks, and you want the finished product to have visible chunks. This is more spiced than spicy; if you are a heat lover, at the end of cooking feel free to add more cayenne or hot sauce. If at the end of cooking your satay is already very thick and creamy, don't add the tapioca—the peanut butter will provide enough extra thickening.

1. Place the garlic through the stock in the slow cooker. Stir well.
2. Cover, set heat to LOW, and cook for 10 hours, or until the chickpeas are tender.
3. In a small measuring cup or bowl, combine the peanut butter through the water to make a smooth paste. Scoop out about ¼ cup of the liquid from the slow cooker and add to the bowl. Combine well so the paste stays smooth. Add the paste to the slow cooker and stir well to thicken.
4. Taste and season with the salt and pepper as required.
5. Let stand covered for 10 minutes prior to serving, then sprinkle with the roasted peanuts, if using.

SERVES 4 TO 6

PREPARATION TIME:
15 MINUTES

3 garlic cloves, minced
2 shallots, finely chopped
1 tablespoon minced fresh ginger
1 celery stalk, finely chopped
1 sweet potato, chopped into 1-inch cubes, peeling optional
1 cup red lentils
½ cup dry chickpeas, soaked overnight, drained, and rinsed
1½ teaspoons cumin
1 teaspoon fenugreek
1 teaspoon paprika
1 teaspoon cardamom
½ teaspoon salt
¼ teaspoon black pepper
¼ teaspoon turmeric
¼ teaspoon allspice
⅛ teaspoon nutmeg
⅛ teaspoon cinnamon
¼ teaspoon cayenne
1½ cups canned coconut milk
2½ cups vegetable stock, store-bought or homemade (page 43)

2 tablespoons natural peanut butter, preferably smooth
1 tablespoon tapioca flour, or cornstarch
2 tablespoons water

Salt and black pepper

Roasted peanuts, optional

*Please check all packaged ingredients, as noted on page 39.

Black Bean Beans

SERVES 4 TO 6

PREPARATION TIME:
20 MINUTES, DIVIDED

 *

1 tablespoon canola oil
1 jalapeño pepper, minced
1 tablespoon minced fresh
    ginger
3 garlic cloves, minced
¼ cup cilantro, leaves and
    stalks finely chopped,
    packed

1 teaspoon coriander
2 tablespoons store-
    bought black bean
    sauce (see Note)
½ cup adzuki beans, or
    black beans, soaked
    overnight, drained, and
    rinsed
3 cups vegetable stock,
    store-bought or
    homemade (page 43)

2 tablespoons rice wine
    vinegar
1 tablespoon soy sauce
1 or 2 tablespoons maple
    syrup, to taste
1 pound green beans,
    sliced ¼-inch thick

Salt and black pepper

*Please check all packaged
ingredients, as noted on
page 39.

I HAVE A CONTAINER of black bean sauce, a pungent paste made from fermented black soybeans, in my fridge that I often use for sautéing tofu or green beans—I love the combination of flavors. I've taken that theme further with this slow cooker variation, discarding the tofu in favor of a favorite Asian bean, the adzuki, and infusing it with all the savory deliciousness of the black bean sauce. Wonderful served over rice, or as part of an Asian meal.

1. Heat the oil in a medium skillet over medium-high heat and sauté the jalapeño, ginger, garlic, and cilantro until sizzling and aromatic, 2 minutes. Transfer to the slow cooker.

2. Add the coriander through the stock and stir well.

3. Cover, set heat to LOW, and cook for 6 hours, or until the beans are tender.

4. Add the vinegar through the green beans, cover, and cook for 2 hours, or until the beans are tender.

5. Taste, season with the salt and pepper, and add maple syrup, if required.

NOTE: Black bean sauce is usually found in the ethnic foods aisle with the Asian cooking sauces and marinades.

Potato and White Bean Curry

OH, HAPPY ACCIDENT! In my original planning for this dish, there were not supposed to be any caraway seeds. I just grabbed the wrong spice jar in error and didn't realize until too late. I felt the seeds worked with the other flavors, so I assumed the universe was speaking to me. A word of warning: This dish is not very saucy. If you think more is better when it comes to liquid, after the beans are cooked add more coconut milk to reach your desired consistency.

1. Combine the potatoes through the stock in the slow cooker.
2. Cover, set heat to LOW, and cook for 7 hours, or until the beans and potatoes are just tender.
3. Stir in the peas and cook for 1 hour.
4. Remove the bay leaf. Taste and season with the salt, pepper, and hot sauce as required. Adjust the liquid to reach your desired consistency, if necessary.

SERVES 6 TO 8

PREPARATION TIME:
10 MINUTES

6 medium white potatoes, peeling optional, cut into ½-inch cubes
1½ teaspoons cumin
1½ teaspoons curry powder, your preferred heat
1 teaspoon dried oregano
½ to 1 teaspoon chile flakes, or more to taste
¼ teaspoon garlic powder
¼ teaspoon onion powder
⅛ teaspoon caraway seeds
¼ teaspoon salt
1 bay leaf
¾ cup dry navy beans (or any other white beans besides cannellini or white kidney), soaked overnight, rinsed, and drained
½ medium onion, finely chopped
3 garlic cloves, minced
1¼ cups canned coconut milk
3 cups vegetable stock, store-bought or homemade (page 43)

¾ cup frozen peas

Salt, black pepper, and hot sauce
Additional stock or water, as required

*Please check all packaged ingredients, as noted on page 39.

Cauliflower and Cashew Korma

SERVES 4 TO 6

PREPARATION TIME:
20 MINUTES

½ cup raw cashews,
    unsoaked (see Note)

1 tablespoon coconut oil
1 onion, finely chopped
2 garlic cloves, minced
1 tablespoon minced fresh
    ginger
1 teaspoon mustard seeds

1 teaspoon coriander
1 teaspoon cumin
1 teaspoon cardamom
2 teaspoons Tandoori
    Spice Mix (page 53), or
    other mild or medium
    curry powder
½ teaspoon salt
½ teaspoon black pepper

1 cup raw cashews,
    soaked at least 8 hours
    or overnight, drained,
    and rinsed

¾ cup vegetable stock,
    store-bought or
    homemade (page 43)
1½ cups canned coconut
    milk
2 tablespoons cornstarch

½ medium head
    cauliflower, cut into
    medium florets

3 tablespoons finely
    chopped cilantro

Salt and black pepper

*Please check all packaged
ingredients, as noted on
page 39.

AH, CHICKEN KORMA, a favorite for Indian takeout. A very nonauthentic curry—English rather than Indian—it is a mildly spiced, rich, creamy (usually using both coconut cream and heavy cream) dish, often with added nuts, that just cries out for being made vegan. No meat substitute—I allowed the cauliflower and the cashews to really star. It is every bit as heavy and delicious as the original, or so I have been told. Although this ingredient is farther down the ingredients list, remember to soak 1 cup of cashews the night before you make this dish. If your food processor or blender doesn't get the cashews entirely smooth, don't despair; the sauce is fine with a little texture, especially when served over rice. Use the remaining cauliflower to make a soup such as Lentil, Cauliflower, and Potato (page 79).

1. In a large skillet over medium heat, toast the ½ cup of cashews until golden brown, 5 to 7 minutes. Remove from the skillet and reserve.
2. In the same skillet, heat the coconut oil over medium heat and sauté the onion through the mustard seeds for 5 minutes, or until they are soft and very aromatic. Add the coriander through the black pepper and sauté for 1 minute. Transfer to the slow cooker.
3. Meanwhile, pulse the 1 cup of soaked cashews in a food processor or powerful blender until they reach a paste-like consistency. Add the stock through the cornstarch and blend until smooth and creamy.
4. Add the cauliflower and blended nut mix to the slow cooker and stir well to combine. Cover, set heat to LOW, and cook for 5 hours, or until the cauliflower is tender and the sauce has thickened.
5. Stir in the toasted cashews and the cilantro, taste, and season with the salt and pepper as required.

NOTE: You can use roasted cashews and skip step 1.

116

Shiitake and Chickpea Curry

NOT A TRUE curry in the sense that it contains no curry spices, but this lightly heat-spiced coconut-based stew fits better in this section than any other. It's also wonderful if served over rice, just like a curry. The mushrooms, retaining a little chewiness, provide an interesting texture contrast to the tender beans and rich, creamy sauce. Add thawed frozen green peas or other vegetables along with the oyster mushrooms if you'd like to add some vegetable love. If you're a mushroom hater, don't write this recipe off just yet; you can make it without them and call it Sweet Potato and Chickpea Curry instead.

1. Combine the chickpeas through the water in the slow cooker. Cover, set heat to LOW, and cook for 8 hours, or until the chickpeas are tender.

2. Turn off the slow cooker, drain, and discard the ginger and lemongrass. Return the chickpeas to the slow cooker.

3. Add the garlic through the coconut milk to the slow cooker, cover, set heat to LOW, and cook for 4 hours, or until the sweet potato and shiitake mushrooms are tender.

4. Add the oyster mushrooms and salt, stir well, and cook 1 hour.

5. Make a slurry of the cornstarch and a little water. Stir into the curry to thicken.

6. Serve garnished with mung bean sprouts, if desired, and season with salt, pepper, and hot sauce to taste.

NOTE: To use cooked chickpeas instead, add 3 cups cooked chickpeas (drained and rinsed if canned) with the garlic through the coconut milk, and cook the curry for only 4 hours.

SERVES 4

PREPARATION TIME:
30 MINUTES, DIVIDED

1 cup dry chickpeas, soaked overnight, drained, and rinsed (see Note)
One 1-inch piece fresh ginger, peeling optional
1 stalk lemongrass, trimmed and crushed
4 cups water

3 garlic cloves, minced
3 stalks lemongrass, finely chopped (1 tablespoon)
1 tablespoon minced fresh ginger
1 red Asian chile pepper, seeds removed, minced
1 teaspoon tamarind paste
1 teaspoon agave
¼ teaspoon chile flakes, optional
¼ medium finely chopped sweet potato
6 ounces shiitake mushrooms, stalks removed, caps cut into ½-inch dice
½ cup vegetable stock, store-bought or homemade (page 43)
1½ cups canned coconut milk

4 ounces oyster mushrooms, thinly sliced
½ teaspoon salt

1 tablespoon cornstarch

Mung bean sprouts, optional
Salt, black pepper, and Asian hot sauce

*Please check all packaged ingredients, as noted on page 39.

Tandoori Baked Tofu

SERVES 4 TO 6

PREPARATION TIME:
15 MINUTES

 *

⅔ cup vegan mayonnaise
⅔ cup vegan sour cream
2 shallots, finely chopped
2 tablespoons grated fresh
    ginger
2 tablespoons canola oil
2½ tablespoons Tandoori
    Spice Mix (page 53), or
    other mild or medium
    curry powder
1 teaspoon curry powder,
    mild or medium
2 tablespoons lemon juice
1 tablespoon agave
½ teaspoon salt

1 pound extra-firm regular
    water-packed tofu
    (pressing not required),
    cut into ½-inch cubes

*Please check all packaged
ingredients, as noted on
page 39.

I'LL GIVE YOU the warning first: This is *not* a low-fat dish, but it is so very, very good—and creamy and rich enough that you need only a little to be satisfied! The tofu is soft, with a melt-in-your-mouth texture created by the rich and creamy sauce it is cooked in. As the sauce cooks, it forms a creamy crust that is a little heavy but very good. Serve with Coconut Rice (page 216), or any aromatic long-grain rice, with a hefty serving of vegetables such as Peppered Kale (page 225). If desired, cover the tofu smothered in the sauce and marinate in fridge at least 1 hour, maybe even overnight to really infuse with flavor prior to cooking.

1. Combine the mayonnaise through the salt in the slow cooker. Mix until smooth.
2. Add the tofu and gently coat with the sauce, ensuring the tofu pieces are completely covered.
3. Cover, set heat to LOW, and cook for 4 hours, or until the sauce is thickened and golden and the tofu is soft and creamy.

Laksa-Inspired Tofu and Noodles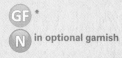

THIS TASTY TOFU dish makes a wonderful meal in a bowl, and you can add more vegetables at the end to liven it up if you wish. It's influenced by the flavors and spice profile of traditional Malaysian laksa. Although nowhere near traditional, this laksa is inspired by, and pays homage to, that wonderful spicy soup. You'll need the juice and zest of 1 large lime. I don't recommend freezing this dish.

1. Combine the garlic through the lime juice in the slow cooker. Add the tofu and toss.
2. Cover, set heat to LOW, and cook for 6 hours, or until the tofu is very tender and completely infused with the flavors of the broth.
3. Taste and season as required. It will look very liquid-y, but you will be adding noodles.
4. Put the noodles in a bowl of boiling water, cover, and leave for about 5 minutes, or until they are flexible but not fully cooked. Drain, discarding the water. Add the noodles to the slow cooker, stir carefully so as not to break up the tofu too much, and cook for 10 minutes, or until the noodles are tender but not gummy.
5. Garnish with the bean sprouts, a sprinkle of peanuts, and a lime wedge, if desired. Season to taste with the salt and pepper.

NOTES:

If you like less heat use a jalapeño; if more, add a second chile.

Rice noodles are in the ethnic aisle of local supermarkets as well as in Asian stores.

SERVES 4

PREPARATION TIME:
20 MINUTES, DIVIDED

GF *

N in optional garnish

2 garlic cloves, minced
1 shallot, finely chopped
1 serrano chile pepper, minced (see Notes)
¼ cup finely chopped cilantro leaves and stalks
1 tablespoon brown rice syrup
3 stalks fresh lemongrass, minced (1 tablespoon)
1 tablespoon minced fresh ginger
1 teaspoon lime zest
1 teaspoon cumin
2 teaspoons curry powder, your choice of heat
¼ teaspoon chile flakes, or to taste
½ teaspoon salt
⅛ teaspoon turmeric
1½ cups canned coconut milk
1½ cups vegetable stock, store-bought or homemade (page 43)
2 tablespoons lime juice

1 pound extra-firm tofu, drained and pressed, cut into ½-inch cubes

½ pound medium-width rice noodles (see Notes)

1 cup mung bean sprouts
Roasted peanuts
Lime wedges
Salt and black pepper

*Please check all packaged ingredients, as noted on page 39.

Thai BBQ Tofu

SERVES 4

PREPARATION TIME:
25 MINUTES

GF *

1 tablespoon canola oil
¼ cup finely chopped
  cilantro, packed
3 tablespoons Thai basil
  leaves, finely chopped
  (see Note)
1 tablespoon minced fresh
  ginger
2 garlic cloves, minced
3 stalks lemongrass, finely
  chopped (1 tablespoon)
½ teaspoon chile flakes
½ teaspoon cumin seeds

1 pound extra-firm tofu,
  crumbled
½-inch piece fresh ginger,
  crushed, peeling
  optional
1 stalk lemongras,
  trimmed and crushed
½ cup vegetable stock,
  store-bought or
  homemade (page 43)
½ cup tomato juice
2 tablespoons tomato paste
2 tablespoons lime juice
2 tablespoons soy sauce
2 tablespoons sweet Thai
  chili sauce
1 tablespoon rice wine
  vinegar

2 tablespoons tapioca
  starch or cornstarch

2 tablespoons minced
  cilantro leaves
2 tablespoons minced Thai
  basil leaves

Salt, black pepper, and
  Asian hot sauce

*Please check all packaged
ingredients, as noted on
page 39.

THIS IS FUSION Thai and as such requires an open mind and adventurous taste buds. The tofu is so very tender and the aromatic flavors burst and zing, really livening up the meal. It's best served over rice or even a slice of cornbread.

1. Heat the oil in a large skillet and sauté the cilantro through the cumin seeds until aromatic, 2 minutes. Transfer to the slow cooker.
2. Add the tofu through the vinegar; stir to combine.
3. Cover, set heat to LOW, and cook for 6 hours, or until the tofu is tender and the sauce has reduced a little.
4. Remove the whole ginger and lemongrass from the slow cooker. Make a slurry of the tapioca starch and a little water; add to the slow cooker and stir to thicken.
5. Taste and season with the salt, pepper, and hot sauce as required.
6. Serve garnished with a mix of the chopped cilantro and basil leaves.

NOTE: If you can't find Thai basil with its purplish leaves, use regular basil.

Soy Curl Vindaloo

ALTHOUGH MANY VERSIONS of vindaloo contain potatoes, the traditional kind does not, so I don't feel bad about not putting them in mine. I've thickened the rich, spicy sauce using red lentils and added sour notes (in the form of both wine and vinegar) so the heat isn't too over the top. It may seem that the amount of cayenne you're adding is extreme, but remember that the power of ground spice decreases somewhat throughout the long cooking time. If you are a real hot food lover, you'll need to add a little more heat at the end. Serve with rice and an Indian bread such as a roti, naan, or chapatti to soak up the spice and make it a little easier on your tummy.

1. Heat the oil in a small skillet over medium-high heat; add the garlic, ginger, chiles, and shallots and allow to sizzle for 2 minutes. Add the coriander through the turmeric; sauté for 1 minute. Transfer to the slow cooker.

2. Deglaze the skillet with the wine; add to the slow cooker with the soy curls through the tomato paste. Stir to combine.

3. Cover, set heat to LOW, and cook for 6 hours, or until the vindaloo is very tender and thick.

4. Taste and season with the salt, pepper, and hot sauce as required.

NOTE: If you like more heat, go with serrano chiles; otherwise, use jalapeño chiles. Alternatively, add as much as you think you can handle, or leave out completely.

SERVES 4 TO 6

PREPARATION TIME:
20 MINUTES

 *

1 tablespoon canola oil
4 garlic cloves, minced
1½ tablespoons minced
   fresh ginger
3 serrano or jalapeño
   peppers, minced (see
   Note)
3 shallots, minced

1½ teaspoons coriander
1½ teaspoons paprika
¾ to 1 teaspoon cayenne,
   or to taste
¼ teaspoon turmeric

¼ cup plus 2 tablespoons
   red wine or vegetable
   stock, store-bought or
   homemade (page 43)

3 cups soy curls
¾ cup red lentils
3 tablespoons balsamic
   vinegar
6 cups vegetable stock
1½ tablespoons tomato
   paste

Salt, black pepper, and hot
   sauce

*Please check all packaged
ingredients, as noted on
page 39.

Tempeh Tikka Masala

SERVES 4 TO 6

PREPARATION TIME:
10 MINUTES

GF *

8 ounces tempeh, cut into
  ½-inch cubes
¾ cup canned crushed
  tomatoes
¾ cup canned coconut
  milk
2 garlic cloves, minced
1 tablespoon lemon juice
1 tablespoon minced fresh
  ginger
1 tablespoon tomato paste
1½ teaspoons cumin
1½ teaspoons smoked
  paprika
1½ teaspoons paprika
1 tablespoon cane sugar
½ teaspoon cinnamon
½ teaspoon cardamom
½ teaspoon salt
¼ teaspoon turmeric
¼ to ½ teaspoon chile
  flakes, to taste

¼ cup vegan sour cream

Salt and black pepper

1 seeded tomato, finely
  chopped
Vegan sour cream,
  optional

*Please check all packaged
ingredients, as noted on
page 39.

THIS IS MY nonauthentic take on chicken tikka masala, itself a nonauthentic take on traditional Indian curries! This curry is rich and heavy. The serving size is small, but you don't need much to be satisfied. There may not be any oil in the recipe, but it is certainly not low fat! If you're not a huge tempeh fan or don't have any, feel free to substitute pressed extra-firm tofu or any seitan (store-bought or homemade), though results may vary. If you're using tofu, be aware that it will absorb more of the marinade and you may have to add a little extra liquid if you want a saucier end result. If you'd like more sauce, stir in more vegan sour cream at the end of the cooking time. If you like heat in everything, increase the amount of chile flakes or add ¼ to ½ teaspoon cayenne with the spices. You can also always add hot sauce to taste at the end.

1. Combine the tempeh through the chile flakes in the slow cooker.
2. Cover, set heat to LOW, and cook for 6 hours, or until the tempeh is very tender and the sauce has thickened.
3. Stir in the vegan sour cream. Taste and season with the salt and pepper as required.
4. Serve hot, garnished with the tomato and vegan sour cream, if using.

Pineapple Sweet and Sour Seitan 📷

THICK, GLOOPY, AND sticky, just like your favorite Chinese takeout. Wonderful served with Coconut Rice (page 216) or any aromatic long-grain rice. This is lovely, mostly sweet and spicy with a just hint of sour, and loaded with all the vegetables you'd find in takeout sweet and sour. Most of the sweetness (and liquid) comes from the pineapple, so canned pineapple really doesn't work. I'm sure you'll be able to find a delicious use (like eating as is) for the remaining pineapple. Adjust the amount of jalapeño to your heat preference.

1. Combine the pineapple through the broth in the slow cooker. Stir well.
2. Cover, set heat to LOW, and cook for 5 hours, or until the liquid is released and the seitan is tender.
3. Mix the arrowroot with a little water to make a slurry, add to the slow cooker, and stir for 2 minutes, or until thick.
4. Taste and season with the salt and pepper as required.

NOTE: If you don't have arrowroot powder, use tapioca starch because cornstarch will make the sauce cloudy.

SERVES 4 TO 6

PREPARATION TIME:
20 MINUTES

SF if using vegetable stock

½ large fresh pineapple, peeled, cored, and cut into ½-inch chunks
½ medium red pepper, cut into ½-inch chunks
¼ medium green pepper, finely chopped
½ medium red onion, finely chopped
2 tablespoons agave
1 teaspoon minced fresh ginger
¼ teaspoon chile flakes
2 tablespoons seasoned rice wine vinegar
2 tablespoons lime juice
½ to 1 jalapeño pepper, minced
½ pound (2 cups) seitan, preferably light, store-bought or homemade (page 47, ½ recipe), cut into ½-inch chunks
½ cup seitan cooking broth or vegetable stock, store-bought or homemade (page 43)

1½ tablespoons arrowroot powder or tapioca starch (see Note)

Salt and black pepper

Red Seitan Curry

SERVES 4 TO 6

PREPARATION TIME:
30 MINUTES

1 celery stalk, finely
    chopped
1 onion, half finely
    chopped, half in ½-inch
    chunks
2 garlic cloves, minced
1 tablespoon finely
    chopped sun-dried
    tomatoes
1 tablespoon tomato paste
1 to 1½ teaspoons Thai red
    curry paste, more or
    less to taste
One 15-ounce can diced
    tomatoes
2 cups vegetable stock,
    store-bought or
    homemade (page 43)

½ cup vegetable stock, at
    room temperature
1 teaspoon tomato paste
1 teaspoon soy sauce
1 teaspoon Thai red curry
    paste

½ teaspoon coriander
½ teaspoon cumin
3 tablespoons chickpea
    flour, sifted if lumpy
½ teaspoon onion powder
½ teaspoon garlic powder

½ cup plus 2 tablespoons
    vital wheat gluten

¼ cup all-purpose flour

2 tablespoons canola oil

1 cup green beans,
    trimmed and cut in
    ½-inch lengths
1 cup frozen peas, thawed

1 tablespoon arrowroot
    powder or cornstarch,
    optional

Salt, black pepper, and
    Asian hot sauce

THIS CURRY IS Thai inspired, aromatic, thick, and perfect with rice, though I do cheat and use premade vegan chili paste. The raw seitan pieces are tossed in flour and seared to give a nice crust, which holds the color and shape for the remainder of the cooking time. The little flour left after searing also acts as a partial thickener, so you may find the curry plenty thick enough without the arrowroot slurry at the end. If so, omit that step. Make and sear the seitan pieces up to a day ahead of time if you wish, holding in the fridge until required. If you'd prefer to use store-bought seitan, please see the variation. This curry is not too over the top heat-wise, so feel free to use more of the paste if you know you like it hot. If you are spice phobic, start off with only ½ teaspoon with the stock; you can always stir in more later. If you prefer a green curry, check out the Green Seitan Curry (page 126).

1. Combine the celery through the 2 cups stock in the slow cooker.
2. In a medium bowl whisk together the ½ cup stock through the curry paste.
3. Add the coriander through the garlic powder and whisk in.
4. Stir in the wheat gluten and mix to form a stiff dough. Knead in the bowl for about 3 minutes to develop the gluten.
5. Let the seitan mixture rest while you place the flour in a large resealable plastic bag or shallow bowl and heat the oil over medium-high heat in a large skillet.
6. Cut the seitan into no more than ½-inch pieces (they will expand as they cook) and toss in the flour to coat and keep the pieces from sticking to one another.
7. Sear all sides of the seitan until the outsides are browned and firm, about 5 minutes in total. Transfer the seitan and any excess flour in the skillet to the slow cooker.

8. Cover, set heat to LOW, and cook for 6 hours, or until the seitan is cooked through and no longer tastes like raw chickpea flour.
9. Add the beans and peas; cook for 1 hour, or until tender.
10. If necessary, make a slurry with the arrowroot and a little water. Add to the pot and stir in to thicken the mix.
11. Taste and season with the salt, pepper, and hot sauce as required.

VARIATIONS:

If you want a coconut-style red curry, replace ½ cup of the vegetable stock with coconut milk when you add it to the slow cooker.

To use store-bought seitan in the recipe above or in the Green Seitan Curry (page 126), first complete step 1, reducing the stock by 1 cup. Skip ahead to step 8, adding the seitan to the slow cooker. Complete the recipe as written. Adjust spices to taste prior to serving, since the seitan may not be as infused with the spices and curry paste as in the original version.

Green Seitan Curry

SERVES 4 TO 6

PREPARATION TIME:
30 MINUTES

1½ cups canned coconut
    milk
1½ cups vegetable stock,
    store-bought or
    homemade (page 43)
1 lemongrass stalk,
    crushed
1 teaspoon lime zest
2 garlic cloves, minced
1 tablespoon minced
    ginger
1 tablespoon finely
    chopped cilantro stalks
1½ teaspoons green Thai
    curry paste, or to taste

½ cup vegetable stock, at
    room temperature
1 teaspoon soy sauce
1 teaspoon green Thai
    curry paste

(see Red Seitan Curry,
    page 124)

2 tablespoons finely
    chopped cilantro leaves
2 spring onions, sliced

THIS MILDER, CREAMIER, Thai-inspired curry variation is similar to its red counterpart but uses the more fragrant green Thai curry paste.

1. Combine the coconut milk through the curry paste in the slow cooker.
2. In a medium bowl whisk together the ½ cup stock through the curry paste.
3. From this point forward, follow the instructions for Red Seitan Curry (page 124), starting with step 3.
4. Just prior to serving remove the lemongrass stalk and discard, then stir cilantro and spring onions into the curry.

Curried Sausages with Apricots, Squash, and Pistachios

I HAVE VAGUE MEMORIES of my mother making a curried sausage dish with dried fruit in it when I was a child. I think she used raisins. I took that memory, played around with the ingredients, and created this fragrant, not too spicy, flavorsome curry to use up leftover sausages. I like to use sausages with a little spice in them, but you can use whichever sausages take your fancy. Pretoast the nuts or buy roasted unsalted for quickest combining. Use the rest of your squash in a recipe such as the Squash and Cranberry Bake (page 209).

1. Combine the sausages through the coconut milk in the slow cooker; stir well.
2. Cover, set heat to LOW, and cook for 4½ to 5 hours, until the squash is tender.
3. Add the vegan mayonnaise and stir well. Taste and season with the salt and pepper as desired.
4. Garnish with the toasted nuts, if desired.

SERVES 4 TO 6

PREPARATION TIME:
20 MINUTES

2 links vegan sausage, store-bought or homemade (page 49, ½ recipe), cut into ¼-inch pieces (about 4 cups)
1 shallot, minced
2 garlic cloves, minced
1 jalapeño pepper, seeds removed, minced
1 tablespoon curry powder, your choice of heat
1 tablespoon Tandoori Spice Mix (page 53), or other mild or medium curry powder
¼ teaspoon cayenne, optional
¼ cup dried apricots, finely chopped
¼ cup toasted pistachio nuts
½ medium butternut squash or any winter squash, cut into ½-inch dice
¾ cup plus 2 tablespoons vegetable stock, store-bought or homemade (page 43)
½ cup canned coconut milk

¼ cup vegan mayonnaise
Salt and black pepper

2 tablespoons toasted pistachio nuts, optional

Chilies and BBQ-Inspired Dishes

BOLD, VIBRANT FLAVORS, with lots of beans. Is that what you are expecting from this chapter? If so, the recipes won't disappoint. They include chilies, chili-inspired dishes, and those with a BBQ theme because I feel there is a kinship between the two. Vegan hot dog off the barbecue loaded with chili from the slow cooker, anyone?

The dishes in this chapter are really easy to serve with almost anything, and leftovers are easy to use in new and interesting ways:

Make Cornbread Scones (page 243), or any cornbread you fancy, because they make a wonderful dipper for chili.

Cut up flour tortillas, brush one side with a little Garlic Infused Oil (page 54), sprinkle with salt and pepper, and broil (oil side up) until golden for a simple, flavorful dipper.

Make a side of Pineapple Kale-Slaw (page 232) or some Green Guacamole (page 237) to dollop on the top. Super yum.

You can serve these dishes over steamed rice, with Baked Garlic Potatoes (page 214), or as a filling for tacos, tamales, enchiladas, burritos, or chimichangas.

You can even spread chili between corn tortillas and bake for a chili lasagna, or make a pasta lasagna or a shepherd's pie with a twist.

If you have any leftovers, please note that these chilies do tend to thicken as they are stored so you may need to add additional liquid (either water or vegetable stock) as you reheat them. All the dishes in this chapter freeze well.

A note about chilies and chile peppers: I aimed for a middle-of-the-road spiciness, and as such the recipes will be too spicy for some and nowhere near spicy enough for others. On each recipe I added "or to taste" when chile powder, chile flakes, hot sauce, or even chile peppers are listed. If you know how much heat you can tolerate, adjust prior to cooking. If you are unsure or would rather taste the finished dish first, adjust the level of spice when cooking is complete. Remember, you can always add more heat (and other seasonings), but it is very hard to reduce the amount if you have been overgenerous.

Kidney Bean and Sweet Potato Chili

THERE SEEMS TO be a consensus among cookbooks that black beans and sweet potatoes love each other. I tend to disagree and think that the chunkier, heartier, red kidney beans are sweet potatoes' true love. Try this mild, slightly sweet chili and see what you think. Start with only ¼ teaspoon of cayenne unless you are a spice lover and want a spicier chili. You can easily add more spice later to taste. Remember, for safety's sake, not to cook the kidney beans in the slow cooker (see page 24).

1. Combine the onion through the creamed corn in the slow cooker.
2. Cover, set heat to LOW, and cook for 6 hours, or until the sweet potato is very tender.
3. Taste and season with the salt, pepper, and hot sauce as required. If desired, roughly mash some of the sweet potato pieces with a potato masher or a fork to thicken the chili a little more. If you prefer thinner chili, add more stock as needed.

SERVES 4 TO 6

PREPARATION TIME: 15 MINUTES

½ onion, finely chopped
3 garlic cloves, minced
2 celery stalks, finely chopped
½ cup finely chopped cilantro stalk and leaves
1 medium yellow-fleshed sweet potato, peeled and cut into ½-inch cubes
1½ teaspoons cumin
1½ teaspoons smoked paprika
½ teaspoon salt
½ teaspoon dried basil
½ teaspoon dried oregano
¼ teaspoon garlic powder
¼ to ½ teaspoon cayenne, to taste
One 15-ounce can tomato sauce
1¼ cups vegetable stock, store-bought or homemade (page 43)
2 cups cooked red kidney beans (see warning on page 24)
1 cup canned creamed corn

Salt, black pepper, and hot sauce, to taste

Additional stock, optional

*Please check all packaged ingredients, as noted on page 39.

Pepper and Cherry Chili

SERVES 4

PREPARATION TIME:
30 MINUTES, DIVIDED

(GF) *

2 cups fresh dark sweet
   cherries (such as Bing),
   pitted and roughly
   chopped
2 medium red peppers,
   finely chopped
1 medium yellow pepper,
   finely chopped
2 serrano or jalapeño
   peppers, seeded and
   minced
½ medium red onion,
   finely chopped
¼ cup finely chopped fresh
   parsley
½ teaspoon smoked
   paprika
½ teaspoon paprika
½ teaspoon ancho chile
   powder
¾ cup dry pinto beans,
   soaked overnight,
   drained, and rinsed
2½ cups vegetable stock,
   store-bought or
   homemade (page 43)

1 tablespoon lime juice
1 tablespoon soy sauce
1 tablespoon balsamic
   vinegar
1 tablespoon regular
   molasses
1 tablespoon tomato paste
1 tablespoon cornstarch

Salt, black pepper, and hot
   sauce

*Please check all packaged
ingredients, as noted on
page 39.

I ADORE CHERRIES AND every year look forward to the local season. There's nothing I like better than gorging myself on ripe cherries until the juice stains my hands and my tummy hurts. I wanted to use cherries in a savory setting for a summer-inspired dish to see if it would shine. Boy, does it ever! The pairing of the sweet cherries with the sweet pepper and the heat from the hot peppers really works. It is, of course, fruity but not to the point of being sweet—there's a nice balance. If you don't have a cherry pitter, prepare the cherries almost in a production line: Cut around the middle of each with a paring knife, then pull each cherry in half and remove the pit, then roughly chop the big pile of halved cherries with a chef's knife. If you have access to frozen cherries you can make this dish year-round.

1. Combine the cherries through the stock in the slow cooker. The liquid will only just cover the other ingredients. You may need to push everything down with clean hands to ensure it is just covered, but please don't be tempted to add more liquid since the cherries and bell peppers will release liquid as they cook.

2. Cover, set heat to LOW, and cook for 8 hours, or until the beans are tender.

3. In a small bowl, whisk together the lime juice through cornstarch. Stir into the cooked chili to thicken; combine well.

4. Taste and season with the salt, pepper, and hot sauce as required.

Mock-a-Leekie "Chicken and Leek" Soup (page 84)

Butternut Squash and Pear Soup (page 68)

Laksa-Inspired Tofu and Noodles (page 119)

Pineapple Sweet and Sour Seitan (page 123)

Mediterranean Vegetable and Bean Stew (page 95)

Thai-Inspired Green Quinoa (page 201)

Sort-of-Succotash (page 206)

Lima Bean and Shiitake Stew (page 90)

South American Chili (page 140)

Soy Curl and Soybean Chili (page 141)

**Smoky Chickpea Tofu Pasta
(page 176)**

**Israeli Couscous with
Almonds and Parsley
(page 218)**

Nutty Wild Rice (page 207)

Peppered Kale (page 225)

Mushroom, Green Pepper, and Black Bean Chili

MEDIUM SPICED AND loaded with lots of yummy mushrooms, this chili is for the fungi lover in your life. I think black beans are the perfect bean to go with mushrooms as they both have an earthy quality. If you feel otherwise or have another bean you need to use up, by all means substitute. If you don't have dried porcini mushrooms, substitute another dried mushroom, or just omit from the recipe. The final result won't have the same deep earthy quality but will still be loaded with mushroomy goodness. This isn't the thickest of chilies, although it's not thin either. If you like it thicker, after it has finished cooking make a slurry, add to the slow cooker, and cook for 5 minutes to thicken. The recipe does make a lot of chili! Plan to use the leftovers in other ways—see my examples (page 88).

1. In the bowl of a food processor or blender, combine the porcini mushrooms through the boiling water. Cover and let stand to soak at least 20 minutes. When soaked add the Marmite through the liquid smoke; pulse until somewhat smooth. Transfer to the slow cooker.
2. Add the onion through the stock and stir to combine.
3. Cover, set heat to LOW, and cook for 10 hours, or until the beans are tender.
4. Taste and season with the salt, pepper, and hot sauce as required. Let stand for 10 minutes prior to serving.

NOTES:

Cut mushrooms to different sizes for interest in the final dish. You can use all cremini, all button, or a mixture, or even add in some shiitake or other mushrooms if you have them.

The long cooking time and heartiness of the mushrooms counteracts the usual bitterness of green pepper in a slow cooker.

SERVES 6 TO 8

**PREPARATION TIME:
20 MINUTES**

½ cup dried porcini mushrooms
¼ cup sun-dried tomatoes
1 cup boiling water

1 tablespoon Marmite
2 tablespoons tomato paste
1½ teaspoons liquid smoke

1 onion, finely chopped
1 celery stalk, finely chopped
14 medium mushrooms, roughly chopped (see Notes)
1 portobello cap, halved and sliced ¼-inch wide
3 garlic cloves, minced
1 medium green pepper, chopped (see Notes)
2 jalapeño peppers, minced, to taste
2 teaspoons cumin
1 teaspoon coriander
1 teaspoon smoked paprika
1 teaspoon dried oregano
½ teaspoon ground fennel seeds
½ teaspoon chile flakes or to taste
One 19-ounce can diced tomatoes, undrained
1 cup dry black beans, soaked overnight, drained, and rinsed
2½ cups vegetable stock, store-bought or homemade (page 43)

Salt, black pepper, and hot sauce

*Please check all packaged ingredients, as noted on page 39.

Spicy Beets and Beans

SERVES 2 TO 4

PREPARATION TIME:
30 MINUTES, DIVIDED

¾ cup dry black beans,
   soaked overnight,
   drained, and rinsed
2 medium beets, peeled
   and cut into ¼-inch
   pieces
2 chipotles in adobo,
   seeded and minced
1 bay leaf
1 teaspoon cumin
1 teaspoon onion powder
1 teaspoon garlic powder
½ teaspoon dried oregano
¼ teaspoon ground fennel
   seeds
2 cups water or vegetable
   stock, store-bought or
   homemade (page 43)

1 tablespoon canola oil
2 garlic cloves, minced
½ red onion, thinly sliced

2 cups lightly packed
   shredded beet greens
   from 1 bunch beets
   (see Note)

Salt, black pepper, and hot
   sauce

*Please check all packaged
ingredients, as noted on
page 39.

THERE ARE SOME foods I find so comforting that just thinking about eating them will warm and relax me. Almost. This recipe combines two of them—beans and beets—and highlights their earthiness with smoky, spicy chipotle. Serve with some plain brown rice and refreshing Pineapple Kale-Slaw (page 232) as a meal for four, or by itself for two hungry people. It's not the most vibrantly colored dish, though the greens do provide a welcome lift and contrast. The recipe uses both the beets and the beet greens. Buy them attached but store them separately. The recipe needs finishing after cooking but just prior to serving, so the slow cooker portion can be done in advance and held in the refrigerator.

1. Combine the beans through the stock in the slow cooker.
2. Cover, set heat to LOW, and cook for 8 hours, or until the beets and beans are tender.
3. Drain, discarding the cooking liquid and bay leaf and reserving the beets and beans.
4. Heat the oil in a medium skillet over medium-high heat.
5. Add the garlic and allow to sizzle; add the onion and sauté until soft and translucent, 4 to 5 minutes.
6. Add the shredded greens, and sauté to wilt, 2 to 3 minutes.
7. Stir through the reserved beets and beans until well combined. Taste and season with the salt, pepper, and hot sauce as required.

NOTE: If you don't have access to beet greens use another quick-cooking green such as fresh spinach or arugula.

Seitan and Vegetable Chili

NOT EAT-IT-FOR-DESSERT SWEET, just sweet as opposed to being spicy and overly savory. The vegetables are all what I call sweet vegetables, and the addition of molasses and chocolate gives the chili a depth of flavor that accentuates the sweetness while definitely leaving it a main course. It's great served with the usual chili accompaniments. If you don't believe *mild* and *chili* should ever be used in the same sentence, feel free to use chipotle (or another, hotter) chile powder instead of the ancho, and add some hot peppers with the bell peppers. The amount of corn kernels is roughly the amount you get from one decent-sized cob, so if you have access to fresh, please use it because it will be sweeter.

1. Combine the celery through the stock in the slow cooker and stir well.
2. Cover, set heat to LOW, and cook for 8 hours, or until the beans are tender.
3. Taste and season with the salt, pepper, and hot sauce as required.

NOTE: You can replace up to half the vegetable stock with seitan cooking broth if you made your own.

SERVES 4 TO 6

PREPARATION TIME:
20 MINUTES

2 stalks celery, finely chopped
¼ cup sun-dried tomatoes, finely chopped
2 tablespoons tomato paste
½ teaspoon cinnamon
1 teaspoon cumin
1 teaspoon coriander
1 teaspoon paprika
1 teaspoon ancho chile powder
1½ tablespoons semisweet vegan chocolate chips
2 tablespoons regular or fancy molasses
1 medium red pepper, roughly chopped
1 medium yellow pepper, roughly chopped
¾ cup corn kernels, fresh, frozen, or canned, drained, and rinsed
½ cup dry pinto beans, soaked overnight, drained, and rinsed
½ pound (2 cups) seitan, preferably light, store-bought or homemade (page 47, ½ recipe), chopped into ¼-inch cubes
⅓ cup white wine, not too dry, or vegetable stock, store-bought or homemade (page 43)
1 cup canned crushed tomatoes
2 cups vegetable stock, (see Note)

Salt, black pepper, and hot sauce

Pigeon Pea and Plantain Chili

SERVES 4 TO 6

PREPARATION TIME:
15 MINUTES, DIVIDED

1 cup dry pigeon peas,
  soaked overnight,
  drained, and rinsed
  (see Notes)
1 ripe plantain, peeled,
  quartered lengthwise,
  and cut into ¼-inch
  pieces (see Notes)
1 habanero or Scotch
  bonnet pepper, whole
  and only scored (see
  Notes)
½-inch piece fresh ginger,
  peeled and scored
1 bay leaf
½ medium onion, finely
  chopped
2 garlic cloves, minced
2 teaspoons cumin
2 teaspoons oregano
⅛ teaspoon allspice
2¾ cups vegetable stock,
  store-bought or
  homemade (page 43)

1 tablespoon lime juice
1 tablespoon tomato paste
1 tablespoon cane sugar
1½ tablespoons arrowroot
  powder or cornstarch

Salt, black pepper, and hot
  sauce

*Please check all packaged
ingredients, as noted on
page 39.

DON'T BE FRIGHTENED of the habanero! Although this chili is spicy, it has a wonderful fruity flavor and is not at all palate killing. I think that leaving the pepper whole, scoring it, and allowing it to infuse the chili yields the best balance of heat and flavor. The flavor is lifted further by the late sweet and sour additions, leading to a balanced, wholesome, and filling chili. I like it served with brown rice and a refreshing pile of Pineapple Kale-Slaw (page 232) on the side. If even after thickening you would like a thicker chili, make a little cornstarch slurry and stir through.

1. Combine the peas through the stock in the slow cooker.
2. Cover, set heat to LOW, and cook for 8 hours, or until the peas and plantain are tender.
3. Remove the habanero and bay leaf.
4. In a small bowl, whisk together the lime juice through arrowroot until smooth. Stir into the chili, cover, and cook for 1 hour on LOW to meld flavors and thicken.
5. Taste and season with the salt, pepper, and hot sauce as required.

NOTES:

To find pigeon peas, try an Asian spice store or anywhere that stocks a range of Latin products. If you can find only canned, reduce the stock by ½ cup and cook for only 6 hours, or until the plantain is perfectly tender. If you have trouble finding even canned pigeon peas, use either chickpeas or black-eyed peas in the same quantity.

Buy the plantain when it is green and a few days in advance of making this recipe; allow it to ripen in your fruit bowl alongside bananas. For this recipe it is best when it is completely yellow and just starting to have black specks.

To score the habanero, make vertical slits with a sharp knife on the sides of the pepper to allow the flavor to come out when cooking. If you like less spice, make fewer slits, even making only one if you really don't want lots of heat. I usually make four slits around the sides of the pepper.

Coffee'd Tempeh Chili

SERVES 4 TO 6

PREPARATION TIME:
10 MINUTES

 *

8 ounces tempeh, cut into
  ½-inch pieces
2 cups cooked red kidney
  beans or one 19-ounce
  can, drained and rinsed
½ medium onion, finely
  chopped
2 garlic cloves, minced
1 teaspoon ancho chile
  powder
1 teaspoon cumin
1 teaspoon smoked
  paprika
½ teaspoon chipotle chile
  powder
2 teaspoons tomato paste
2 tablespoons agave
½ cup strong coffee or
  espresso (see Note)
One 15-ounce can diced
  tomatoes, undrained
¾ cup vegetable stock,
  store-bought or
  homemade (page 43)

2 tablespoons semisweet
  vegan chocolate chips

Salt and black pepper

*Please check all packaged
ingredients, as noted on
page 39.

IN THIS BEAUTIFULLY intense chili the chocolate provides a little hint of sweetness and depth of flavor that accentuates the coffee nicely, as in a café mocha. It's all about balance, and the chocolate helps to achieve that. It cooks down to quite a thick chili, so if you'd like to add a little more liquid at the end, feel free. Serve with a side of Cornbread Scones (page 243) or just a big pile of tortilla chips for dunking and scooping.

1. Combine the tempeh through the stock in the slow cooker. The tempeh won't be completely covered.
2. Cover, set heat to LOW, and cook for 5½ to 6 hours, until the tempeh is tender and sauce thickened.
3. Stir in the chocolate; cover and let stand for 10 minutes.
4. Taste and season with the salt and pepper as required.

NOTE: To make strong coffee without a coffeemaker, dissolve 4 tablespoons of instant coffee granules in ½ cup boiling water.

VARIATION:

Not a tempeh fan? Double the beans to 4 cups (or two 19-ounce cans) and proceed as directed.

Maple-Infused Sausage Chili

THIS RECIPE WAS originally devised to use up that half-recipe of sausages left in the fridge, but you'll find yourself making (or buying) the sausages to be able to make this chili! Yes, it is that good. With developed flavors that call out spicy, smoky, and just a little sweet, I like to serve it simply, with Corn-bread Scones (page 243) or Baked Garlic Potatoes (page 214) as the only accompaniment. Adjust the number of chipotles to taste. If you'd like your chili thicker, use a cornstarch slurry at the end of the cooking time.

1. In the slow cooker combine the beans through the stock.
2. Cover, set heat to LOW, and cook for 6 hours, or until the beans are just tender.
3. Add the sausages through the liquid smoke; stir well.
4. Cover and cook for 1 hour, or until the flavors are well melded and the beans are very tender.
5. Taste and season with the salt, pepper, and hot sauce as required.

VARIATION:

Instead of grating all the sausages, grate only half and cut the rest into ½-inch chunks for a texture variation.

SERVES 4

PREPARATION TIME:
20 MINUTES, DIVIDED

 depending on sausages used

¾ cup dry black beans, soaked overnight, drained, and rinsed
1 teaspoon onion powder
1 teaspoon garlic powder
1 teaspoon smoked paprika
1 chipotle in adobo, seeded and minced, or more to taste
1 tablespoon maple syrup
3 cups vegetable stock, store-bought or homemade (page 43)

½ pound vegan sausage or seitan, store-bought or homemade (Seitan, page 45, or Chipotle Lentil Sausages, page 49), grated (about 3 cups after grating)
1 cup Simple Tomato Sauce (page 55), or canned
1 tablespoon maple syrup
1 teaspoon liquid smoke

Salt, black pepper, and hot sauce

South American Chili

½ red onion, finely
   chopped
1½ cups corn kernels,
   from 2 cobs, frozen, or
   canned
2 jalapeño peppers, or
   serrano peppers,
   seeded and minced
2 finely chopped bell
   peppers, red, orange,
   or yellow (not green)
1 teaspoon oregano
2 teaspoons cumin
1 teaspoon ancho chile
   powder, or chipotle
   chile powder
½ teaspoon chile flakes,
   optional, or more to
   taste
1 bay leaf
2 medium peeled white
   potatoes, cut into
   ¼-inch dice (see Note)
¾ cup dry pinto beans or
   Columbian red beans,
   soaked overnight,
   drained, and rinsed
4½ cups vegetable stock,
   store-bought or
   homemade (page 43)

½ cup quinoa
¼ cup amaranth
1 tablespoon tomato paste
½ teaspoon salt

Salt, black pepper, and hot
   sauce

*Please check all packaged
ingredients, as noted on
page 39.

A TRUE MEAL IN a bowl! Vegetables, beans, and grains together add up to a yummy meal, served, if you wish, with a little something to dip. It's a thin, saucy chili perfect for eating from a bowl; it will thicken as it stands, so the next day it will be great with nachos or in a burrito. If you've never eaten amaranth, this is a gentle introduction. It provides a cute "popping" texture to the dish as well as a little thickening.

1. Combine the onion through the stock in the slow cooker.
2. Cover, set heat to LOW, and cook for 10 hours, or until the beans and potatoes are tender. At this stage the chili will look very liquid-y.
3. Add the quinoa through the salt, cover, and cook for 1 to 1½ hours, until the grains are cooked.
4. Remove the bay leaf, taste, and season with the salt, pepper, and hot sauce as required.

NOTES:

If you have access to purple potatoes, use them for an interesting color contrast.

Choose serrano peppers instead of jalapeño and chipotle chile powder instead of ancho chile powder for more intense spice.

Soy Curl and Soybean Chili

GF *

THIS ASIAN-INFLUENCED CHILI is a bit chunky textured, so good for eating as a bowl of goodness alongside Cornbread Scones (page 243) or another favorite dipper. I made it a little spicy (though not too much); as always, reduce or increase the heat level to taste. The black soybeans won't be to everyone's taste, but I like the fusion hints they bring to the chili.

1. Combine the soy curls through the tomato juice in the slow cooker.
2. Cover, set heat to LOW, and cook for 6 hours, or until the soy curls are very tender.
3. Taste and season with the salt, pepper, and hot sauce as required.

NOTE: Use already-cooked canned soybeans; using dry soybeans takes a very long time to cook. If you can't find them, or don't like them, substitute 3 cups cooked adzuki beans or even black beans.

1 cup soy curls
Two 15-ounce cans cooked black soybeans, drained and rinsed (see Note)
1½ tablespoons soy sauce
1 teaspoon minced fresh ginger
2 garlic cloves, minced
1 serrano chile, seeded and minced
1 teaspoon liquid smoke
1½ teaspoons hot sauce, or to taste
5 fresh Roma tomatoes, seeded and roughly chopped
1½ cups tomato juice

Salt, black pepper, and hot sauce

*Please check all packaged ingredients, as noted on page 39.

Three Bean and Whole Grain Chili

SERVES 6 TO 8

PREPARATION TIME:
15 MINUTES

(GF) *

1 medium onion, finely
   chopped
3 garlic cloves, minced
1 celery stalk, finely chopped
¼ cup cilantro stalks and
   leaves, finely chopped
1½ cups corn kernels
1 medium chopped red pepper
2 teaspoons cumin
1 teaspoon coriander
1½ teaspoons smoked
   paprika
1½ teaspoons chipotle chile
   powder
¼ teaspoon black pepper
2 teaspoons liquid smoke
½ cup dry navy beans,
   soaked, drained, and
   rinsed
½ cup dry black beans, soaked,
   drained, and rinsed
½ cup dry pinto beans,
   soaked, drained, and
   rinsed
¾ cup steel-cut oats
2½ cups dark vegetable
   stock, store-bought or
   homemade (page 43)

1 cup diced tomatoes in
   juice, undrained
3 tablespoons tomato paste
2 tablespoons semisweet
   vegan chocolate chips
1 tablespoon soy sauce
1 teaspoon blackstrap
   molasses
1 teaspoon lime zest
1 or 2 chipotles in adobo,
   seeded and minced
½ teaspoon chile flakes
½ teaspoon salt

¼ cup cilantro leaves,
   chopped
2 tablespoons lime juice

Salt, black pepper, and hot
   sauce to taste

OH MY, THIS is a hearty, almost meaty thick chili without a fake meat product in sight. Hooray! Don't be put off by the length of the ingredients list: The recipe is very simple, and everything comes together really quickly. If you would like to use a different type of bean, like chickpeas, then go right ahead; just ensure you have at least three types of beans (for the title) and a total of 1½ cups. Changing the beans may change the cooking time, however, so be warned—you may have to cook the chili longer to get the beans tender. Soaking works best using separate containers so that the black beans don't turn everything purple (sorry to fill your fridge with containers overnight). The first part of this recipe, where the beans and oats are cooked together, is perfect for overnight cooking if serving this dish for lunch.

1. Combine the onion through stock in the slow cooker. Stir well.
2. Cover, set heat to LOW, and cook for 8 hours, or until the beans and oats are just tender. The chili will be thick.
3. Add the tomatoes through the salt, stir well, and cook for 2 hours, still on LOW, or until flavors meld.
4. Stir in the cilantro and lime juice, taste, and season with the salt, pepper, and hot sauce as required.
5. Let stand 10 minutes prior to serving.

*Please check all packaged
ingredients, as noted on
page 39.

Smoky BBQ Chili

A VEGETABLE-LESS CHILI FOR those who prefer their chili to be just "meat and beans," though in this case, it's meatless too! I made this one smoky, rich, and thick. I like to serve it as the filling for nachos topped with some melted vegan cheese, vegan sour cream, and Classic Guacamole (page 236), but it is great used wherever you'd use chili. The cooking time is long because I added all the acidic ingredients with the beans, so they need this extra time to become tender. On the other hand, the cooking time also thickens the sauce nicely, so don't worry when you see how liquid-y it is as you put everything in the slow cooker. I like it as it is, but if you feel it needs a little something to cut through the heaviness, add a tablespoon of lime juice just prior to serving.

1. Combine the tomato paste through the stock in the slow cooker; stir well.
2. Cover, set heat to LOW, and cook for 10 hours, or until the beans are very tender and the sauce has thickened.
3. Taste and season with the salt, pepper, and hot sauce as required.

NOTE: I am a huge fan of liquid smoke. If you aren't, perhaps start with half the amount and add more later.

SERVES 4

PREPARATION TIME:
10 MINUTES

 *

2½ tablespoons tomato
    paste
2 tablespoons maple
    syrup
2 tablespoons soy sauce
1 tablespoon balsamic
    vinegar
1 tablespoon liquid smoke
    (see Notes)
1½ teaspoons blackstrap
    molasses
1½ teaspoons hot sauce,
    more to taste
1 teaspoon onion powder
1 teaspoon garlic powder
1 teaspoon cumin
1 teaspoon smoked
    paprika
½ cup TVP granules
½ cup dry black beans,
    soaked overnight,
    drained, and rinsed
½ cup dry pinto beans,
    soaked overnight,
    drained, and rinsed
One 15-ounce can crushed
    tomatoes
3 cups vegetable stock,
    store-bought or
    homemade (page 43)

Salt, black pepper, and hot
    sauce

*Please check all packaged
ingredients, as noted on
page 39.

Orange Pumpkin BBQ Lentils

SERVES 4 TO 6

PREPARATION TIME:
15 MINUTES

2 garlic cloves, minced
¼ cup maple syrup
½ cup canned pumpkin
    puree
¼ cup finely chopped fresh
    cilantro
2 teaspoons orange zest
½ teaspoon chile flakes
½ teaspoon liquid smoke
1 pound butternut squash,
    other winter squash,
    or pumpkin, cut into
    ½-inch pieces
¾ cup red lentils
¾ cup brown lentils
2 cups vegetable stock,
    store-bought or
    homemade (page 43)
1½ cups orange juice

Salt, black pepper, and hot
    sauce

*Please check all packaged
ingredients, as noted on
page 39.

THIS DISH EVOLVED from an orange pumpkin BBQ marinade I like to make for tofu. This dish is both sweet and savory, very orange-y, and not too spicy, but you can adjust it to taste. Be warned, if you're not a big fan of orange in savory dishes, this one may not be for you. Use the other half of the squash in a soup such as Butternut Squash and Pear Soup (page 68).

1. In the slow cooker combine the garlic through the orange juice and stir well.
2. Cover, set heat to LOW, and cook for 8 hours, or until the lentils are soft and thick.
3. Taste and season with the salt, pepper, and hot sauce as required.

Baked Beans

NAMED SUCH ONLY because *Baked* Beans sounds better than "Cooked Overnight for 12 Hours Beans" (which is exactly what I did to make them). I also thought about "Better than the Store-Bought Beans" because that is what I—and my husband—think they are! These beans are not as sweet as commercial baked beans, but if you like your beans really sweet, adjust to taste at the end of the cooking time. To score the ginger and onion, use a paring knife to cut some marks just deep enough to allow the flavor to escape. If you poke the cloves into the scored onion, you won't have to search for them later.

1. Combine the beans through the molasses in the slow cooker.
2. Cover, set heat to LOW, and cook for 12 hours, or until the beans are very tender and the sauce is thickened.
3. Remove the bay leaf, onion, cloves (if you can find them—otherwise warn the diners), and cinnamon stick.
4. Taste and season with the salt and pepper as required.

SERVES 6 TO 8

PREPARATION TIME:
10 MINUTES

1½ cups dry navy beans,
  soaked overnight,
  drained, and rinsed
1 cup vegetable stock,
  store-bought or
  homemade (page 43)
1½ cups Simple Tomato
  Sauce (page 55), or one
  15-ounce can
1 bay leaf
½ onion, peeled and
  scored
3 whole cloves
One 3-inch cinnamon stick
1 teaspoon dry mustard
  powder
One 1-inch piece peeled
  whole ginger, scored
1 tablespoon tomato paste
1 tablespoon liquid smoke
1 tablespoon agave
1 tablespoon maple syrup
1 tablespoon blackstrap
  molasses

Salt and black pepper

*Please check all packaged
ingredients, as noted on
page 39.

Franks'n'Beans

SERVES 4 TO 6

PREPARATION TIME:
15 MINUTES

½ cup dry navy beans,
    soaked overnight,
    drained, and rinsed
½ medium onion, finely
    chopped
1 shallot, finely chopped
2 garlic cloves, minced
1 celery stalk, finely
    chopped
¼ cup sun-dried tomatoes,
    finely chopped
1 bay leaf
½ cup red lentils
One 15-ounce can diced
    tomatoes, undrained
1½ cups tomato juice
2 tablespoons tomato
    paste
1 tablespoon soy sauce
1½ teaspoons blackstrap
    molasses
1 teaspoon liquid smoke
1¼ cups vegetable stock,
    store-bought or
    homemade (page 43)

6 veggie dogs, chopped
    into ½-inch chunks

Salt and black pepper

IF YOU HAVE children, you may be familiar with the cartoon *Timothy Goes to School,* based on the books by Rosemary Wells. Timothy (a raccoon) is in kindergarten; two of his class-mates are Frank and Frank (bulldogs) who live with their dad (Big Frank). Big Frank is always making franks'n'beans for the Franks, and it seems to be all they eat. I made this recipe originally to try to get my children to eat franks'n'beans, associating it with the cartoon, but I had no luck: "It's got beans in it, Mum. I never knew franks'n'beans meant beans." If you aren't bean-phobic yourself, I'm sure you'll love this one!

Although you can make the whole recipe ahead of time, the contrast in textures is better served if you make only the stew and refrigerate, without the hot dogs added. Sauté the hot dogs while the stew reheats and add just prior to serving.

1. Combine the beans through the stock in the slow cooker.
2. Cover, set heat to LOW, and cook for 8 hours, or until the beans and lentils are tender. The stew will be quite thick.
3. Remove the bay leaf.
4. Heat a little oil in a skillet and fry the veggie dog pieces until browned, 5 minutes. Add to the stew, mix through, and serve immediately.

VARIATION:
BANGERS'N'BEANS

Replace the veggie dogs with homemade sausages for a totally homemade variation.

Chipotle'd Black-Eyed Pea Stew

YOU CAN MAKE this smoky, spicy, tomato-laden, hearty stew with any bean you care to substitute, but keep in mind it won't be as lucky on New Year's Day! Not that I am superstitious, mind. Serve it with potatoes, rice, pasta, cornbread, tortilla chips, in tacos—whatever you want, though make sure you've some greens on the side if you really want to be lucky! If you want greens *in* the stew, see the variation.

1. Combine the black-eyed peas through the celery in the slow cooker.
2. Cover, set heat to LOW, and cook for 7 hours, or until the peas are tender and the liquid is reduced.
3. Add the tomato paste through the mixed vegetables, cover, and cook on LOW for 2 hours, or until the peas and vegetables are very tender and the flavors are well melded.
4. Taste and season with the salt, pepper, and hot sauce as required.

NOTES:

If you are heat averse and can't even handle a chipotle, reduce the amount by half or even leave it out. The stew won't be chipotle'd anymore, but it will still be tasty.

Use frozen mixed vegetables, green peas, or cooked leftovers. Adjust cooking times if needed; precooked leftovers will require less time than frozen vegetables.

VARIATION:
QUICK GREEN'D AND CHIPOTLE'D BLACK-EYED PEA STEW
  Add 1 cup finely shredded kale when you add the vegetables.

SERVES 4 TO 6

PREPARATION TIME:
20 MINUTES, DIVIDED

¾ cup dry black-eyed peas, soaked overnight, drained, and rinsed
2½ cups vegetable stock, store-bought or homemade (page 43)
½ onion, finely chopped
2 shallots, finely chopped
3 garlic cloves, minced
1 celery stalk, finely chopped

3 tablespoons tomato paste
1½ tablespoons soy sauce
1½ teaspoons liquid smoke
1 or 2 chipotles in adobo, seeded and minced (see Notes)
¾ teaspoon dried thyme
¾ teaspoon dried oregano
¾ teaspoon cumin
½ teaspoon salt
½ teaspoon paprika, preferably smoked
¼ teaspoon black pepper
1½ cups Simple Tomato Sauce (page 55), or one 15-ounce can
1½ cups frozen mixed vegetables (see Notes)

Salt, black pepper, and hot sauce

*Please check all packaged ingredients, as noted on page 39.

Red Wine Refried Beans

SERVES 4

PREPARATION TIME:
5 MINUTES

GF * SF

1 medium onion, finely
   chopped
4 garlic cloves, minced
2 teaspoons cumin
1 teaspoon ancho chili
   powder
1 bay leaf
1 cup dry pinto beans,
   soaked overnight,
   drained, and rinsed
5 cups vegetable stock,
   store-bought or
   homemade (page 43)

2 tablespoons tomato
   paste
½ cup red wine or
   vegetable stock
1 cup canned diced
   tomatoes, undrained

¼ cup finely chopped
   cilantro, or to taste
Salt, black pepper, and hot
   sauce

*Please check all packaged
ingredients, as noted on
page 39.

REFRIED BEAN PURISTS will be chasing me down the street and throwing things at me, but I like my refried beans with more stuff in them. I find standard refried beans (although perfectly nice and edible) a little simplistic, so I add to them to bring more flavors into play and enhance the depth of flavor in the beans. Use these beans any way you would "normal" refried beans—over tortilla chips covered with vegan cheese as simple nachos; as a warm dip; with rice and a vegetable side; on toast, burgers, or hot dogs; or layered into tacos or burritos. For a change of pace, leave them a little saucy and serve over pasta. You can cook the beans in advance and make the refried beans later.

1. Combine the onion through the stock in the slow cooker.
2. Cover, set heat to LOW, and cook for 8 hours, or until the beans are tender.
3. Drain the beans, remove the bay leaf, and return the mixture to the slow cooker. Mash with a potato masher until no whole beans remain.
4. Add the tomato paste through the diced tomatoes; mash well to combine.
5. Cover, set heat to HIGH, and cook for 1 hour for the flavors to meld. Uncover and continue to cook on HIGH for 30 to 45 minutes, stirring occasionally until the beans reach your preferred consistency. The top of the mixture may have liquid pooling, but the bottom may be sticking. Cook a shorter time for saucier beans, a longer time for a firmer consistency. The time will vary due to your preference and the amount of juice in the tomatoes.
6. Stir the cilantro through, taste, and season with the salt, pepper, and hot sauce as required.

Bean Taco Filling

THIS IS A little like refried beans but with no frying (or refrying) in sight, and no mashing, either. It's a thick, comforting, aromatic bean dish, perfect for loading on your tacos or in your burritos. There's not many veggies, so I expect you to be loading your tacos or burritos with lots of fresh raw goodness and maybe even some Pineapple Kale-Slaw (page 232). The first step of cooking the beans can be done in advance and the second step (when the kidney beans are added) at a later time in a skillet on the stovetop, if preferred. If you use the stovetop to finish the dish, everything will need to cook for about 20 minutes over medium heat.

1. Heat the oil in a medium skillet over medium-high heat, add the cumin seeds through the chile flakes, and toast until brown and very aromatic, 1 to 2 minutes. Take care not to burn them.

2. Add the onion through the cilantro stalk and sauté until the onion just starts to brown, about 4 minutes. Transfer to the slow cooker and add the black beans and water. Stir to combine.

3. Cover, set heat to LOW, and cook for 8 hours, or until the beans are tender.

4. Drain the slow cooker contents, reserving ½ cup cooking liquid. Transfer everything back into the slow cooker, including the reserved ½ cup cooking liquid.

5. Add the kidney beans through the black pepper; stir well to combine.

6. Uncover, set heat to HIGH, and cook, stirring every ½ or ¾ hour if possible for 2½ hours, or until all the liquid is absorbed or evaporated and the flavors are well melded.

7. Taste and season with the salt, pepper, and hot sauce as required.

VARIATION:

Add ¼ cup chopped cilantro leaves with the kidney beans, or stir through just prior to serving if you are a cilantro lover.

SERVES 4

PREPARATION TIME:
20 MINUTES, DIVIDED

 GF * SF

1 tablespoon olive oil

1 teaspoon cumin seeds
1 teaspoon crushed
  coriander seeds
¾ teaspoon chile flakes, or
  to taste

1 medium onion, finely
  chopped
2 garlic cloves, minced
2 tablespoons finely
  chopped cilantro stalk

¾ cup dry black beans,
  soaked overnight,
  drained, and rinsed
2½ cups water

2 cups cooked red kidney
  beans, or one 19-ounce
  can, drained and rinsed
  if canned (see warning
  on page 24)
2 roasted red peppers
  (page 20), finely
  chopped
2 tablespoons tomato
  paste
1 teaspoon dried oregano
½ teaspoon smoked paprika
½ teaspoon paprika
½ teaspoon dried
  marjoram
½ teaspoon salt
¼ teaspoon black pepper

Salt, black pepper, and hot
  sauce

*Please check all packaged
ingredients, as noted on
page 39.

Casseroles and Roasts

151

I N THIS CHAPTER I included dishes that mostly could have been cooked conventionally in the oven. The slow cooker is essentially a casserole dish, and the surrounding heat is like the heat of an oven (though longer, slower, and less likely to heat your house). Many of these recipes need the slow cooker to be lined (instructions will be in each recipe) because the items would stick otherwise and be difficult to remove for serving, especially if the result is meant to be firm and sliceable.

The sliceable recipes, made by lining the slow cooker before filling, will often accumulate a little water under the lining as the food cooks. This is normal and is due to the moist cooking environment that doesn't let the excess water escape. Just discard as directed in each recipe.

I like to serve these recipes with lots of the dishes from To Serve With (page 211). I give suggestions with many of the recipes since they all suit different dishes—potatoes, grains, gravies, salads, vegetables, even savory baking. One quick hint: Nut Roast (page 164) and "Not-Meat" Loaf (page 162) are really delicious sliced, pan fried, and sandwiched between whole grain bread with some ketchup!

A lot of the casseroles are good served hot or cold, which makes using leftovers a breeze. Take them to work for lunch because there is no need to reheat. If you do reheat, however, in an oven or microwave, make sure the item is piping hot before eating. All the firmer, sliceable items can be sliced, cooled, and then frozen in slices for easy portion control when retrieving from the freezer.

Lemon Tofu and Beans

A LOVELY GARLIC AND lemon pairing, perfect if served over plain rice, polenta, or Coconut Rice (page 216). I have also been known to eat it, by itself, as lunch! I haven't used much salt in the recipe because the lemon pepper seasoning I have is salty enough. If yours isn't salted or you are a real salt fiend, add ½ teaspoon with the dry ingredients and taste and season just prior to serving. Speaking of taste, how much do you like green beans? I often add more, sometimes up to a pound (but that is a little excessive), so add as much as you think will work for you. Leftovers are great cold in a wrap or heated through in a hot skillet to crisp a little.

1. Combine the zest through the salt in the slow cooker.
2. Add the tofu and toss to combine.
3. Cover, set heat to LOW, and cook for 6 hours, or until the tofu is very tender.
4. Add the beans, stir, cover, and set heat to HIGH. Cook for 45 minutes, or until the beans are tender but still have a little bite.

SERVES 4

PREPARATION TIME:
15 MINUTES

Zest from 2 lemons (2 tablespoons)
Juice from 1 to 2 lemons (3 to 4 tablespoons, or more to taste)
1 cup canned coconut milk
4 garlic cloves, minced
2 teaspoons lemon pepper seasoning
1 teaspoon garlic powder
1 teaspoon dried thyme
½ teaspoon salt

1 pound extra-firm tofu, well drained, pressed, and cut into ½-inch cubes

10 to 12 ounces green beans, trimmed and cut into 1-inch lengths

Salt and black pepper

Leek, Potato, and Celeriac Crumble

SERVES 4 TO 6

PREPARATION TIME:
30 MINUTES, DIVIDED

2 tablespoons olive oil
2 tablespoons water
3 medium white potatoes
cut into ¼-inch dice,
peeling optional
½ medium celeriac (celery
root), peeled and cut
into ¼-inch dice
4 medium leeks, trimmed,
rinsed, cut in half
lengthwise then into
½-inch slices
4 sprigs fresh thyme
2 tablespoons finely
chopped fresh dill, or 1
teaspoon dried
1 teaspoon salt
¼ teaspoon black pepper

SAUCE
2 tablespoons vegan
margarine
1 shallot, finely chopped
2 garlic cloves, minced

2 tablespoons all-purpose
flour
1 teaspoon prepared
yellow mustard
1 tablespoon finely
chopped fresh parsley

1 cup plain soymilk
½ cup vegetable stock,
store-bought or
homemade (page 43)

Salt and black pepper

CELERIAC (A.K.A. CELERY root), has a mild, celery-like flavor, dense off-white flesh, and a creamy texture once cooked. The knobbly, somewhat tough outer skin needs to be sliced off and discarded prior to use. If you don't like celeriac, or can't see yourself using the other half, use an equal weight of parsnips instead, peeled and with any hard woody middle bits removed. Celeriac is also great, however, in a mixed root vegetable roast or Winter Vegetables and Quinoa (page 202).

For this recipe I use the high setting to get the vegetables a little caramelized prior to topping and again for the crumble to cook and the sides to brown. Serve with gravy such as Mushroom Gravy (page 238) on the side and you have dinner, unless you want to be a little fancier and add more vegetable sides. Or you can make the crumble your side, along with, for example, a seared tofu.

1. Combine the oil through the black pepper in the slow cooker, cover, set heat to HIGH, and cook for 4 hours, or until tender and starting to caramelize, stirring hourly if possible.

2. At the end of the cooking time, prepare the sauce and topping.

3. To prepare the sauce, melt the margarine in a medium saucepan over medium heat; add the shallot and garlic. Sauté until the shallot is translucent, 3 to 4 minutes.

4. Add the flour through the parsley and cook for about 2 minutes, stirring constantly. Add the soymilk ¼ cup at a time, stirring almost constantly each time until thick. Remove from the heat and stir in the stock, but don't cook to thicken.

5. Taste and season with the salt and pepper as required.

6. To prepare the topping, mix the flour through the dill in a large bowl. Cut or rub in the margarine until the mix resembles coarse bread crumbs.

7. When the vegetables are cooked, remove the thyme sprigs (the leaves should have magically cooked off), stir the sauce into the slow cooker, and mix with the vegetables to coat evenly.

8. Sprinkle the topping evenly over the mixture, cover, set heat to HIGH, and cook for 2 hours or until the edges of the topping are golden brown.

TOPPING
½ cup whole wheat pastry flour
½ cup all-purpose flour
1 cup quick-cooking rolled oats (not instant)
½ teaspoon salt
¼ teaspoon black pepper
2 tablespoons finely chopped fresh parsley
1 tablespoon finely chopped fresh dill, or 1 teaspoon dried
⅓ cup vegan margarine

Potato Casserole

SERVES 4 TO 6

PREPARATION TIME:
30 MINUTES

GF * N

Canola oil or vegan
  margarine

¾ cup vacuum-packed
  firm silken tofu
1 cup almond milk
2 tablespoons ground
  almonds
2 tablespoons nutritional
  yeast
1 tablespoon cornstarch
2 garlic cloves, minced
1 shallot, minced
½ teaspoon prepared
  yellow mustard
½ teaspoon salt
½ teaspoon black salt
¼ teaspoon turmeric
¼ teaspoon black pepper
Salt and black pepper

4 medium Yukon gold
  or other firm white
  potatoes, peeling
  optional, cut into
  ⅛-inch-thick slices

½ cup grated vegan
  cheese, optional

*Please check all packaged
ingredients, as noted on
page 39.

THIS IS COMFORT food at its best: tender potatoes enveloped in a slightly tangy, creamy sauce. Earlier versions had double the amount of mustard, and while others preferred the dish that way, I found it too piquant. If you're a mustard lover you can easily increase the amount suggested. If you have a food processor with a slicing blade or a mandoline, you can make quick work of the potato slicing and guarantee even slices. Some slow cookers will brown the edges more than others, but so long as the potatoes are tender, the level of browning you have is fine.

1. Grease the inside of the slow cooker insert with the oil.
2. In a blender combine the tofu through the pepper and pulse until smooth and thick. Taste and adjust the seasoning as required. Pour into the slow cooker.
3. Toss the potatoes into the slow cooker. Smooth the top; they will be almost covered by the liquid.
4. Cover, set heat to LOW, and cook for 6 hours, or until the potatoes are tender and a little browned around the edges.
5. Let stand covered for 15 minutes.
6. If the insert is broiler safe and if desired, sprinkle the top with the cheese and broil lightly for 2 to 3 minutes to brown.

Potato and Kale Frittata

SPANISH FRITTATAS ARE like big, fat omelets loaded with potatoes and cooked in a skillet, sliced, and served. I've taken the basic idea, added lots of kale for extra color, nutrition, and flavor, then cooked up an egg-free omelet mix. Served hot or cold with a green salad, this is perfect for lunch, especially outdoors on a sunny day. For best time management, make the component parts ahead (including cutting the kale), assemble as required, then finish the final cooking. If desired, cook the potatoes in a steamer basket on the stovetop.

1. Place the potatoes and the water into the slow cooker. Cover, set heat to LOW, and cook for 4 hours, or until tender. Drain and transfer to a large mixing bowl.

2. Line the slow cooker insert with 2 sheets of foil placed in opposite directions, leaving enough foil at both ends to serve as handles. Spray with nonstick spray.

3. Blend the tofu through the pepper in a blender or food processor until smooth. Transfer to the bowl with the potatoes; add the garlic and kale.

4. Mix until well combined. Transfer to the slow cooker and spread out evenly, smoothing the top.

5. Cover, set heat to LOW, and cook for 4 hours, or until the potatoes are fully tender and the edges of the frittata are firm with the center a little softer.

6. If the insert is broiler safe and if desired, broil the top of the frittata until lightly golden and firm, 8 to 10 minutes.

7. Grasp the foil handles and remove from the slow cooker. Let stand 10 minutes prior to cutting and serving.

VARIATION:

Use an equal amount of chard in place of kale for a slightly different but still good frittata.

SERVES 4 TO 6

PREPARATION TIME:
25 MINUTES, DIVIDED

 *

3 medium white potatoes, peeling optional, cut into ¼-inch dice
3 cups water

6 ounces firm, vacuum-packed silken tofu
1 cup soy milk
½ cup canned coconut milk
¼ cup chickpea flour, sifted if lumpy
¼ cup cornstarch
1 tablespoon nutritional yeast
1 tablespoon prepared yellow mustard
1 teaspoon salt
1 teaspoon cumin
½ teaspoon turmeric
½ teaspoon black salt
¼ teaspoon white pepper

3 garlic cloves, minced
1 bunch kale, stems removed, shredded

*Please check all packaged ingredients, as noted on page 39.

No-Crust Southwestern Onion Quiche

SERVES 6 TO 8

PREPARATION TIME:
30 MINUTES

2 tablespoons olive oil
1 large cooking onion,
    quartered and finely
    sliced
1 medium red onion,
    halved and finely sliced
½ cup finely chopped
    cilantro stems and
    leaves
3 garlic cloves, minced
1 jalapeño, minced
1½ teaspoons salt
1 teaspoon cumin
¼ to ½ teaspoon chile
    flakes, or to taste
½ teaspoon oregano
¼ teaspoon black pepper

¾ cup quick-cooking rolled
    oats, not instant

1½ cups raw cashews,
    soaked in water for at
    least 10 hours, drained,
    and rinsed

8 ounces firm regular
    water-packed tofu,
    crumbled
6 ounces firm silken
    vacuum-packed tofu,
    crumbled

2 tablespoons lime juice

½ cup corn kernels, if
    canned, drained and
    rinsed

Salt and black pepper

*Please check all packaged
ingredients, as noted on
page 39.

WITH FLAVORS REMINISCENT of southwestern cooking, this firm quiche is perfectly tasty hot or cold, and just right for dinner, lunch, potlucks, and picnics. When making a quiche without a crust you need to ensure it firms up really well so it can be sliced and served. The rolled oats ensure this one does. If you taste the mix before you bake it, you may find it is a little reminiscent of savory oatmeal, but during baking that flavor goes away. You can make the mix, including sautéing the vegetables and blending everything together, ahead of time, place in the insert, and refrigerate until required, but remember to plan ahead to soak the nuts for 10 hours.

1. Line the slow cooker insert with 2 sheets of foil placed in opposite directions, leaving enough foil at both ends to serve as handles. Spray with nonstick spray.
2. In a large skillet over medium heat, combine the oil through the pepper, stir well, cover, and cook, stirring occasionally until everything is soft and translucent and has released its liquid, 10 minutes.
3. Turn the heat to medium high and sauté, stirring frequently until the liquid has evaporated, the volume has reduced by half, and the onions are lightly golden, 3 to 4 minutes.
4. While the onion mix is sautéing, pulse the oatmeal in a food processor to a coarse flour.
5. Add the drained cashews to the oatmeal and pulse well to combine. The mix will look like wet bread crumbs.
6. Add the tofu and blend until well combined, smooth, and thick.
7. When the onions are cooked, add the lime juice to deglaze the skillet, scraping up any coated-on pieces.
8. Transfer half the onions to the food processor and blend until smooth.
9. Add the remaining onions and corn; gently pulse, leaving them textured. Alternatively, stir them in.

158

10. Taste and season with the salt and pepper as required.
11. Transfer the mixture to the lined slow cooker insert.
12. Cover, set heat to LOW, and cook 5½ to 6 hours, until the edges are browned and the center is firm.
13. Uncover and let stand in the slow cooker for 10 minutes. Remove from the insert using the foil handles.
14. For ease of slicing, let stand for 10 minutes prior to serving.

VARIATION:
CORNMEAL RED ONION AND PEPPER QUICHE
Replace the oatmeal with coarse cornmeal, add a teaspoon of agave, and use roasted red onion and red pepper instead of the sliced sautéed onions in the filling.

No-Crust Roast Fennel and Red Pepper Quiche

SERVES 4 TO 6

PREPARATION TIME:
40 MINUTES, INCLUDING
VEGETABLE ROASTING

1 large or 2 small fennel
    bulbs, trimmed and
    chopped into no more
    than ½-inch pieces
2 red peppers, trimmed
    and chopped into no
    more than ½-inch
    pieces
2 tablespoons olive oil
Salt and black pepper

½ cup raw cashews
¼ cup plus 2 tablespoons
    ground almonds
2 tablespoons cornstarch
1 teaspoon salt
1 teaspoon marjoram
½ teaspoon ground fennel
    seeds
¼ teaspoon nutmeg
¼ teaspoon black pepper

12 ounces extra-firm
    water-packed Chinese-
    style tofu, crumbled
1½ teaspoons lemon juice

2 shallots, finely chopped
2 garlic cloves, minced
1 celery stalk, finely
    chopped

Salt and black pepper

THIS CRUSTLESS QUICHE dish uses ground almonds to aid with the setting of the quiche, which also gives it a slightly nutty background flavor. I love the vibrant Mediterranean-inspired flavors of fennel and pepper, softened and lightly caramelized prior to being smothered in a rich mix that is sliceable for serving once cooked. You may roast the vegetables ahead of time and hold until required.

1. Preheat the oven to 425°F. Toss the fennel, peppers, and oil in a 9 by 13-inch baking pan, season with the salt and pepper, and roast uncovered for 30 minutes, or until the vegetables are soft and just golden, stirring once during roasting.

2. Meanwhile, using a food processor, pulse the cashews until they are a fine meal. Add the almonds through the pepper and pulse to combine.

3. Add the tofu and lemon juice and blend until smooth and well mixed with the nut mix. Stop frequently to scrape down the sides.

4. Place the shallots through the celery in a large bowl. Add the roasted vegetables.

5. Add the tofu mix to the vegetables and mix well to evenly distribute the vegetables. Taste and season with the salt and pepper as required.

6. Line the slow cooker insert with 2 pieces of foil placed in opposite directions, leaving enough foil at both ends to serve as handles. Spray with nonstick spray.

7. Transfer the mix to the slow cooker and smooth the top.

8. Cover, set heat to LOW, and cook for 4 hours, or until the edges are browned and firm, with the center set but less firm.

9. Uncover, turn off the heat, and let stand in the slow cooker for 10 minutes. Remove using the foil handles.

10. Let stand for 10 minutes prior to slicing and serving.

Bobotie

THIS IS A South African casserole for which, according to a South African friend of mine, there are as many recipes as there are South African grandmothers. I don't feel bad about throwing my spiced and fruity nonauthentic recipe into the ring! I used different types of lentils because when they are cooked they have slightly different textures. Try looking for the puy, French, or beluga lentils in a natural foods store. If you can't find one of these options, use more brown lentils; the recipe will still work fine. If you find turmeric bitter, reduce the amount to ¾ teaspoon—you can always add a little more later if you feel the finished dish needs it. Serve with brown rice, mashed potatoes, or even a baked sweet potato.

1. Combine the onions through the cinnamon in the slow cooker.
2. Cover, set heat to LOW, and cook for 4 hours, or until the lentils are tender and the liquid is absorbed.
3. Taste and season with the salt and pepper as required.

SERVES 4

PREPARATION TIME:
25 MINUTES

½ medium onion, finely chopped
2 garlic cloves, minced
3 cups vegetable stock, store-bought or homemade (page 43)
1 medium carrot, finely chopped
½ cup brown lentils
½ cup puy, French, or beluga lentils
¼ cup raisins
¼ cup chopped almonds
¼ cup canned crushed pineapple, drained
1½ teaspoons grated fresh ginger
1½ teaspoons lemon zest
1 teaspoon turmeric
1 teaspoon cumin
1 teaspoon coriander
½ teaspoon white pepper
½ teaspoon cardamom
¼ teaspoon cloves
¼ teaspoon cinnamon

Salt and black pepper

*Please check all packaged ingredients, as noted on page 39.

"Not-Meat" Loaf

SERVES 6 TO 8

**PREPARATION TIME:
30 MINUTES**

½ medium onion, finely
    chopped
1 celery stalk, finely
    chopped
2 garlic cloves, minced
1 shallot, finely chopped
1 medium carrot, peeled
    and grated
1 tablespoon seeded Dijon
    mustard
2 tablespoons soy sauce
1 teaspoon liquid smoke
1 teaspoon Marmite
1 tablespoon tomato paste
1 teaspoon dried thyme
1 teaspoon dried rubbed
    sage
1 cup cooked millet,
    packed (see Note)
1 pound seitan, preferably
    dark, store-bought
    or homemade (page
    46, 1 recipe), grated,
    or commercial soy
    crumbles (about 4
    cups)
¾ cup vegetable stock,
    store-bought or
    homemade (page 43)
¾ cup Simple Tomato
    Sauce (page 55), or
    canned
Salt and black pepper

½ cup vital wheat gluten

STILL MOIST, AS a good meatloaf should be, yet hearty and satisfying, this traditionally flavored loaf is made extra "meaty" by the inclusion of grated seitan. It is great served with Garlic and Onion Mashed Potatoes (page 215), Maple-Touched Chili Brussels Sprouts (page 224), and Mushroom Gravy (page 238). Even real meat-and-potatoes people will go back for seconds of this loaf. Try one of the flavor variations for a less "old-school" meatloaf taste. It is truly delicious served hot, or cold at a picnic. The slices reheat well, and it is freezer friendly. The longer it stands the easier it is to slice.

1. Line the slow cooker insert with 2 sheets of foil placed in opposite directions, leaving enough foil at both ends to serve as handles. Spray with nonstick spray.
2. Combine the onion through the tomato sauce in a large bowl. Taste and season with the salt and pepper as required.
3. Stir in the wheat gluten. The mixture will look damp but will not feel wet and will hold together when pressed.
4. Transfer to the slow cooker and press in the mixture evenly, smoothing the top.
5. Cover, set heat to LOW, and cook for 8 hours, or until firm and browned.
6. Uncover, cool for 10 minutes, remove using the foil handles, and let stand 10 minutes prior to serving.

NOTE: If you are cooking millet specifically for this dish, start with ⅓ cup dry; it will triple in volume when cooked.

MEXICAN-INSPIRED "NOT-MEAT" LOAF

Substitute ketchup for the Dijon mustard, reduce the soy sauce to 1 tablespoon, and add 1 tablespoon hot sauce (as hot as you like). Reduce the carrot by half and add ½ cup corn kernels when you mix everything together. Substitute equal amounts of cumin and coriander for the thyme and sage.

ASIAN-INSPIRED "NOT-MEAT" LOAF

Add 1 tablespoon grated fresh ginger and ¼ cup finely chopped cilantro with the onion. Instead of the thyme and sage, substitute ½ teaspoon each of coriander, ground ginger, and cardamom, plus a pinch of turmeric.

ITALIAN-INSPIRED "NOT-MEAT" LOAF

Substitute ketchup for the Dijon mustard, reduce the soy sauce to 1 tablespoon, and add a tablespoon of homemade or store-bought pesto. Reduce the carrot by half and add ½ cup finely chopped black olives, capers, or both when you mix everything together. Instead of the thyme and sage, substitute equal amounts dried basil and oregano.

Nut Roast

3 cups roughly chopped
mixed nuts of your
choice, such as
almonds, pecans,
pistachios, hazelnuts,
cashews, Brazil nuts,
and even peanuts (see
Note)

1 medium onion, finely
chopped
4 garlic cloves, minced
2 stalks celery, finely
chopped
1 medium carrot, finely
chopped
1 tablespoon plus 1
teaspoon poultry
seasoning mix, store-
bought or homemade
(page 52)
2 bay leaves
1 teaspoon salt
½ teaspoon black pepper
¼ cup ground chia seeds
1 cup ground almonds
1 cup ground pecans
1 cup chickpea flour, sifted
if lumpy
¼ cup cornstarch

2 cups vegetable stock,
store-bought or
homemade (page 43)

*Please check all packaged
ingredients, as noted on
page 39.

THIS IS A mildly seasoned loaf with the nut flavors really shining through, so be sure to use nuts you like. It is impressive warm with Garlic and Onion Mashed Potatoes (page 215), Peppered Kale (page 225), and Mushroom Gravy (page 238). You can even pair it with cranberry chutney for a Thanksgiving centerpiece that is sure to delight. Leftovers are great cold in sandwiches, or sliced and pan fried in a little oil to reheat and crisp the outsides; serve with ketchup. Toast nuts in advance and hold until required, or chop and have them toasting while you chop the vegetables for best time management. Use the largest bowl you have; if you have a bread-rising bowl try that one because there is a lot to mix.

1. Line the slow cooker insert with 2 sheets of foil placed in opposite directions, leaving enough foil at both ends to serve as handles. Spray with nonstick spray.

2. Toast the nuts in a large skillet over medium heat, stirring frequently until aromatic and golden, 7 to 8 minutes. Remove from the heat.

3. While the nuts are toasting, combine the onions through the cornstarch in a large bowl; mix well. Add the nuts and stir. Mix in the stock, ensuring that all the mix is evenly dampened.

4. Transfer to the slow cooker and smooth the top. The mix will reach about 2 inches up the sides.

5. Cover, set heat to LOW, and cook for 6 hours, or until the sides are dark brown and the center is just firm and a lighter brown.

6. Uncover, let stand for 10 minutes, and remove from the slow cooker using the foil handles.

7. Let stand another 10 minutes, slice with a serrated knife, and serve. Take care to warn diners there are 2 bay leaves somewhere!

NOTE: Use a food processor or a knife to chop the nuts. They should be in random yet small pieces, no large chunks but not so small as to appear like a nut meal. Take care not to process too long or you could end up with nut butter.

Stuffed and Rolled Seitan Roast

SERVES 4 TO 6

PREPARATION TIME:
45 MINUTES

STUFFING

6 slices fresh bread, crusts
    removed, cut into
    ½-inch cubes
½ medium dessert apple
    such as Gala, peeled,
    cored, and finely
    chopped
½ teaspoon dried thyme
1 teaspoon dried rubbed
    sage
1 teaspoon onion powder
1 teaspoon garlic powder
¼ cup finely chopped fresh
    parsley
¼ cup dried apricots, finely
    chopped

2½ tablespoons vegetable
    stock, store-bought or
    homemade (page 43)
1 teaspoon lemon juice

Salt and black pepper

SEITAN

1½ cups vital wheat gluten
½ cup nutritional yeast
1 teaspoon onion powder
1 teaspoon garlic powder
½ teaspoon powdered
    sage
½ teaspoon dried thyme,
    crumbled
½ teaspoon paprika
¼ teaspoon black pepper
½ cup dry bread crumbs

OKAY, SO THIS isn't all that quick, but I promise it's easier than it seems! This is a pork loin–style roast, sans the pork, of course. This cruelty-free roast is a fancy-looking dish, with moist and tender seitan enclosing a sweet and savory soft stuffing, but is actually very simple to make. The texture is perfectly tender and less firm than other baked seitan dishes, and the flavors are those usually associated with nonvegan roasts, including sage, apple, and apricots in the stuffing. Please don't leave this recipe cooking much longer than the stipulated time, or you may be in for an explosion in your slow cooker! You can also freeze slices of the roast, thawing it overnight in the fridge and then reheating on a small sheet pan at 300°F for 40 minutes, covering it loosely in foil and turning it halfway through. Prior to shaping the seitan dough, measure the widest part of your slow cooker to ensure that when it is rolled and stuffed it will fit. A little extra work, but worth it for the cursing it will save later on if you've rolled your roast and then realize it doesn't fit.

1. For the stuffing, in a large bowl mix the bread through the apricots until well combined.
2. Add the stock and lemon juice; mix until the stuffing is a uniform dampness.
3. Taste and season with the salt and pepper as required.
4. Have ready two 16-inch pieces of foil.
5. For the seitan, in a large bowl whisk together the gluten through the bread crumbs.
6. Using a blender or immersion blender and the cup that comes with it, combine the tofu through the stock, pulsing to ensure the mixture is very smooth with no lumps. Scrape down the sides as required.
7. Pour the blended mix into the seitan ingredients and mix well. Knead in the bowl for 3 to 4 minutes to activate the gluten.
8. Place the short side of one of the pieces of foil in front of you. Spread the dough, press, and roll (with a rolling pin as necessary) into a 6 by 12-inch rectangle, filling any gaps in the seitan so no foil shows through.

166

9. Spread the stuffing on top of the seitan, leaving a ½-inch border of bare seitan along each edge.

10. Roll the seitan over the stuffing toward you, using the foil as a guide to help keep everything tight as you would when making sushi.

11. Place the rolled seitan in the center of the foil. Fold the long sides of the foil up toward the center; they will just meet. Fold the remaining sides up to form a seitan parcel. Roll the seitan parcel in the other 16-inch piece of foil, covering the seal from the first piece and scrunching the ends to seal.

12. Place in the slow cooker; it may be snug if yours is circular in shape. Add the water.

13. Cover, set heat to LOW, and cook for 4 to 4½ hours, until the seitan is aromatic and firm.

14. Using tongs, carefully remove from the slow cooker and remove the foil.

15. For the basting sauce, mix the stock through the liquid smoke in the slow cooker, add the unwrapped roast, and baste with a pastry brush.

16. Uncover, set heat to HIGH, and cook for 45 minutes, basting frequently.

17. Remove the roast from the slow cooker and let stand for at least 5 minutes prior to cutting. The longer it stands the firmer and easier to slice it will become.

18. Cut the finished roast with a serrated knife.

VARIATION:

When you are finished cooking, use the leftover basting liquid to make gravy. Heat the leftover liquid in a saucepan with 2 cloves minced garlic until the garlic sizzles. Add 2 tablespoons all-purpose flour and mix well to form a thick roux. Add soymilk or other nondairy milk ⅓ cup at a time and whisk well after each addition so the sauce thickens smoothly. Add enough milk to make the gravy to your desired thickness.

6 ounces vacuum-packed firm silken tofu
8 ounces regular water-packed firm tofu
1 teaspoon liquid smoke
3 tablespoons soy sauce
2 garlic cloves, minced
1½ teaspoons Dijon mustard
1½ teaspoons prepared yellow mustard
2 teaspoons apple cider vinegar
2 tablespoons unsweetened applesauce
½ cup plus 2 tablespoons vegetable stock, store-bought or homemade (page 43)

1 cup water

BASTING SAUCE
¼ cup vegetable stock
2 tablespoons soy sauce
2 tablespoons olive oil
2 teaspoons liquid smoke

Pasta Bakes and Sauces

OR THIS CHAPTER I adapted both oven-cooked pasta bakes and stovetop-cooked pasta sauces for the slow cooker. I recommend using wheat-based pasta for these recipes because some nonwheat pastas (like corn and rice) don't hold up to the cooking all that well. If you use nonwheat pasta, be aware you'll need to keep a closer eye on it as it cooks and use trial and error to determine which pasta works best and how much you'll need to adjust the cooking times.

Also, each baked pasta recipe has a specific pasta shape noted, but there is no reason why you can't use differently shaped but similarly sized pasta—perhaps what you have in the cupboard.

Pasta cooked in the slow cooker is quite soft, not with a firm al dente bite. If you prefer your pasta al dente, the easiest—though more hands-on—way to achieve it is to put the sauce ingredients in the slow cooker and allow them to cook for 1 hour, then add the pasta and cook for the remaining time. The pasta will retain some bite, and the sauce will thicken and meld as it should.

Sometimes the pasta cooking on the top remains a little crunchier than the rest. If you find this is the case, a quick stir to move that pasta to the bottom about two-thirds of the way through the cooking time will fix the problem and ensure even cooking.

These recipes make a substantial amount to feed the whole family and reheat well in the oven or microwave. The sauces, but not the actual pasta, are also suitable for freezing.

I like the recipes in this chapter best when served with a green salad or salads such as Bean and Olive Salad (page 227) and with vegetable dishes like Peppered Kale (page 225). Also, these dishes are wonderful with baked dishes, in particular Oregano and Sun-Dried Tomato Rolls (page 244).

If I haven't noted so on the recipe, feel free to top each pasta dish with a little grated vegan cheese and broil to melt. If your slow cooker insert is broiler safe then do this in the slow cooker; otherwise serve the pasta onto broiler-safe individual serving plates and broil one at a time.

Pasta with Sun-Dried Tomato, Red Wine, and Sweet Pepper "Pesto"

THIS DECONSTRUCTED SUN-DRIED tomato and pepper pesto is served hot, tossed through pasta. It's a rich, nutty dish lovely for a summer meal with a green salad and some fresh bread such as Oregano and Sun-Dried Tomato Rolls (page 244). The red wine provides a depth of background flavor and quite a lift, but if you don't do wine, use more vegetable stock. To make ahead, roast and chop the peppers, reconstitute and chop the tomatoes, and keep in the fridge.

1. Place the tomatoes in a small bowl, pour the water over them, cover, and let stand for about 15 minutes, until soft. Drain, transfer the liquid to the slow cooker, finely chop the tomatoes, and add to the slow cooker.

2. Pulse the nuts through the basil in a food processor until quite a smooth paste is formed. Add to the slow cooker with the pasta through the stock; mix to combine.

3. Cover, set heat to LOW, and cook for 3 hours, or until the pasta is tender.

4. Stir through the shredded basil, taste, and season with the salt and pepper as required.

5. Sprinkle with a little Dry Chees-y Mix and toasted nuts, if desired.

VARIATION:

PASTA WITH SUN-DRIED TOMATO, RED WINE, BLACK OLIVES, AND SWEET PEPPER "PESTO"

Roughly chop ½ cup black olives and add to the slow cooker with the pasta.

SERVES 4

PREPARATION TIME:
15 MINUTES

½ cup dried sun-dried tomatoes (not oil packed)
1 cup boiling water

½ cup skinned raw almonds
½ cup walnut pieces
¾ cup fresh basil, packed

2 cups uncooked large (about 1-inch long) shell-shape pasta
2 shallots, finely chopped
2 garlic cloves, minced
2 medium roasted red peppers (page 20), finely chopped
2 medium roasted yellow peppers (page 20), finely chopped
½ cup red wine or vegetable stock, store-bought or homemade (page 43)
1 cup vegetable stock, store-bought or homemade

¼ cup shredded fresh basil

Salt and black pepper

Dry Chees-y Mix (page 51), optional
Toasted walnut and almond pieces, optional

Fusilli Puttanesca Style

SERVES 4

PREPARATION TIME:
15 MINUTES

½ medium onion, finely
   chopped
2 garlic cloves, minced
1 jalapeño pepper, seeded
   and minced
1 teaspoon dried oregano
1 teaspoon paprika
¼ teaspoon chile flakes, or
   to taste
1½ cups Simple Tomato
   Sauce (page 55), or one
   15-ounce can
1½ cups tomato juice
½ cup sliced black olives
¼ cup sliced green olives
2 tablespoons capers
¼ cup finely chopped
   fresh basil
2 cups uncooked fusilli
   pasta
1 cup vegetable stock,
   store-bought or
   homemade (page 43)

Salt, black pepper, and hot
   sauce

INSPIRED BY PASTA puttanesca, the southern Italian classic, this is savory, salty, a teensy bit spicy, and a really, really good way to eat pasta. If you love olives, expect to love this dish.

1. Combine the onion through the stock in the slow cooker.
2. Cover, set heat to LOW, and cook for 3 hours, or until the pasta is tender and the sauce is thickened.
3. Taste and season with the salt, pepper, and hot sauce as required.

Tomato Salsa Pasta Bake

THIS IS A little bit of a cheater's dinner—using store-bought salsa to spice up a tomato-based pasta bake—but the addition gives depth of flavor to a simple dish that's paired with vegetables often found in commercial tomato salsa. It's still quite saucy, so it's more suitable for serving in bowls than on plates.

1. Combine the stock though the cilantro in the slow cooker. Add the pasta and mix well. The sauce will look very runny but will be absorbed as it cooks.
2. Taste and season with the salt, pepper, and hot sauce as required.
3. Cover, set heat to LOW, and bake for 2½ to 3 hours, until the pasta is tender and the sauce is somewhat thickened.
4. If the insert is broiler safe, top with vegan cheese, panko, or bread crumbs if desired and broil for 2 to 3 minutes to brown and crisp. Alternatively, transfer individual servings to broiler-safe plates, top, and broil as desired.

SERVES 4 TO 6

PREPARATION TIME:
15 MINUTES

2½ cups vegetable stock, store-bought or homemade (page 43)
One 15-ounce can crushed tomatoes
1½ cups store-bought chunky tomato salsa, your choice of heat
12 cloves Poached Garlic (page 54), mashed if desired
½ cup finely chopped red pepper
¼ cup finely chopped green pepper
½ cup corn kernels, from 1 cob if fresh, frozen, or canned, drained
¼ cup finely chopped red onion
¼ cup finely chopped cilantro

3 cups uncooked fusilli pasta

Salt, black pepper, and hot sauce

Vegan cheese, panko, bread crumbs, or a combination, optional

Southwestern Pasta

SERVES 4

PREPARATION TIME:
20 MINUTES, DIVIDED

½ cup dry pinto beans,
    soaked overnight,
    drained, and rinsed
½ red onion, finely
    chopped
3 garlic cloves, minced
1 bay leaf
1 teaspoon oregano
½ teaspoon chile flakes
2¼ cups vegetable stock,
    store-bought or
    homemade (page 43)

½ red pepper, finely
    chopped
¾ cup corn kernels, 1
    cob if fresh, drained
    and rinsed if canned,
    thawed if frozen
1½ cups uncooked rotini
    pasta
1 cup soymilk

¼ cup vegan sour cream
½ red onion, quartered
    and sliced
¼ cup cilantro, finely
    chopped
2 tablespoons lime juice

Salt and black pepper

Avocado, optional

THIS IS SURPRISINGLY good when it all comes together: creamy beans and tender vegetables with pasta in a tangy creamy sauce, what's not to like? Some of the red onion is added quite late so it retains some crunch and color. If you're not a raw onion fan, add it with the corn and pepper. For extra carbs at dinner, serve topped with slightly crushed corn chips.

1. Combine the beans through stock in the slow cooker.
2. Cover, set heat to LOW, and cook for 6 hours, or until the beans are tender.
3. Add the red pepper through the soy milk and cook for 3 hours, or until the pasta is tender and the liquid is reduced.
4. Stir in the vegan sour cream through the lime juice. Remove the bay leaf.
5. Season with the salt and pepper as required.
6. Serve garnished with slices of avocado, if using.

Penne with Mushrooms and Pine Nuts

I**F YOU LIKE** the earthy, rich taste of mushrooms and the creamy bite of pine nuts, this is the recipe for you! Add ½ cup frozen green peas to the mix about 1 hour before the end of cooking time if you would like a hit of green vegetables. If you find the dish ends up a little too liquid-y for your taste (it will depend on the mushrooms you use and how much liquid they release), thicken with either a cornstarch slurry or a little Dry Chees-y Mix (page 51) stirred through.

1. Heat the nuts in a small skillet over medium heat until toasted and golden, 5 minutes. Stir frequently to ensure even toasting. They should be golden; remove from the heat if they start to turn darker. Transfer ¼ cup of the nuts to a small bowl.

2. In a spice grinder or small blender, blend the remaining ¼ cup of nuts into a powder. In the lid of the spice grinder or in a small bowl, mix the powder with the wine to form a paste.

3. Combine the garlic through the stock in the slow cooker. Add the nut paste and stir to combine.

4. Cover, set heat to LOW, and cook for 3 hours, or until the mushrooms are very tender, the pasta is cooked, and the sauce is partially absorbed and reduced.

5. Stir through the basil and reserved toasted pine nuts. Taste and season with the salt and pepper just prior to serving.

SERVES 4 TO 6

PREPARATION TIME:
20 MINUTES

½ cup pine nuts, or more to taste

¼ cup white wine or vegetable stock, store-bought or homemade (page 43)

2 garlic cloves, minced
1 shallot, minced
4 cups mixed mushrooms such as portobello, cremini, shiitake, white, or oyster, cut into ¼-inch pieces
1 teaspoon dried basil
½ teaspoon salt
Freshly ground black pepper
3 cups uncooked penne pasta
1¾ cups almond milk
1¼ cups vegetable stock

¼ cup shredded fresh basil

Salt and black pepper

Smoky Chickpea Tofu Pasta

SERVES 4 TO 6

PREPARATION TIME:
10 MINUTES

GF *

1 cup dry chickpeas,
  soaked overnight,
  drained, and rinsed
4 cups vegetable stock,
  store-bought or
  homemade (page 43)
¼ cup soy sauce
2 tablespoons maple
  syrup
2 teaspoons liquid smoke
1 teaspoon ancho chile
  powder
1 teaspoon cumin
1 teaspoon smoked
  paprika
1 teaspoon paprika
1 teaspoon garlic powder
1 teaspoon onion powder
¼ teaspoon chile flakes,
  optional, or to taste

2 cups uncooked rotini or
  fusilli pasta
8 ounces smoked tofu, cut
  into ½-inch dice

2 tablespoons olive oil

Salt and black pepper

*Please check all packaged
ingredients, as noted on
page 39.

THIS PASTA BAKE is not your usual pasta dish. It's not overly saucy, just moist and full of smoky flavor. It tastes great hot or cold but has a tendency to get dry after it cools. If you want to serve it cold, toss in a little extra olive oil or stock to help maintain some moisture. If you do end up with extra liquid at the end of the cooking time after removing the pasta, tofu, and chickpeas from the slow cooker, mix a slurry, add to the liquid, and stir for a few minutes while it thickens.

1. Combine the chickpeas through the chile flakes in the slow cooker.
2. Cover, set heat to LOW, and cook for 8 hours, or until the chickpeas are tender.
3. Just prior to the chickpeas being tender, cook the pasta according to package directions until just al dente. Dry sauté the tofu cubes in a nonstick skillet until golden on all sides, about 8 minutes.
4. Add the pasta, tofu, and oil to the slow cooker; stir to combine. Cover and cook on LOW for 15 minutes, or until the flavors have melded.
5. Taste and season with the salt and pepper as required.

Baked Artichoke Pasta

SERVES 4 TO 6

PREPARATION TIME:
10 MINUTES

I CONSIDERED CALLING THIS Baked Tapas Pasta because several additions are classic tapas ingredients: artichoke hearts, capers, olives, and red peppers. It really is comfort food, a touch reminiscent of a traditional tuna noodle casserole (a happy accident!) with a twist from the flavors of those wonderful tapas ingredients. I've also added in an optional topping of cheese and panko or bread crumbs, so use that if you like.

1. In a blender or food processor, blend the artichoke hearts through the pepper until thick, creamy, and smooth. Taste and season with the salt and pepper as required. Place in the slow cooker.

2. Add the pasta through the capers to the slow cooker. The sauce will look runny, but the pasta will absorb liquid as it cooks.

3. Cover, set heat to LOW, and cook for 3 hours, or until the pasta is tender and has absorbed most of the liquid.

4. If desired and if the insert is broiler safe, top with vegan cheese, bread crumbs, and/or thinly sliced vegetables and broil for 2 to 3 minutes until brown and crisp. Alternatively, transfer individual servings to broiler-safe plates, top, and broil as desired.

One 14-ounce can artichoke hearts, drained and rinsed
1 cup vegetable stock, store-bought or homemade (page 43)
6 ounces vacuum-packed firm silken tofu
½ cup plain soy yogurt
½ cup canned coconut milk
½ cup soymilk
2 garlic cloves, roughly chopped
1 teaspoon dried tarragon
1 teaspoon dried rubbed sage
½ teaspoon salt
¼ teaspoon black pepper

Salt and black pepper

3 cups uncooked fusilli pasta
¼ cup sliced green or black olives, or a combination
½ red pepper, finely chopped
1½ tablespoons capers

Vegan cheese, panko or bread crumbs, thinly sliced vegetables such as tomato or red pepper, optional

Creamy Leek and Almond Pasta

SERVES 4 TO 6

PREPARATION TIME:
20 MINUTES

2 tablespoons slivered
almonds or chopped
skinned almonds

1 tablespoon olive oil

4 large leeks, washed
and trimmed, halved
lengthwise and finely
sliced

2 cups almond milk
½ cup vegan mayonnaise
½ cup vegan unsweetened
plain yogurt
¼ cup ground almonds
1¼ cups vegetable stock,
store-bought or
homemade (page 43)
½ teaspoon salt
¼ teaspoon black pepper
2 tablespoons fresh dill,
finely chopped, or 2
teaspoons dried dill

3 cups uncooked small
shell-shaped pasta

Salt and black pepper

YOU'RE GETTING BOTH vegetables and a little protein in this dish, so you *could* pretend it is healthy. After one bite you'll more likely be thinking about how incredibly good and satisfying this creamy and filling super comfort food is. Very quick and easy to prepare, and just right for a cool autumn evening.

1. Toast the almonds in a large, dry skillet over medium heat until golden, 3 to 4 minutes. Remove from the heat and place in a small bowl.
2. In the same skillet, heat the oil over medium heat, add the leeks, and sauté until they are soft and bright green, 5 minutes. Transfer to the slow cooker.
3. Add the almond milk through the dill; stir until well combined. Stir in the pasta.
4. Cover, set heat to LOW, and cook for 2½ to 3 hours, until the pasta is tender.
5. Garnish with the toasted almonds.

VARIATION:

SPICED LEEK AND ALMOND PASTA

Add a pinch of nutmeg as a slight flavor variation. Taste and season as required.

"GREENED" LEEK AND ALMOND PASTA

Add cooked green peas or asparagus to the final dish for a springtime lift.

Autumn Baked Macaroni

A WONDERFULLY WARMING DISH that screams "harvest time." Perfect for a fall evening after a day jumping in piles of leaves! Don't be frightened of the cranberries in the ingredients list: They add a burst of flavor and a splash of color that is very welcome in this autumnal pasta bake. The hint of sweetness they provide really lifts the natural sweetness in the squash and provides an intense contrast to the herbs and savory base. This dish has been called "Fall in a Bowl" and is nice served with a dollop of vegan sour cream on top to really make it more delicious. If you don't have access to fresh sage, that is fine; it just adds a further depth of sage flavor to the finished dish.

1. Preheat the oven to 425°F. In a 9 x 13-inch baking pan, toss together the squash through the sage leaves, if using. Season with the salt and pepper to taste.

2. Roast the squash for 20 minutes, turning halfway through the cooking time, until soft and just a little caramelized. Remove the sage leaves. Transfer squash to the slow cooker, scraping in any cooked-on bits.

3. Add the shallot through the macaroni to the slow cooker. Stir well to combine.

4. Cover, set heat to LOW, and cook for 3 hours, or until the pasta is tender and the sauce is very thick.

5. Taste and season with the salt and pepper as required.

6. If the insert is broiler safe and if desired, sprinkle with a little cheese and melt under the broiler just prior to serving. Alternatively, transfer individual servings to broiler-safe plates, top, and broil as desired.

SERVES 4 TO 6

PREPARATION TIME:
30 MINUTES, INCLUDING
ROASTING THE SQUASH

 in the Dry Chees-y Mix

½ medium butternut squash cut into ¼-inch pieces
1 tablespoon Garlic Infused Oil (page 54) or olive oil
½ teaspoon dried thyme
½ teaspoon powdered dried sage
Fresh sage leaves, optional

Salt and black pepper

1 shallot, finely chopped
2 garlic cloves, minced
6 cloves Poached Garlic (page 54), mincing optional
2 tablespoons Dry Chees-y Mix (page 51)
1 teaspoon dried rubbed sage
½ teaspoon dried thyme
½ teaspoon salt
¼ teaspoon black pepper
2¼ cups vegetable stock, store-bought or homemade (page 43)
1 cup canned pumpkin puree
¼ cup dried cranberries, sweetened or unsweetened
3 cups uncooked macaroni elbows

Salt and black pepper

Vegan cheese, optional

"Not-Meat" Balls and Spaghetti

SERVES 4

PREPARATION TIME:
20 MINUTES

SF

 N if using the Dry
Chees-y Mix

1½ cups Simple Tomato
    Sauce (page 55), or one
    15-ounce can
1½ cups tomato juice
¾ cup vegetable stock,
    store-bought or
    homemade (page 43)
½ teaspoon garlic powder
½ teaspoon onion powder
½ teaspoon dried basil

¾ cup (½ recipe) Chipotle
    Lentil Pâté (page 50)
1 cup cooked millet
2 tablespoons olive oil
1 tablespoon tomato paste
½ teaspoon dried oregano
½ teaspoon dried
    marjoram
⅛ teaspoon ground fennel
    seeds
¼ teaspoon salt

¾ cup vital wheat gluten

Olive oil

Uncooked spaghetti for 4
    servings

Dry Chees-y Mix (page
    51), optional
Vegan Parmesan

SING WITH ME: "On top of Spaghetti, all covered with Teese, I lost my 'Not-Meat' Ball, when somebody sneezed." Or just eat these luscious balls on your spaghetti instead! A hint of the chipotle remains in the finished balls, enough for your tongue to be trying to figure out what the delicious back note is. If you are cooking millet specifically for this dish, start with ⅓ cup dry millet; it will triple in volume when cooked. This dish is inclined to stick a little, so be prepared to soak the insert in some hot soapy water for ease of cleanup.

1. Combine the tomato sauce through the basil in the slow cooker.
2. In a large bowl, with a fork, mix the pâté through the salt.
3. Add the gluten and mix well with the fork. With your hand knead in the bowl for 3 to 4 minutes to activate the gluten. Shape into 16 equal-sized balls and allow to rest. Discard any millet that is not incorporated in the balls.
4. Heat a little oil in a large skillet over medium-high heat. Sear the balls to brown the outsides and form a crust, 4 to 5 minutes total, turning as required. The millet may spit a little, so keep out of the way.
5. Transfer the balls to the sauce mix in the slow cooker. The balls should form a single layer with some gaps (they will expand as they cook) and be completely submerged in the liquid.
6. Cover, set heat to LOW, and cook for 4 hours. The balls will have expanded and will be firm yet moist and cooked all the way through. The liquid will have been absorbed and reduced until thick and coating the balls.
7. As the end of the slow cooking time approaches, cook the spaghetti according to package directions; drain and place in individual bowls.
8. Serve the balls and sauce over the spaghetti with a sprinkling of Dry Chees-y Mix or vegan Parmesan, if desired.

180

Penne with Sausage and Tomato Sauce

THE SAUSAGE YOU use will determine the final flavor profile of the dish, so ensure you choose one you like to pair with the creamy tomato sauce. Any sausage (homemade or store-bought) will be yummy; each time the result will be slightly different.

1. Combine the shallots through the tomatoes in the slow cooker.
2. Stir in the pasta.
3. Cover, set heat to LOW, and cook for 3 hours, or until the pasta is tender.
4. Taste and season with the salt and pepper as required.
5. Serve hot with the cheeses sprinkled on top, if desired.

VARIATION:

SUPER SPICY PASTA WITH SAUSAGE AND TOMATO SAUCE

Use Chipotle Lentil Sausages (page 49) as your sausage, and if you're looking for a real kick, mince a jalapeño and add with the garlic and shallots. Add some chile flakes with the spices, too, if you really want it hot.

SERVES 4

PREPARATION TIME: 10 MINUTES

 if using the Dry Chees-y Mix

2 finely chopped shallots, about ¼ cup
2 garlic cloves, minced
½ pound vegan sausages, store-bought or homemade (page 49, ½ recipe), cut into ½-inch pieces (about 2 cups)
1 teaspoon dried rubbed sage
½ teaspoon salt
1 teaspoon dried oregano
1 teaspoon dried basil
1 teaspoon smoked paprika
½ cup plus 2 tablespoons soy creamer, store-bought or homemade (page 56)
½ cup vegetable stock, store-bought or homemade (page 43)
One 15-ounce can diced tomatoes, fire roasted if possible

1 cup uncooked penne pasta

Salt and black pepper

Dry Chees-y Mix (page 51), vegan Parmesan, or grated vegan cheese, optional

Lasagna

SERVES 6 TO 8

PREPARATION TIME:
25 MINUTES, DIVIDED

N in the Dry Chees-y Mix

1 cup TVP granules
1½ cups tomato juice
1 cup vegetable stock,
    store-bought or
    homemade (page 43)
3 tablespoons tomato
    paste
1 teaspoon oregano
1 teaspoon basil
1 teaspoon paprika
1 teaspoon garlic powder
1 teaspoon onion powder
1 teaspoon salt
½ teaspoon black pepper
⅛ teaspoon nutmeg

Salt and black pepper

12 ounces lasagna
    noodles, cooked 2
    minutes less than
    package directions to
    be very al dente

1½ cups Dry Chees-y Mix
    (page 51)
1 cup soymilk
1 cup soy creamer, store-
    bought or homemade
    (page 56)
½ cup water
1 tablespoon cornstarch

¼ cup grated vegan
    cheese, optional

¼ cup canned crushed
    tomatoes or tomato
    sauce

Salt and black pepper

Vegan cheese, optional

THIS RECIPE COMBINES tender pasta layered with a spiced savory "meat" sauce and a creamy "cheese" sauce, just as the traditional version does. I love to serve this with a green salad and garlic bread on the side. If I don't feel up to making actual garlic bread, I like to make an impromptu variation: Take a wheat tortilla, spread with some mashed Poached Garlic (page 54), and bake for 8 to 10 minutes until crisp. Alternatively, I drizzle the top of the finished lasagna with a little homemade or store-bought pesto for an extra Italian flavor. Cook the lasagna noodles and prepare the sauce at the end of the TVP cooking time, or prepare the TVP in advance and assemble when required.

1. Combine the TVP through the nutmeg in the slow cooker. Cover, set heat to LOW, and cook for 4 hours, or until the TVP is tender.

2. Turn off the slow cooker and transfer the TVP mix to a large bowl. Taste and season as required.

3. Cook the noodles while making the sauce. Combine the Dry Chees-y Mix through the cornstarch in a small saucepan. Heat over medium heat, stirring frequently until thickened, about 8 to 10 minutes.

4. Stir in grated vegan cheese, if desired.

5. Place the tomatoes in the bottom of the slow cooker and spread to a thin, even layer, which will stop the bottom layer from drying too much.

6. Layer the lasagna on top of the tomato: ½ of the TVP sauce, ⅓ of the noodles, ½ of the chees-y sauce, ⅓ of the noodles, the remaining TVP sauce, the remaining noodles, and finish with the remaining chees-y sauce.

7. Cover, set heat to HIGH, and cook for 1½ to 2 hours, until the pasta is tender.

8. Top with vegan cheese if desired, and if the insert is broiler safe, broil until bubbly and the chees-y sauce is browned. Alternatively, transfer individual servings to broiler-safe plates, cover each with a little vegan cheese, and broil.

VARIATIONS:

Add a layer of fresh basil leaves or mashed Poached Garlic (page 54) between the layers of the lasagna.

Chees-y Mac

SERVES 6 TO 8

PREPARATION TIME:
20 MINUTES

Ⓝ in the Dry Chees-y Mix

1 tablespoon vegan
    margarine
1 tablespoon grapeseed
    oil

3 garlic cloves, minced
1 shallot, finely chopped
¾ cup finely chopped
    canned artichoke
    hearts, drained and
    rinsed (4 hearts)

3 tablespoons all-purpose
    flour
¼ cup plus 2 tablespoons
    Dry Chees-y Mix (page
    51)
¼ teaspoon turmeric
¼ teaspoon salt

1 cup plus 2 tablespoons
    canned coconut milk
1½ teaspoons Dijon or
    other mild mustard

2 cups soymilk
1 cup vegetable stock,
    store-bought or
    homemade (page 43)
3 cups uncooked macaroni
    elbows

Salt and black pepper

½ cup grated vegan
    cheese or to taste,
    optional

A SIMPLE, ONE-POT MACARONI and "cheese" that is rich, creamy, and thick. The coconut milk provides a rich creaminess without a coconut taste. The artichoke hearts provide an integral background salty creaminess, so they're not just vegetables! Be warned, however: The dish does look slightly green from the artichoke—not a vibrant green, just a little off the usual mac and cheese color. If you like a crust, top with vegan cheese and a sprinkle of panko. Broil until the cheese is melted and the panko toasted, either in the insert if it is broiler safe or on individual serving plates. You can even add sliced tomatoes or peppers to broil. This is a dish that grows on you—you may start off unsure about it, but you'll take another bite, then another, until suddenly you've eaten the whole bowl!

1. Heat the margarine and oil in a medium skillet over medium heat until melted and combined.
2. Sauté the garlic through the artichokes until soft and lightly browned, 5 minutes.
3. To make a light roux, add the flour through the salt and cook for 1 to 2 minutes, stirring well.
4. Add the coconut milk and mustard; stir until a thick paste-like consistency is formed. Add ½ cup of the soymilk and stir until smooth.
5. Transfer the sauce, remaining soy milk, stock, and pasta to the slow cooker. Stir well to combine.
6. Cover, set heat to LOW, and cook for 3 hours, or until the pasta is tender and the sauce is thick.
7. Taste and season with the salt and pepper as required.
8. Stir in the cheese, if using. Let stand for 10 minutes to allow the cheese to melt.

VARIATION:

Add thawed frozen green peas or cooked broccoli florets for the last 15 minutes of cooking, if you like your cheesy mac with more veggies.

Green Pasta Sauce

MAINLY, BUT NOT only, for tossing through your cooked pasta—perhaps alongside some other vegetables (broccoli, anyone?) and tossed with some toasted pine nuts. This delicious and vibrantly green sauce is a wonderful change from tomato- and cream-based sauces. If you don't like or can't find arugula, use only spinach.

1. Place the margarine in the slow cooker and set heat to HIGH, allowing the margarine to soften. Stir in the flour and salt until well combined, about 1 minute.

2. Add the stock and stir until it is incorporated; repeat with the soymilk.

3. Add the onions through the cilantro; stir to combine. The greens will fill the slow cooker and not be completely covered by the liquid.

4. Cover, set heat to LOW, and cook for 1 hour. Stir the now-wilted greens into the liquid. Cover and cook, still on LOW, for 2 hours, or until the mixture is thickened and bright green.

5. Use an immersion blender to blend until smooth, creamy, and green. Add the lemon juice.

6. Taste and season with the salt, pepper, and lemon juice as required. Add stock or even pasta cooking water if the sauce is too thick.

7. Refrigerate in a covered container for up to 1 week. When reheating, do so gently.

MAKES ABOUT 3 CUPS

**PREPARATION TIME:
10 MINUTES**

¼ cup vegan margarine

¼ cup plus 1 tablespoon
 all-purpose flour
½ teaspoon salt

1 cup vegetable stock,
 store-bought or
 homemade (page 43)
1 cup soy milk

6 spring onions, green
 onions, or scallions,
 white and green parts
 finely chopped
4 garlic cloves, minced
1 teaspoon agave
¼ cup plus 2 tablespoons
 finely chopped fresh
 parsley
4 cups baby arugula,
 packed
2 cups baby spinach,
 packed
½ cup cilantro leaves,
 packed

1 teaspoon lemon juice

Salt, black pepper, and
 lemon juice
Vegetable stock, optional

Creamy Garlic Pasta Sauce

MAKES ABOUT 5 CUPS

**PREPARATION TIME:
10 MINUTES**

4 heads garlic, separated
  into cloves, bases
  removed and peeled
  (about 45 cloves)
1 cup canola or grapeseed
  oil

1½ cups raw cashews,
  soaked overnight,
  drained, and rinsed

2 cups vegetable stock,
  store-bought or
  homemade (page 43)
1 cup almond milk
¼ cup Dry Chees-y Mix
  (page 51)
2 tablespoons cornstarch

Salt and black pepper

*Please check all packaged
ingredients, as noted on
page 39.

ALTHOUGH THE GARLIC is mellow and smooth thanks to
the poaching, this dish really is for garlic lovers. It's also not
a low-fat recipe, but the result is so thick, rich, and creamy that
it is worth the splurge. Use this sauce not only to toss with
pasta but to replace a béchamel or chees-y sauce in Lasagna
(page 182), or anywhere else you'd like an extra garlic lift. If
you're using a regular food processor to pulse the nuts, remember
to give the motor rests so it doesn't overheat. The result may
not be completely smooth, but it will still be good.

1. Combine the garlic and oil in the slow cooker. The garlic
   should be covered by the oil.
2. Cover, set heat to LOW, and cook for 2 hours until garlic
   is soft.
3. In a powerful blender or food processor pulse the cashews
   until finely chopped.
4. Add the garlic and oil from the slow cooker and process
   until smooth and creamy.
5. Add the stock through the cornstarch; blend until well
   combined and silky smooth.
6. Return to the slow cooker, stir to combine. Cover, set heat
   to LOW, and cook for 2 hours, or until thick and smooth.
7. Taste and season with the salt and pepper as required.

Lentil "Spag Bol" Sauce

A TOMATO-PACKED, VIBRANTLY FLAVORED, protein-rich topping for your spaghetti. Not exactly what you'd be eating in Bologna, but very good all the same. For a thicker sauce, cook a while longer. For a thinner sauce, add stock.

1. Combine the garlic through the whole tomatoes in the slow cooker.
2. Cover, set heat to LOW, and cook for 6 hours, or until the lentils are tender and the sauce is thick.
3. Taste and season with the salt and pepper as required.

SERVES 4

PREPARATION TIME: 15 MINUTES

3 garlic cloves, minced
1 stalk celery, finely chopped
½ medium onion, finely chopped
2 teaspoons dried basil
1½ teaspoons paprika, preferably smoked
1 teaspoon dried oregano
2 tablespoons balsamic vinegar
2 tablespoons tomato paste
1 teaspoon liquid smoke
1 cup red lentils, picked over and rinsed
2 cups vegetable stock, store-bought or homemade (page 43)
One 15-ounce can crushed tomatoes
One 15-ounce can whole tomatoes, fire roasted if possible

Salt and black pepper
Additional stock as required

*Please check all packaged ingredients, as noted on page 39.

Grains and Sides

LTHOUGH "SIDES" IS part of this chapter's name, several of these grain dishes are hearty and substantial enough to be meals in their own right, maybe with a side of vegetables or salad. Many recipes are versions of stovetop and oven-baked dishes I love and really are main meals loaded with proteins and veggies. I like them as lunch dishes, but you can make that call for yourself.

However, feel free to use the heavier recipes as side dishes to chilies, stews, or curries; just take care you match the flavors or you may end up with menu discord. The more obvious side dishes suit all sorts of menus and are especially good for the holidays, when having the side in the slow cooker makes for easy transport and less stress. Mix and match as you will.

If you are worried about cooking the grains evenly, when at least half the cooking time has elapsed, give the dish a quick stir to move things around if you can. Otherwise, don't worry; all will be okay.

For leftover grains, store in the fridge for up to 3 days and reheat in a skillet, oven, or microwave until piping hot all the way through. For risotto-based dishes, you can form leftovers into balls, coat with panko or bread crumbs, and fry to make risotto balls, as good as any restaurant makes.

Italian Barley

I LIKE THIS DISH as a lunch; it's not overly herby, instead nicely balanced and quite hearty. I like to have a little something on the side, such as Chees-y Crackers (page 240). Leftovers can be served cold as a salad. Please soak the barley in advance. This softens the grain, shortens the cooking time, and rinses out some of the starch that would otherwise leave cooked barley a bit slimy.

1. Combine the onion through the wine in the slow cooker.
2. Cover, set heat to LOW, and cook for 4 hours, or until the barley is tender and the liquid is mostly absorbed.
3. Add the basil, taste, and season with the salt and pepper as required.

VARIATION

SOUTHWESTERN BARLEY

Combine the following in the slow cooker. Cover, set heat to LOW, and cook for 4 hours. Season with salt, black pepper, lime juice, and hot sauce just prior to serving.

1 cup pearl barley, soaked overnight, drained and rinsed
2¼ cups vegetable stock, store-bought or homemade (page 43)
2½ tablespoons lime juice
1 tablespoon agave
1 teaspoon liquid smoke
1 teaspoon garlic powder
1 teaspoon onion powder
½ teaspoon salt
¾ cup corn kernels, if canned, drained and rinsed, from 1 cob if fresh
½ medium red onion, finely chopped
½ medium red pepper, finely chopped
1 jalapeño pepper, seeded and minced
½ cup cilantro, finely chopped

SERVES 6 TO 8

PREPARATION TIME:
5 MINUTES

½ onion, finely chopped
2 garlic cloves, minced
2 tablespoons tomato
    paste
1 teaspoon dried basil
1 teaspoon dried oregano
½ teaspoon salt
¼ teaspoon black pepper
1½ cups pearl barley,
    soaked overnight,
    drained, and rinsed
One 15-ounce can white
    kidney or cannellini
    beans, drained and
    rinsed, or 1½ cups
    cooked
2 cups plus 2 tablespoons
    vegetable stock, store-
    bought or homemade
    (page 43)
¾ cup canned diced
    tomatoes in juice,
    undrained
½ cup tomato juice
¼ cup red wine or
    vegetable stock

¼ cup fresh basil or flat-
    leaf (Italian) parsley,
    shredded

Salt and black pepper

Classic Polenta

SERVES 4 TO 6

PREPARATION TIME:
25 MINUTES

1 tablespoon olive oil
2 garlic cloves, minced

½ medium onion, finely
    chopped

1 tablespoon white
    wine, or vegetable
    stock, store-bought or
    homemade (page 43)

4½ cups boiling vegetable
    stock

1 cup fine cornmeal

Salt and black pepper

*Please check all packaged
ingredients, as noted on
page 39.

POLENTA WORKS REALLY well in the slow cooker, becoming smooth and luscious, which was a surprise to me the first time I tried it because I thought it had to be stirred and stirred, then stirred some more to get the texture right. Not so. I love using this cooking method with all sorts of flavor combinations. Following the basic recipe are some ideas for delicious variations, or you can make up your own. Some are similar to the options given for risotto (page 196); I find the flavor combinations work well with both.

1. Heat the oil in a large skillet over medium-high heat. Add the garlic and allow to sizzle briefly.
2. Add the onion, toss to coat, and cook, stirring occasionally until soft and lightly browned, about 10 minutes.
3. Deglaze the skillet with the wine, and transfer the contents of the skillet to the slow cooker.
4. Add the stock to the slow cooker. Stir.
5. While stirring, pour in the cornmeal in a continuous stream, ensuring no lumps form. The cornmeal will thicken a little.
6. Cover, set heat to LOW, and cook for 5 hours until all the liquid is absorbed and the polenta is tender.
7. Taste and season as required.

VARIATIONS

FRIED POLENTA
Instead of serving the polenta directly from the slow cooker, spread in a 9 by 13-inch baking pan, refrigerate for at least one hour until firm (which may be done well in advance), slice and pan fry in a little oil in a large skillet until golden and crisp.

FENNEL AND ROSEMARY
Sauté 1 finely chopped fennel bulb with the onion, and add 1 teaspoon of finely chopped fresh parsley with the stock.

192

SUN-DRIED TOMATO AND OLIVE

Add 2 tablespoons finely chopped sun-dried tomatoes and ¼ cup finely chopped green olives with the onion. Stir ¼ cup of black olives into the polenta just prior to serving to avoid discoloration.

POACHED GARLIC AND BROCCOLI

Sauté 2 cups finely chopped broccoli with the onion in a little Garlic Infused Oil (page 54), add with 4 to 6 cloves Poached Garlic (page 54) to the slow cooker.

SPINACH AND SMOKY TOFU

Add ½ cup Smoked Tofu, homemade (page 27) or commercially prepared, and 2 finely chopped shallots to the skillet in place of the onion. Sauté for only 5 minutes. Add 1 packed cup of baby spinach with 30 minutes cooking time remaining and allow to wilt.

ASPARAGUS

Use Asparagus Stock (page 44) instead of the vegetable stock. Just prior to serving, lightly sauté 1 cup asparagus cut into ½-inch lengths; allow to sizzle briefly until the asparagus is bright green but still crisp, then stir through the cooked polenta.

PEPPER AND CAPER

For a puttanesca-style polenta, sauté 1 finely chopped red pepper with the garlic and onion. Add chile flakes to taste and 2 tablespoons of capers before adding to the slow cooker.

GARLIC AND HERB

Sauté 3 cloves of minced garlic and 1 shallot in olive oil, instead of the garlic and onion as above, then add finely chopped fresh herbs of your choice to the stock.

DECONSTRUCTED PESTO

Use Garlic Infused Oil (page 54) and Poached Garlic (page

54) to taste instead of the olive oil and garlic as above; when finished cooking, stir through at least ¼ cup fresh basil and at least ¼ cup toasted pine nuts.

MEXICAN ROASTED CORN

Roast 1 cob of corn either on the grill or under the broiler until lightly charred, remove the kernels from the cob, and add to the slow cooker with the polenta. Also add ½ teaspoon oregano and a pinch of chile flakes. At the end of the cooking time, stir through 1 or 2 tablespoons lime juice (to taste) and 2 tablespoons finely chopped cilantro. Serve with Simple Tomato Sauce (page 55), vegan sour cream, or both.

Classic Risotto

RISOTTO CAN WORK really well in the slow cooker, which was a surprise the first time I tried it because generally speaking, you have to take a lot of care when using rice in the slow cooker, and risotto is renowned for being a little finicky. Be sure to choose a specific risotto rice, such as Arborio or Carnaroli, because regular short grain rice doesn't have the starch content to work in this application. I thought I'd give you a basic method, followed by some ideas so you can make your own slow cooker risotto variations however you like; check out my suggestions on the next page.

1. Heat the oil in a large skillet over medium-high heat. Add the garlic and allow to sizzle briefly.
2. Add the shallot, toss to coat, and cook, stirring occasionally until soft and lightly browned, about 5 minutes.
3. Add the rice and toss to coat.
4. Use the wine to deglaze the skillet, cook until mostly absorbed, and transfer to the slow cooker.
5. Add the stock to the slow cooker and stir.
6. Cover, set heat to LOW, and cook for 1½ to 2 hours.
7. Remove from the slow cooker when done so the residual heat doesn't overcook the rice.
8. Taste and season with the salt and pepper as required.

NOTE: You may need to adjust the cooking time to suit your slow cooker and your preferred texture. If you do, make sure to note down the new time for future reference.

SERVES 4 TO 6

PREPARATION TIME:
20 MINUTES

1 tablespoon olive oil
2 garlic cloves, minced
1 shallot, finely chopped

1 cup risotto rice, such as Arborio or Carnaroli

2 tablespoons white wine, or vegetable stock, store-bought or homemade (page 43)

3¼ cups vegetable stock

Salt and black pepper

*Please check all packaged ingredients, as noted on page 39.

RISOTTO VARIATIONS:

Don't limit yourself to these ideas, but use them to create your own dishes when you are comfortable with the basics. And when these become second nature, try some even fancier variations, like my Asparagus and Pine Nut Vodka Risotto (page 197) or Tomato and Walnut Risotto (page 198).

POACHED GARLIC AND BROCCOLI

Use Poached Garlic (page 54) in place of the minced garlic. Sauté 1½ cups of broccoli in a little Garlic Infused Oil (page 54) in a medium skillet over medium-high heat until bright green and still crisp, 3 to 4 minutes. Add to the slow cooker with some more Poached Garlic once the risotto is cooked.

SPINACH AND SMOKY TOFU

Add commercially prepared or homemade Smoked Tofu (page 27) and sautéed shallots to the slow cooker with the rice. Add 1 packed cup baby spinach in the last 15 minutes to wilt.

MUSHROOM

Saute ½ cup finely chopped mushrooms with the garlic and shallot. Use Mushroom Stock (page 44) as your liquid and stir in ½ cup sautéed mushrooms at the end of the cooking time. I like shiitakes for the chewiness they add.

PUTTANESCA STYLE

Sauté one finely chopped red pepper with the garlic and shallot; add finely chopped olives, chile flakes to taste, and 2 tablespoons capers before adding to the slow cooker with the rice.

HERBED RISOTTO

Add ½ teaspoon dried basil, ½ teaspoon dried oregano, or any other herbs you wish along with the rice to the slow cooker. Finish with ½ cup shredded fresh basil stirred through once the rice is cooked.

Asparagus and Pine Nut Vodka Risotto

INSTEAD OF WHITE wine, which is the liquid you'd expect to see in risotto, I made this one with vodka, which, while subtle, really allows the flavors of the asparagus to shine. Don't discard the hard ends of the asparagus; freeze for making stock. See Classic Risotto (page 195) for hints on making your own risotto variations.

1. Toast the pine nuts in a medium skillet over medium heat until aromatic and golden, taking care not to burn, about 5 minutes. Transfer ½ cup to the slow cooker and the remaining ¼ cup to a spice grinder or small food processor.

2. Grind the nuts to a fine powder. In the lid of the spice grinder or a small bowl, combine the nuts with the water and mix to form a paste.

3. Place the oil in the same skillet and sauté the onion through the pepper until the onion is translucent, about 5 minutes.

4. Add the rice and toss to coat.

5. Use the vodka to deglaze the skillet, cook until mostly absorbed, 2 minutes, and transfer to the slow cooker.

6. Add the stock and nut paste to the slow cooker and stir to combine.

7. Cover, set heat to LOW, and cook for 1 hour, or until the rice is almost tender and the liquid nearly absorbed.

8. Add the asparagus, cover, and cook for 1 hour, or until both the rice and asparagus are tender. Remove from the slow cooker so the residual heat doesn't overcook the rice or asparagus.

9. Taste and season with the salt and pepper as required.

SERVES 4

PREPARATION TIME: 20 MINUTES

 GF * SF N

¾ cup pine nuts

2 tablespoons water

1 tablespoon Garlic Infused Oil (page 54) or olive oil

½ medium onion, finely chopped

4 cloves Poached Garlic (page 54), minced

½ teaspoon salt

¼ teaspoon black pepper

1 cup Arborio (risotto) rice

½ cup vodka, white wine, or vegetable stock, store-bought or homemade (page 43)

2¾ cups Asparagus Stock (page 44), vegetable stock, or a combination

One bunch (½ pound) asparagus, hard ends removed, chopped into ¼-inch lengths

Salt and black pepper

*Please check all packaged ingredients, as noted on page 39.

Tomato and Walnut Risotto

SERVES 4

PREPARATION TIME:
45 MINUTES

3 tablespoons untoasted
   walnuts
1 tablespoon water

2 tablespoons olive oil
½ medium onion, finely
   chopped
2 garlic cloves, minced
1 shallot, minced
1 celery stalk, finely
   chopped

1 cup Arborio (risotto) rice
1 teaspoon dried oregano
¼ teaspoon salt
¼ teaspoon black pepper

1 cup vegetable stock,
   store-bought or
   homemade (page 43)

1 cup vegetable stock
One 15-ounce can crushed
   tomatoes, undrained
⅓ cup sun-dried tomatoes,
   finely chopped

½ cup toasted walnut
   pieces

Salt and black pepper

*Please check all packaged
ingredients, as noted on
page 39.

THIS ONE IS so very good even though at first glance you'd be forgiven for wondering how on earth it works. The nutty walnuts combine well with the tart-sweet vibrancy of the tomatoes and elevate both flavors to the sublime. The nuts can be toasted in advance and held until required, or done first, before the skillet is used for sautéing the vegetables. Other nuts—pecans, almonds, or hazelnuts—can be substituted for the walnuts if necessary.

1. In a mini food processor or spice grinder, grind the untoasted walnuts into a fine meal, taking care not to grind into walnut butter. Using the lid of the spice grinder or a small bowl, mix with the water until a smooth paste forms. Place in the slow cooker.

2. Heat the oil in a large skillet, over medium heat, and sauté the onion through the celery until soft but not browned, 5 minutes. Add the rice through the pepper and sauté for 2 minutes.

3. Add the 1 cup vegetable stock to the rice, stirring constantly until most of the liquid is absorbed.

4. Transfer the rice mix to the slow cooker, and add the remaining stock through the sun-dried tomatoes. Stir well.

5. Cover, turn heat to LOW, and cook for about 2½ hours, until the rice is tender and liquid absorbed.

6. Reserve 1½ tablespoons of the toasted walnuts to use as garnish; add the remaining toasted nuts to the risotto. Stir in, turn off the heat, cover, and stand for 10 minutes.

7. Taste and season with the salt and pepper as required.

8. Garnish, if desired, with the reserved toasted walnuts sprinkled on top of each bowl and serve.

Red Rice and Beans

IF YOU'VE EVER seen red rice in your grocery store and wondered how to use it, here's a recipe to get you started. When cooked the rice is quite chewy, with an earthy flavor that combines really well with the beans and paprika. And yes, the beans are red, the rice is red, the spices are red, the peppers are red, and the tomatoes, which accent everything at the end, are red, so that is where the name came from. Inspired, right? If you don't have access to red rice, use a long-grain brown rice without soaking and reduce the cooking time to 3 to 3½ hours. Check that everything is cooked toward the end of the cooking time and extend if required.

1. Combine the rice through the stock in the slow cooker.
2. Cover, set heat to LOW, and cook for 4 to 4½ hours, until the rice is tender and the liquid is absorbed.
3. Stir in the tomato and cilantro just prior to serving. Taste and season with the salt and black pepper as required.

SERVES 4

PREPARATION TIME:
20 MINUTES

1 cup red rice, soaked overnight, drained, and rinsed
One 15-ounce can red kidney beans (see warning on page 24), or 1½ cups cooked
1 teaspoon smoked paprika
1 teaspoon paprika
1 teaspoon cumin
¾ teaspoon salt
½ red onion, finely chopped
2 garlic cloves, minced
1 roasted red pepper (page 20), finely chopped
1¾ cups plus 2 tablespoons vegetable stock, store-bought or homemade (page 43)

2 Roma tomatoes, seeds removed and finely chopped
¼ cup cilantro, finely chopped

Salt and black pepper

*Please check all packaged ingredients, as noted on page 39.

Rice and (Pigeon) Peas

SERVES 4

PREPARATION TIME:
20 MINUTES, DIVIDED

½ cup dry pigeon peas, soaked overnight, drained, and rinsed (see Note)
2½ cups water
1 bay leaf

1 tablespoon Garlic Infused Oil (page 54) or canola oil
1 cup long-grain brown rice
1 teaspoon cumin seeds
1 teaspoon crushed coriander seeds

½ medium onion, finely chopped
4 cloves Poached Garlic (page 54), minced
2 tablespoons cilantro stalk and leaves, finely chopped

1½ cups plus ⅓ cup vegetable stock, store-bought or homemade (page 43)
½ teaspoon cumin
½ teaspoon coriander
½ teaspoon salt

Salt and black pepper

*Please check all packaged ingredients, as noted on page 39.

THE FIRST TIME I tasted pigeon peas I fell in love. These legumes are creamy, earthy, and very satisfying. Here I have paired them with rice, though my pairing is certainly less authentic than traditional Jamaican rice and peas (usually baked). I like this as a lunch with nothing added, but I have also used leftovers as a side dish for chili or Latin-inspired baked tofu. Look for dried pigeon peas in Indian spice stores or wherever you buy Latin foods. If you are concerned about crunchy rice, stir the dish after 2 hours so the rice is moved around the slow cooker. At this stage you can add up to ¼ cup more stock if you feel your rice is absorbing it too quickly. There are whole and ground versions of the same spices in this recipe; it is not a mistake!

1. Combine the peas through the bay leaf in the slow cooker.
2. Cover, set heat to LOW, and cook for 8 hours, or until just tender. Drain, discarding the bay leaf and cooking water. Keep the peas in the slow cooker.
3. Heat the oil in a large skillet over medium heat; toast the rice and seeds until aromatic, the seeds start popping, and rice is lightly golden, 3 to 4 minutes.
4. Add the onion through the cilantro to the skillet and sauté to combine and soften the onion, 3 minutes.
5. Transfer to the slow cooker with the stock through the ½ teaspoon salt.
6. Cover, set heat to LOW, and cook 2½ to 3 hours, until the rice is tender, stirring after 2 hours, if desired
7. Taste and season with the salt and pepper as required, fluff with a fork, and let stand 10 minutes prior to serving.

NOTE: If you have trouble finding pigeon peas, use either chickpeas or black-eyed peas.

VARIATION

Use canned pigeon peas, drained and rinsed; add with the rice to the slow cooker, skipping the first slow-cooking step.

Thai-Inspired Green Quinoa

I LOVE THIS COMBINATION of flavors, and it is for me one of the perfect ways to serve quinoa. It's easy and looks pretty to mold it into a cup, ramekin, or small bowl and turn out onto a serving plate, especially if using as a side. If allowed to cool it makes a great quinoa salad. If you're not a super quinoa fan, skip it and just cook the chickpeas as written, and use them as a snack or side dish on their own; they are so flavorful. This is a great dish to make while at work—start the chickpeas before you leave, then when you come home you can add the remaining ingredients and still have some time to do other things before dinner is ready. The chickpeas can handle a longer cooking time if need be.

1. Combine the chickpeas through the ginger in the slow cooker.
2. Cover, set heat to LOW, and cook for 8 hours, or until the chickpeas are tender. Remove the crushed lemongrass stalk and ginger.
3. Add the quinoa through the salt; stir to combine.
4. Cover and cook 1¼ hours, or until the quinoa and beans are tender and the liquid is absorbed. Stir after ¾ hour, if desired.
5. Stir in the spring onions and cilantro.
6. Just prior to serving, taste and season with the salt and pepper as required.

SERVES 4 TO 6

PREPARATION TIME:
20 MINUTES, DIVIDED

GF * **SF**

½ cup dry chickpeas, soaked overnight, drained, and rinsed
2¾ cups vegetable stock, store-bought or homemade (page 43)
½ medium onion, finely chopped
3 garlic cloves, minced
3 stalks lemongrass, minced, plus 1 stalk, trimmed and crushed
One 1-inch piece fresh ginger, peeled and scored or crushed

1 cup quinoa
2 teaspoons Thai green curry paste
1 cup chopped green beans cut into ¼-inch pieces, or 1 cup frozen peas, thawed
½ teaspoon salt

2 spring onions, finely chopped
¼ cup cilantro, roughly chopped

Salt and black pepper

*Please check all packaged ingredients, as noted on page 39.

Winter Vegetables and Quinoa

SERVES 6

PREPARATION TIME:
35 MINUTES, INCLUDING
ROASTING THE
VEGETABLES

1½ pounds mixed root
vegetables, such as
white potato, sweet
potato, parsnip, carrot,
rutabaga, turnip, or
celeriac, peeled and cut
into ¼-inch pieces
½ medium onion, peeled,
root end on, and cut
into 6 equal pieces (see
Note)
6 garlic cloves, peeled
½ teaspoon ground fennel
seeds
1 teaspoon smoked
paprika
1 teaspoon cumin
1 tablespoon olive oil
½ teaspoon salt
¼ teaspoon pepper

3 tablespoons finely
chopped dried apple
3 tablespoons finely
chopped prunes or
dried plums
3 tablespoons finely
chopped dried apricots
1 cup quinoa
2 cups vegetable stock,
store-bought or
homemade (page 43)

Salt and black pepper

*Please check all packaged
ingredients, as noted on
page 39.

IN THIS HEARTY, stick-to-your-ribs dish, sweet roasted root vegetables are made just a little bit sweeter with the addition of chopped dried fruit. The vegetables are then paired with quinoa for a protein power infusion. There are six pieces of onion and six cloves of garlic in this dish, so (in an ideal world) each person will get one of each. Use whatever leftover root vegetables you have—it will change the flavor profile of the dish slightly every time you make it, which for me is part of its charm. You can substitute raisins or dried cranberries for any of the dried fruit you don't like.

1. Preheat the oven to 425°F and line a large rimmed baking sheet with parchment paper.
2. Toss the vegetables through the oil to coat, spread in a single layer, and sprinkle with the salt and pepper. Roast until the vegetables are tender and beginning to brown, about 25 minutes.
3. Combine the dried fruit through the stock in the slow cooker.
4. Remove the vegetables from oven and place in the slow cooker on top of the quinoa. Distribute evenly but *do not stir.*
5. Cover, set heat to LOW, and cook for 3 to 3½ hours, or until the quinoa is tender and the liquid is mostly absorbed. Stir after 2 hours if possible to allow the quinoa to cook evenly.
6. Taste and season with the salt and pepper as required.

NOTE: Leaving the root end on the onion keeps the layers in each piece together as they cook, making serving the onion easier.

Lemon and Lemongrass Millet Rice

THIS IS A good way to introduce yourself to millet if you've never had it, or to hide it from a skeptic. This is great served with any Southeast Asian, North Asian, or even North African dish, such as Moroccan Spiced Vegetable Stew with Couscous (page 93) in place of the couscous, or Pineapple Sweet and Sour Seitan (page 123). I also like it by itself for lunch (or even breakfast). You can even fry leftovers like standard fried rice and add vegetables and nuts. The lemongrass adds an earthy, mellow lemon taste to the dish, rounding out the sharpness of the actual lemon, but feel free to omit it; the dish will still be tasty.

SERVES 4 TO 6

PREPARATION TIME:
15 MINUTES

1 tablespoon olive oil
2 garlic cloves, minced
2 shallots, finely chopped
4 or 5 stalks minced
    lemongrass (2
    tablespoons)
1 tablespoon lemon zest

⅔ cup millet

¼ cup white wine or
    vegetable stock, store-
    bought or homemade
    (page 43)
3 tablespoons lemon juice

1 cup white basmati or
    jasmine rice
3 cups plus 2 tablespoons
    vegetable stock

3 tablespoons finely
    chopped fresh flat-leaf
    (Italian) parsley

*Please check all packaged
ingredients, as noted on
page 39.

1. Heat the oil in a large skillet over medium heat and sauté the garlic through the lemon zest until aromatic and sizzling, about 2 minutes.
2. Add the millet and stir to coat. Toast, stirring frequently until it smells toasty and looks a little golden, about 5 minutes. Transfer to the slow cooker.
3. Add the wine and lemon juice to the skillet; stir to deglaze the pan. Transfer to the slow cooker.
4. Spread the rice on top of the millet; add the stock. (You want the millet so stay at the bottom as much as possible while cooking so *do not stir*.)
5. Cover, set heat to LOW, and cook for 3 hours, or until the liquid is absorbed and the grains are tender.
6. Just prior to serving stir the parsley through and fluff to distribute the millet evenly through the rice.

VARIATION:

LIME AND LEMONGRASS MILLET RICE
Swap lime juice and zest for the lemon.

Red Pepper and Spinach Millet Risotto

SERVES 4

**PREPARATION TIME:
10 MINUTES**

N in optional garnish

1 tablespoon olive oil
½ red onion, finely
    chopped
2 garlic cloves, minced

⅓ cup millet
1 teaspoon dried basil
1 teaspoon dried oregano

½ cup white wine or
    vegetable stock, store-
    bought or homemade
    (page 43)

2 cups vegetable stock

½ cup Arborio (risotto) rice
2 roasted red peppers
    (page 20), finely
    chopped
1 bunch fresh spinach
    or other quick-wilting
    green such as arugula,
    watercress, or beet
    greens, finely chopped

Salt and black pepper
¼ cup toasted pine nuts,
    optional

*Please check all packaged
ingredients, as noted on
page 39.

NOT AS CREAMY and rich as a traditional risotto, but a good way to try out a different grain that might be intimidating otherwise. The millet adds a slighty nutty flavor and a less creamy texture, but it works with the sweet pepper, slightly bitter spinach, and creamy pine nuts.

1. Heat the oil in a medium skillet over medium heat and sauté the onion and garlic until soft and translucent, about 5 minutes.

2. Add the millet through the oregano and toast until aromatic, about 2 minutes.

3. Add the wine to deglaze the skillet, stirring frequently for 2 minutes.

4. Transfer the contents of the skillet to the slow cooker. Add the stock and stir to combine.

5. Cover, set heat to LOW, and cook for 1½ hours.

6. Add the rice, stir to combine, cover, and cook for 1 to 1½ hours, until the liquid is absorbed and the grains are tender.

7. Stir in the red pepper and spinach and cook uncovered until the spinach is completely wilted.

8. Taste and season with the salt and pepper as required.

9. Let stand 5 minutes, then sprinkle with the pine nuts, if using, and serve.

Smoky Sour and Sweet BBQ Mushrooms

DON'T REMOVE THE gills of mushrooms. I know some people do, for aesthetic reasons, though I don't really see the point. Either way these mushrooms are tender, sour, and sweet with a hint of barbecue smokiness. The sauce is almost overpoweringly flavorful, so be careful when serving. It does make a great dipping sauce, so the best thing to do is remove the mushrooms and serve the sauce on the side so people can add as much or as little as they like. Great served with a baked potato, on a bun, or just on the side. The serving size here is for a side dish; it's rich and filling enough that you can't eat loads of it.

1. Combine the oil through the liquid smoke in the slow cooker and mix well.
2. Add the mushroom slices and toss to coat.
3. Cover, set heat to LOW, and cook for 5 hours.
4. Make the arrowroot into a slurry with the water. Stir in to thicken, mix well, and toss to evenly coat the mushroom slices.

SERVES 4

PREPARATION TIME:
15 MINUTES

 *

1 tablespoon grapeseed oil
3 tablespoons maple syrup
2 tablespoons soy sauce
1 tablespoon pomegranate molasses
2 garlic cloves, grated
1 tablespoon grated fresh ginger
2 teaspoons tamarind paste
1 teaspoon liquid smoke

5 portobello caps, halved, and cut into ½-inch-thick slices, or about 12 white or cremini mushrooms or a combination, equal to 5 cups

1½ tablespoons arrowroot powder or cornstarch
1½ tablespoons water

*Please check all packaged ingredients, as noted on page 39.

Sort-of-Succotash

SERVES 4

PREPARATION TIME:
10 MINUTES

GF * SF

½ cup dry baby or large
lima beans, soaked
overnight, drained, and
rinsed
2 small white potatoes,
peeled and cut into
¼-inch dice
½ small sweet potato,
peeled and cut into
½-inch dice
1 cup vegetable stock,
store-bought or
homemade (page 43)
½ cup canned creamed
corn
½ onion, finely chopped
2 garlic cloves, minced
1 bay leaf

2 corn cobs roughly
stripped, or one 13-
ounce can corn rinsed
and drained, or 1½
cups frozen corn
kernels
½ medium red pepper,
finely chopped
2 tablespoons finely
chopped fresh parsley,
regular or flat leaf

Salt and black pepper

*Please check all packaged
ingredients, as noted on
page 39.

HERE'S A SPIN on succotash—it contains lima beans and corn, but I've added other vegetables to make it more substantial. Serve as a main course over pasta or rice, or alongside leftover chili. This dish will have you falling in love with the creamy delight of lima beans!

1. Combine the beans through the bay leaf in the slow cooker. The liquid will not quite cover the vegetables.
2. Cover, set heat to LOW, and cook for 7 hours, or until the beans and potatoes are tender.
3. Add the corn through the parsley and cook on LOW for a further 2 hours.
4. Taste and season with the salt and pepper as required. Drain excess liquid, if desired.

Nutty Wild Rice

INCLUDE THIS ON your Thanksgiving or Christmas table and really wow the relatives! Packed with goodness from North American native plants and seasonally appropriate items, this is one dish you won't be able to get enough of. Chop and toast the nuts and seeds in advance and hold until required. Use the remaining squash to make Autumn Baked Macaroni (page 179) for another day.

SERVES 6 TO 8

PREPARATION TIME:
20 MINUTES

GF * SF N

1 cup wild rice

1 tablespoon Garlic Infused Oil (page 54) or canola oil
2 garlic cloves, minced
4 cloves Poached Garlic (page 54)
½ medium onion, finely chopped
½ medium winter squash such as butternut, peeled and cut into ¼-inch cubes (about 1 pound)

1 bay leaf
½ teaspoon salt
¼ teaspoon black pepper
½ teaspoon poultry seasoning mix, store-bought or homemade (page 52)
2 cups vegetable stock, store-bought or homemade (page 43)

Salt and black pepper
¼ cup hazelnuts, roughly chopped
¼ cup pecans, roughly chopped
¼ cup sunflower seeds
¼ cup pumpkin seeds

*Please check all packaged ingredients, as noted on page 39.

1. Toast wild rice in a medium skillet over medium heat until golden and aromatic, 5 minutes. Place in the slow cooker.
2. Heat the oil in the same skillet and sauté the garlic through the squash cubes until aromatic and the onion is soft, 5 minutes. Transfer to the slow cooker and wipe the skillet.
3. Add the bay leaf through stock to the slow cooker. *Do not stir*.
4. Cover, set heat to LOW, and cook for 4½ hours, until the rice is tender and the liquid is absorbed.
5. Taste and season with the salt and pepper as required.
6. Using the same skillet, toast the nuts and seeds until golden and aromatic, 5 minutes.
7. Remove from the heat and let stand for 10 minutes.
8. Stir the nuts and seeds into the slow cooker; fluff with a fork just prior to serving.

VARIATION:

For a sweet flavor accent, stir in ⅓ cup dried cranberries with the nuts when the dish has finished cooking.

You can also use this as a stuffing for vegetables, such as red bell peppers, hollowed-out zucchini, or portobello mushrooms. Stuff the rice into the vegetable then top with bread and grated vegan cheese, if desired. Bake for about 30 minutes at 350°F.

Bread Crust Stuffing

SERVES 6 TO 8

PREPARATION TIME:
10 MINUTES

¾ cup mixed salted,
   roasted nuts, roughly
   chopped
¼ cup dried cranberries
2 tablespoons finely
   chopped fresh parsley
1 teaspoon dried rubbed
   sage
½ teaspoon dried thyme
½ teaspoon onion powder
½ teaspoon garlic powder
½ teaspoon dried
   rosemary
¼ teaspoon white pepper
7 cups bread crusts cut
   into ½-inch pieces
   (about 10 slices)

¼ cup olive oil
1 cup vegetable stock,
   store-bought or
   homemade (page 43)

Salt and black pepper

I F YOU ARE anything like me you have bags of bread crusts in your freezer, often left there for ages and in need of using up (bread crumbs to the rescue, but that is another story). This recipe is a perfect holiday-inspired way to do so. You don't have to use just crusts, and the bread can be whatever sort you like, even gluten free. I use mixed salted, roasted nuts since we often have bags of them around at holiday time and it is easier than roasting and salting my own. If you have specific nut likes or dislikes (or allergies), use whatever you prefer, even if you have to roast and salt your own. If your slow cooker has a hot spot, partway through the cooking time turn the insert to avoid an overcooked patch.

1. Line the slow cooker insert with 2 sheets of foil placed in opposite directions with some hanging over the edge to use as handles when removing. Spray with a little nonstick spray.
2. In a large bowl toss together the nuts through the bread crusts.
3. Drizzle the oil and stock over the top and mix well with your hands.
4. Taste and season with the salt and pepper as required. Mix well.
5. Transfer the stuffing mix to the slow cooker and press down until even.
6. Cover, set heat to HIGH, and cook for 3 hours, or until the edges and bottom are firm and crisp with the center still a little moist.
7. Remove the stuffing using the foil handles and let stand for 10 minutes prior to peeling off the foil and serving.

Squash and Cranberry Bake

THIS IS A perfect dish for days like Thanksgiving, when you are running around trying to organize seven dishes so everyone in your family has at least one dish they like. Breathe. Relax. Get this dish started, then get busy with something else. The result is a little sweet, a little tart, and a lovely addition to your meal.

1. Layer the squash in the slow cooker in alternating directions with the dried and fresh cranberries sprinkled between the layers. Use the smaller pieces from the bulbous seed end as the top layers since they won't take as long to cook. Ensure the layers are even and the cranberries well distributed, producing about 5 layers depending on the dimensions of your slow cooker.

2. In a small bowl, mix the juice through the pepper and pour over the squash. It will reach about halfway up the squash.

3. Cover, set heat to LOW, and cook for 3 hours, or until the squash is tender.

4. Sprinkle with the pumpkin seeds, if desired, just prior to serving.

SERVES 4 TO 6

PREPARATION TIME:
15 MINUTES

1 butternut squash, halved
   lengthwise, peeled,
   seeded, and sliced
   widthwise ¼-inch thick
¼ cup fresh or frozen
   cranberries
¼ cup dried cranberries

⅓ cup orange juice
⅓ cup soy creamer, store-
   bought or homemade
   (page 56)
2 teaspoons dried rubbed
   sage
1 teaspoon maple syrup
½ teaspoon orange zest
⅛ teaspoon nutmeg
Pinch each salt and black
   pepper

Toasted pumpkin seeds,
   optional

To Serve With

ALTHOUGH MOST OF the dishes in the preceding chapters stand alone and make a meal in themselves, sometimes it is nice to have a little something on the side—be it a grain, a bread, or additional vegetables. That is where this chapter comes in—dishes made conventionally to complement the wonderful meal you have been lovingly simmering for hours in your slow cooker. Many of these are also one-dish dishes, and very quick and easy, so no excuses after work or the gym! Many recipes that take a little longer can be made in advance and whipped out or reheated when you are ready to serve.

I tried to indicate on each recipe what sorts of meals they would best complement, even if it is just as simple as "best with meals in the Curries and Asian-Inspired Dishes chapter." As always, use your discretion and mix and match to your heart's content!

Starchy Vegetables and Grains

When you want to add more bulk to your meal, head to these recipes. From potatoes to go with a hearty "meaty" stew to rice to accompany a spicy curry, here are tasty options.

Colorful Cooked Vegetables

These are quick-cooking accompaniments from a range of vegetables to add a splash of color, and extra nutrition, to your plate. Casseroles and stews are all very well, but sometimes you need some brightness!

Salads

What would a BBQ-inspired dish be without a side of coleslaw? According to everything I've seen on the Food Network, not worth eating! Here's a range of make-ahead slaws and salads that will be ready when you are.

Sauces and Condiments

What is "Not-Meat" Loaf (page 162) or Nut Roast (page 164) without gravy?

Savory Baked Goods

Fancy something to dunk into your soup or serve alongside your chili or stew? Look no further. From fast and simple quick breads to more time-consuming (but great to make ahead and store) yeast breads, there's something to fill your every craving.

Baked Garlic Potatoes

SERVES 1 TO 2

PREPARATION TIME:
10 MINUTES

COOKING TIME:
1½ HOURS

1 medium baking potato
2 garlic cloves, peeled and
 sliced thinly

WHO'D HAVE THOUGHT two ingredients could create such flavor, such a creamy texture in the simple potato? You need to try this way of baking potatoes; it is so good. Add salt and pepper to taste as you eat them, and, if you would like, a little vegan margarine or vegan sour cream, but I don't think they need anything else. Great served with a chili, so check out your favorite from that chapter. This is our favorite way to bake potatoes on the barbecue in the summertime! Just prepare as directed, heat the barbecue, and cook over indirect heat until tender. For leftovers, fully slice the potato along the partial cuts and panfry in a little oil until crisp and golden.

1. Preheat the oven to 400°F.
2. Scrub the potato and make cuts widthwise along the potato, about ½ inch apart. Cut about ¾ of the way down through the potato; you want the segments still attached at the bottom.
3. Using a thin flexible knife to aid in guiding and opening the cuts, push the slices of garlic into the cuts on the potato. This is a little tricky; just be careful not to force the garlic in or the segments will break all the way through.
4. Wrap tightly in foil and bake for 1¼ to 1½ hours, turning twice if desired, until the potatoes are tender when pierced with a knife.

Garlic and Onion Mashed Potatoes

OFTEN MAKE ROASTED or Poached Garlic (page 54) and add it to my mashed potatoes for a lovely garlic-infused part of dinner. Use whenever you would use mashed potatoes—with stews, casseroles, and even maybe the odd chili.

1. Place the potatoes and enough water just to cover in a large saucepan, bring to a boil, and cook over medium heat uncovered until the potatoes are tender, 12 minutes.
2. Using a colander, drain the potatoes and leave them in the colander.
3. In the same saucepan, toast the mustard seeds over medium heat for 1 minute.
4. Add the oil and garlic until the garlic sizzles, about 1 minute.
5. Add the onion and sauté until lightly browned, 5 minutes.
6. Deglaze the pan with the soymilk. Return the potatoes to the pan. Bring the soymilk to a boil, remove from the heat, and mash potatoes to your desired smoothness.
7. Season to taste with the salt and pepper and serve.

SERVES 4

PREPARATION TIME:
10 MINUTES

COOKING TIME:
20 MINUTES

1 pound white potatoes, cut into 1-inch chunks, skin on for a more rustic version

1 teaspoon mustard seeds, lightly crushed

1 tablespoon olive oil
2 garlic cloves, minced

½ medium onion, quartered and finely sliced

⅔ cup plain soymilk

Salt and black pepper

Coconut Rice

SERVES 4

PREPARATION TIME:
5 MINUTES

COOKING TIME:
55 MINUTES

1 cup brown basmati rice
¼ cup unsweetened
   shredded coconut

1½ cups vegetable stock,
   store-bought or
   homemade (page 43)
½ cup canned coconut
   milk
1 tablespoon coconut oil
½ teaspoon salt, optional

*Please check all packaged
ingredients, as noted on
page 39.

ERE WE HAVE a super coconut rice with layered coconut goodness for the coconut lover in your life. Not sweet at all, just aromatic, this rice is good with any of the Curries and Asian-Inspired Dishes (page 105).

1. Toast the rice and coconut in a medium pot over medium heat, stirring very frequently, for 7 to 8 minutes or until the coconut is golden. Take care not to burn.
2. Add the stock through the salt; stir until the oil is dissolved, bring to a boil, cover, reduce the heat to medium low, and simmer until the liquid is absorbed and the rice is tender, 40 to 45 minutes.
3. Remove from the heat and let stand for 5 minutes; fluff with a fork just prior to serving.

VARIATION:
HERBED COCONUT RICE
Add 1 tablespoon of your choice of chopped fresh herbs (cilantro and mint are good) prior to fluffing and serving.

Couscous with Dried Apricots and Pistachios

READING THIS RECIPE you could be forgiven for thinking that it will taste sweet, with the apricots and cinnamon and all. Calm that concern, as it's just pleasantly accented by a little hint of sweetness. Great to serve warm or cold alongside anything really, but especially dishes with North African– or Ethiopian-influenced flavors such as the Ethiopian Fusion Squash Stew (page 91). It's also good by itself as a very quick and easy lunch.

1. In a medium saucepan bring the stock and oil to a full boil. Remove from the heat, stir in the couscous through the pepper, cover, and let stand until the liquid is absorbed, 10 minutes. Uncover, stir in the pistachios through the parsley, and fluff with a fork.
2. Taste and season with the salt and pepper as required.

NOTE: If toasting the pistachios, use the saucepan you will later be using for the couscous. Cool on a plate, then chop and add as directed.

SERVES 2 TO 4

PREPARATION TIME:
10 MINUTES

COOKING TIME:
15 MINUTES

1½ cups vegetable stock, store-bought or homemade (page 43)
1 tablespoon olive oil

1 cup couscous
¼ cup dried apricots, finely chopped
½ teaspoon coriander
½ teaspoon cardamom
¼ teaspoon allspice
¼ teaspoon cinnamon
¼ teaspoon black pepper

½ cup toasted pistachios, roughly chopped (see Note)
2 or 3 scallions, finely chopped (¼ cup)
2 tablespoons finely chopped fresh flat-leaf (Italian) parsley

Salt and black pepper

Israeli Couscous with Almonds and Parsley

SERVES 2 TO 4

PREPARATION TIME:
10 MINUTES

COOKING TIME:
25 MINUTES

½ cup slivered almonds

1 tablespoon olive oil
1 celery stalk, finely
   chopped
2 medium finely chopped
   shallots

¾ cup Israeli couscous
½ teaspoon marjoram
¼ teaspoon cinnamon
1 bay leaf

1 cup vegetable stock,
   store-bought or
   homemade (page 43)

¼ cup fresh flat-leaf
   (Italian) parsley, packed
   and finely chopped

Salt and black pepper

THIS DISH IS great as a hot side dish or served cold as a salad. I quite like to eat it as a main meal, which serves only 2; as a side dish it should serve 4. It's lovely served with Curries and Asian-Inspired Dishes (page 105) and with the flavors of North Africa, such as Moroccan Spiced Vegetable Stew (page 93). If at the end you find the dish a little dry, add a little more olive oil, maybe 1 tablespoon, and toss.

1. Toast the almonds in a large skillet over medium heat until golden, stirring frequently, about 5 minutes. Remove from the skillet and reserve.

2. Heat the oil in the same skillet and sauté the celery and shallots until soft and lightly browned, 5 minutes. Add the couscous through the bay leaf and sauté until the couscous is lightly golden, 3 to 4 minutes.

3. Add the stock, reduce the heat to medium low, cover, and simmer until the couscous is tender and all liquid is absorbed, about 10 minutes.

4. Stir in the parsley and reserved almonds. Remove the bay leaf, taste, and season with the salt and pepper as required.

Ginger and Garlic Cauliflower

I ADORE THE COMBINATION of cauliflower and ginger. It seems like a match made in heaven, especially in this dish—I added onion and garlic, then let everything caramelize and get sweet and savory. It's simple but really good, especially when served with curries. Use the remainder of the cauliflower for dinner another night in dishes such as Cauliflower and Cashew Korma (page 116) or Roasted Cauliflower and Carrot Dal (page 111).

1. Heat the oil in a large skillet over medium high heat and sauté the onion until softened, about 3 minutes.

2. Add the cauliflower and cook covered, stirring occasionally, until the cauliflower is soft and lightly browned and the onions are mainly caramelized, 8 to 10 minutes. Add splashes of water or stock as required to stop sticking.

3. Add the ginger through the pepper and sauté until very aromatic but not browned, 2 minutes. Use water as required to stop sticking.

SERVES 4 AS A SIDE

PREPARATION TIME:
10 MINUTES

COOKING TIME:
15 MINUTES

2 tablespoons canola oil
¼ cup finely chopped onion
½ head cauliflower cut into small florets

1½ tablespoons grated fresh ginger
3 garlic cloves, minced
Pinch each salt and black pepper, or to taste

Zesty Broccoli with Pine Nuts and Poached Garlic

SERVES 4 AS A SIDE

PREPARATION TIME:
10 MINUTES

COOKING TIME:
15 MINUTES

3 tablespoons pine nuts

2 tablespoons Garlic
   Infused Oil (page 54) or
   olive oil
6 cloves Poached Garlic,
   chopped (page 54)
1 tablespoon fresh ginger,
   minced
2 shallots, finely chopped
Zest of 1 lemon

1 head broccoli cut into
   long-stemmed florets
2 tablespoons water

Salt and black pepper

THIS IS BEAUTIFUL broccoli. Seriously beautiful. Crunchy smooth pine nuts, creamy garlic, and a hit of lemony goodness all combine well with tender broccoli. You can use roasted garlic instead of the poached if that is what you have on hand. This is great served with stews like White Stew (page 101) and with casseroles such as Nut Roast (page 164) or Stuffed and Rolled Seitan Roast (page 166).

1. In a large skillet over medium heat, toast the pine nuts until golden and aromatic, taking care not to let them brown too much, about 5 minutes. Remove and hold.
2. In the same skillet heat the oil and sauté the garlic through the zest until aromatic but not brown, about 2 minutes.
3. Add the broccoli and water; stir to combine, cover, and cook until the broccoli is tender, stirring frequently, about 5 minutes.
4. Add the pine nuts, toss to well combine, ensuring all the crusted-on bits of the garlic mix are incorporated.
5. Taste and season with the salt and pepper as required.

Broccoli in Tahini and Mustard Sauce

A TRULY DELICIOUS WAY to eat broccoli; it looks like a lot more work than it really is. The sauce is good on other green vegetables, too, so feel free to pour it over sautéed kale, wilted spinach, or even other vegetables such as cauliflower (not green but let's not hold that against it). Have broccoli precut and in a bag in the fridge, so all you need to do is cook. Serve with hearty casseroles such as Bobotie (page 161), Nut Roast (page 164), or any "meaty" stew.

1. Fill a medium saucepan with water, bring to a boil, and cook the broccoli until tender, about 5 minutes. Drain, reserving ½ cup cooking water.

2. In the same pan, combine the reserved cooking water with the soymilk through the pepper and whisk until smooth. Heat over medium heat, stirring frequently until thick and smooth, about 5 minutes. Taste and season with the salt as required.

3. Add the broccoli to the sauce and toss to coat. Serve warm.

SERVES 4 TO 6

PREPARATION TIME:
5 MINUTES

COOKING TIME:
15 MINUTES

 *

1 head broccoli cut into
   florets with stalk sliced
   (about 12 ounces)

½ cup soymilk
2 tablespoons tahini
2 tablespoons nutritional
   yeast
1 tablespoon lemon juice
1 tablespoon prepared
   mustard such as Dijon
1 tablespoon cornstarch
¼ teaspoon onion powder
¼ teaspoon garlic powder
¼ teaspoon black pepper

Salt

*Please check all packaged
ingredients, as noted on
page 39.

Citrus and Poppy Seed Green Beans

SERVES 2

PREPARATION TIME:
10 MINUTES

COOKING TIME:
15 MINUTES

1 tablespoon olive oil

8 ounces trimmed green
  beans, cut into 2-inch
  pieces

2 garlic cloves, minced

1½ teaspoons lemon or
  lime zest

3 teaspoons lemon or lime
  juice

1 teaspoon agave

2 teaspoons poppy seeds

Salt and black pepper

WHEN I MADE this for the first time I was a little under-whelmed, but my husband, usually not a green bean fan, could not get enough! He requested I make it the very next day, so I did (with limes instead of lemons, which I found I preferred), and he pronounced it just as delicious. Serve with any of the meat and potatoes–style stews or casseroles to add a little zing and color to your meal. Precut the beans, zest and juice the citrus, and have all in the fridge ready for cooking.

1. Heat the oil in a large skillet over medium heat, add the beans, cover, and cook, stirring occasionally, until the beans are tender and lightly browned in places, about 10 minutes.
2. Add the garlic and zest, toss to coat, and sauté until the garlic is aromatic but not brown, about 2 minutes.
3. Add the juice and agave, toss to coat, add the poppy seeds, and sauté for 1 minute.
4. Taste and season with the salt and pepper as required.

VARIATION:

SESAME CITRUS GREEN BEANS

Substitute sesame seeds (or a combination of sesame and poppy seed) for the poppy seeds and proceed as directed.

Beans and Brussels

I MADE THIS FOR Christmas for the entire extended family and it was loved by everyone, even the veggie-phobic. The dish is just a little spicy; if you are chile sensitive, reduce the amount of chile flakes. This dish is great served alongside Stuffed and Rolled Seitan Roast (page 166) or the Bread Crust Stuffing (page 208) as part of a holiday meal.

1. Heat the oil in a large skillet over medium-high heat and sauté the onion and garlic until aromatic and soft, 3 to 5 minutes.
2. Add the chile flakes through the pepper; stir to combine.
3. Add the beans and Brussels sprouts. Toss well, cover, and allow to steam, stirring occasionally to prevent sticking until bright green and tender with some caramelized patches (these are good, you want them), 5 to 7 minutes. Add splashes of water as required to stop the sticking.

NOTE: To slice the Brussels sprouts, cut into quarters top to bottom; if the sprouts are large enough, cut each quarter in half so there are 8 little wedges from each sprout. No worries if leaves fall off and they don't all stay in wedge form.

SERVES 4

PREPARATION TIME:
15 MINUTES

COOKING TIME:
10 MINUTES

1 tablespoon olive oil
½ medium onion, quartered and thinly sliced.
2 garlic cloves, thinly sliced

½ teaspoon chile flakes
½ teaspoon salt
¼ teaspoon black pepper

4 ounces green beans, trimmed and thinly sliced on a bias into 2-inch lengths
12 ounces Brussels sprouts, outer leaves removed, quartered (see Note)

Maple-Touched Chili Brussels Sprouts

SERVES 2

PREPARATION TIME:
10 MINUTES

COOKING TIME:
7 MINUTES

1 tablespoon olive oil
8 ounces trimmed
   Brussels sprouts,
   halved if small,
   quartered if large

1 shallot, finely chopped
2 garlic cloves, minced
1 tablespoon minced fresh
   ginger
½ teaspoon chile flakes, or
   to taste
Pinch each salt and black
   pepper, or to taste

½ teaspoon maple syrup

I ADORE BRUSSELS SPROUTS, but they have to be cooked right. They can't be mushy, overseasoned, or overcooked in any way. I like them firm, vibrant, and adorned with spices and flavorings that bring out their natural sweetness while adding interest. The maple syrup adds the tiniest touch of smoky sweetness, just enough to lift the spiciness so it's not too overwhelming. These are wonderful with meat and potatoes–style stews such as Seitan in Onion Gravy (page 98).

1. Heat the oil in a medium skillet over medium heat; add the sprouts and toss to coat. Cover and cook, stirring occasionally, until vibrantly green and tender with some darkened and golden patches, about 5 minutes. Add splashes of water as required if they are sticking or browning too quickly.

2. Uncover, add the shallots through the pepper, toss to coat, and sauté until intensely aromatic but before the garlic burns, 1 minute.

3. Sprinkle with the maple syrup and toss.

Peppered Kale

'M A SUPER kale fan and am always looking for new and interesting ways to use it. This one came about on a day when I had loads of kale and bell peppers, and not a lot else, in the fridge. A wonderful side dish for stews and casseroles when you would like more green.

1. Heat the oil in a large skillet over medium heat; add the garlic and allow it to sizzle.
2. Add the onion through the green pepper and sauté until soft, about 5 minutes.
3. Add the kale through the chile flakes, mix, cover, and steam until the kale is just tender, 3 to 4 minutes, stirring occasionally so the onion doesn't stick.
4. Uncover, add the lime juice, taste, and season with the salt as required.

SERVES 4

PREPARATION TIME:
10 MINUTES

COOKING TIME:
10 MINUTES

GF SF

1 tablespoon olive oil

2 garlic cloves, minced

½ medium onion, cut in half and sliced thinly
½ to 1 jalapeño pepper, minced
½ red pepper, sliced into ¼-inch-wide strips
½ green pepper, sliced into ¼-inch-wide strips

3 cups shredded kale, packed
¼ teaspoon black pepper
¼ teaspoon chile flakes, or to taste

1 tablespoon lime juice
Salt to taste

Savoy Cabbage with Raisins and Pecans

SERVES 4

PREPARATION TIME:
10 MINUTES

COOKING TIME:
20 MINUTES

¼ cup pecan pieces

1 tablespoon olive oil
½ red onion, sliced

½ teaspoon salt
¼ teaspoon black pepper
⅛ teaspoon ground fennel
   seeds

½ head savoy cabbage,
   large spines removed,
   shredded

¼ cup golden raisins
2 tablespoons finely
   chopped fresh parsley

Salt and black pepper

SAVOY IS MY favorite cabbage. I find it somewhat less cabbage-y than green or red cabbage, and I like how pretty it looks with its crinkly leaves. This way of cooking and the additions accentuate the cabbage's natural sweetness (the raisins) and its natural earthiness (the fennel seed), and the dish has an added crunch for wonderful texture contrast. Nontraditional but great with the St. Patrick's Day Irish Stew (page 99), and anywhere you're serving mashed potatoes. Use the rest of your cabbage to make the Peasant Vegetable and Sausage Stew (page 97).

1. Heat a large skillet over medium heat and toast the pecan pieces until aromatic and golden, about 5 minutes. Remove from the skillet and hold.

2. In the same skillet, heat the oil and sauté the onion until soft, 4 to 5 minutes.

3. Add the salt through the fennel seeds; stir in the cabbage, distributing the onion and seasonings throughout.

4. Add a splash of water, cover, and cook, stirring occasionally to prevent sticking, until the cabbage is tender and wilted but still bright green, 7 to 8 minutes. Add splashes of water if the cabbage starts to stick.

5. Toss through the pecans, raisins, and parsley.

6. Taste and season with the salt and pepper as required just prior to serving.

Bean and Olive Salad

SOFT AND CRUNCHY at the same time and with plenty of saltiness from the olives, this is a great salad to have as part of a picnic spread, at a barbecue, or alongside a pasta dish. Use any combination of beans you have handy, as long as you end up with 3 cups. Roughly chop the peppers and olives; as long as they are of similar size and not too much bigger than the beans, it will be fine. Use your slow cooker to cook the beans for this salad, following my basic cooking steps for beans (page 24).

1. In a large bowl whisk together the oil through the oregano.
2. Add the beans through the olives and combine well.
3. Taste and season with the salt and pepper as required.
4. Cover and refrigerate for at least 2 hours for the flavors to meld. Keep in the fridge for up to 5 days.

VARIATIONS:

ITALIAN PASTA AND BEAN SALAD

Make this into an impromptu Italian pasta salad with the addition of some leftover cooked small pasta shapes.

SPICY BEAN AND OLIVE SALAD

For a spicier salad, add 1 finely chopped jalapeño and chile flakes to taste.

SERVES 6 TO 8

PREPARATION TIME:
10 MINUTES

3 tablespoons olive oil
3 tablespoons white balsamic vinegar
1 tablespoon agave
½ teaspoon dried oregano

1 cup cooked pinto beans, if canned, drained and rinsed
1 cup cooked chickpeas, if canned, drained and rinsed
1 cup cooked black beans, if canned, drained and rinsed
½ medium green pepper, chopped
½ medium red pepper, chopped
¼ cup chopped green olives, with or without pimientos
¼ cup chopped black olives

Salt and black pepper

Cherry Tomato Salad

SERVES 6 TO 8

PREPARATION TIME:
10 MINUTES

¼ cup olive oil
1 tablespoon balsamic
    vinegar
1 tablespoon red wine
    vinegar
1 teaspoon maple syrup
1 teaspoon dried oregano
1 garlic clove, minced

4 cups cherry tomatoes,
    halved or quartered if
    slightly larger
½ medium green pepper,
    finely chopped
½ to 1 jalapeño pepper,
    minced, or to taste
2 medium spring onions,
    finely chopped

Salt and black pepper

FOR WHEN YOUR garden is producing more cherry tomatoes than you know what to do with or, if like me you don't have a garden, for when the farmers' markets and stores are selling them super cheap. If you can get a variety of colored cherry tomatoes or, even better, heirloom tomatoes, the salad looks ever so much prettier. This salad is even better the next day, so make ahead if you can. Serve with your favorite pasta dishes, or chili, or even on top of a green salad alongside a bowl of soup.

1. In a large bowl whisk together the oil through the garlic until smooth and creamy.
2. Add the tomatoes through the onions and toss to coat.
3. Taste and season with the salt and pepper as required.
4. Chill for at least 1 hour before serving.

Celery and Caper Coleslaw

EVEN IF YOU'VE never been one to fill celery with cream cheese or peanut butter and munch away, sometimes you'll have some left in the fridge that needs using up, so try it in this coleslaw. I prefer this slaw with Coleslaw Dressing (recipe follows), but others prefer it with mayo only. I think this is best the second day, so plan to make ahead if you can. It's great alongside any of the Chilies and BBQ-Inspired Dishes (page 129).

1. Make the Coleslaw Dressing or measure the mayonnaise into a bowl.
2. Add the cabbage through the capers.
3. Mix well, taste, and season with the salt and pepper as required.
4. Refrigerate for at least 1 hour prior to serving.

SERVES 4 TO 6

PREPARATION TIME:
10 MINUTES

 *

1 recipe Coleslaw Dressing (recipe follows) or ½ cup of your favorite vegan mayonnaise

3 cups mixed shredded cabbage, bagged or cut your favorite cabbage
2 small celery stalks, finely sliced on a bias
2 spring onions, finely sliced on a bias
2 tablespoons capers, drained

Salt and black pepper

*Please check all packaged ingredients, as noted on page 39.

Coleslaw Dressing

MAKES ABOUT ½ CUP

PREPARATION TIME:
5 MINUTES

 *

¼ cup your favorite vegan
    mayonnaise
1 tablespoon Dijon, or
    other mild mustard
1 tablespoon lemon juice
1½ teaspoons agave
1 garlic clove, minced

1 to 2 tablespoons water
Salt and black pepper

*Please check all packaged
ingredients, as noted on
page 39.

THIS IS MY basic, all-purpose, mix-and-match coleslaw dressing. Sometimes I jazz it up, as in the Celery and Caper Coleslaw (page 229), Chickpea Slaw (page 231), and Pineapple Kale-Slaw (page 232). At other times I just stir it into shredded cabbage. It's also good as a green salad dressing, so don't reserve it for coleslaw only. Because this dressing can be used in so many salads, it's great to have in the fridge at all times.

1. Whisk the mayonnaise through the garlic together in a large bowl if using for another recipe immediately; otherwise, a small bowl is fine.

2. Add water to get the consistency desired for coating your slaw.

3. Taste and season with the salt and pepper as required.

4. Use as directed in the recipe or cover, refrigerate, and keep for up to 3 days.

Chickpea Slaw

COLESLAW INFUSED WITH creamy avocado, chickpeas, and sweet dried cranberries—oh, how yummy this is! Perfect with any of the Chilies and BBQ-Inspired Dishes (page 129). This is best eaten the day it is made because the avocado will brown after a few days. The lemon juice in the dressing will keep it green, but not forever.

1. In a large bowl make the Coleslaw Dressing; add into that bowl the avocado pieces and toss to coat.
2. Add the cabbage through the cranberries and gently toss to coat with the dressing; try not to break up the avocado too much.
3. Refrigerate for at least 1 hour prior to serving.

SERVES 4 TO 6

PREPARATION TIME:
10 MINUTES

1 recipe Coleslaw Dressing
   (page 230)

½ avocado, roughly
   chopped

3 cups mixed shredded
   cabbage, bagged or
   cut from your favorite
   cabbage
1 cup cooked chickpeas,
   if canned, drained and
   rinsed
½ medium red onion,
   finely chopped
¼ cup dried cranberries

Pineapple Kale-Slaw

SERVES 4 TO 6

PREPARATION TIME:
10 MINUTES

1 recipe Coleslaw Dressing
(page 230)

3 cups mixed shredded
cabbage, bagged or cut
your favorite cabbage
1 cup shredded kale
½ medium red onion,
finely chopped
½ cup canned pineapple
bits, drained
½ cup raisins

I F YOU'RE COOKING for someone who dislikes raw kale, you can hide it in a green mixed salad or try it in a dish like this one. I think it is the sweetness from the pineapple and raisins that does the trick. This kale-slaw is great the next day, and the longer sitting time softens the kale and allows the flavors to really mix. Serve with Chilies and BBQ-Inspired Dishes (page 129) such as Baked Beans (page 145).

1. Make the Coleslaw Dressing in a large bowl; add the cabbage through the raisins and toss to coat.
2. Refrigerate for at least 1 hour prior to serving.

Herbed Chees-y Sauce

YOU CAN MAKE this sauce without the fresh herbs added at the end, but I like the extra flavor lift they add. Perfect for stirring into pasta, over polenta, green vegetables, baked or mashed potatoes, as a dipping sauce with hot appetizers, and just about everywhere! Grating the shallots gives a smoother sauce, if you don't want any texture. For a completely smooth sauce, blend with an immersion blender at the end. You can substitute all-purpose flour and soymilk if you like.

1. Melt the margarine in a small pan over medium heat; sauté the shallots and thyme until soft and aromatic, 2 to 3 minutes.

2. Add the flour and almonds, stir to lightly cook, and add the milk ¼ cup at a time, stirring well between each addition and allowing to thicken prior to adding the next measure.

3. When all the milk is added, stir in the mustard through the salt, heat gently for a few more minutes, taste, and season with the salt and pepper as required just prior to serving.

MAKES ABOUT 1½ CUPS

PREPARATION TIME:
5 MINUTES

COOKING TIME:
15 MINUTES

2 tablespoons vegan margarine

2 shallots, finely chopped or grated
½ teaspoon dried thyme

2 tablespoons chickpea flour, sifted if lumpy
2 tablespoons ground almonds

1¼ cups almond milk

1 tablespoon prepared yellow mustard
2 tablespoons nutritional yeast
1 tablespoon lemon juice
1 tablespoon finely chopped fresh thyme
¼ teaspoon salt
⅛ teaspoon turmeric
⅛ teaspoon paprika
⅛ teaspoon black pepper
⅛ teaspoon black salt

Salt and black pepper

*Please check all packaged ingredients, as noted on page 39.

Garlic "Butter"

MAKES ½ TO ¾ CUP

PREPARATION TIME:
15 MINUTES, MORE FOR
MAKING THE GARLIC
BREAD

 GF "butter" only

SF depending on
margarine

½ to ¾ cup vegan
margarine
4 garlic cloves, finely
minced or grated
1 teaspoon garlic powder
Pinch each salt, black
pepper, thyme, and
rosemary, all to taste

I FEEL A LITTLE silly putting in this recipe, but it is something
I make so often that I thought, "Why not?" Its most common
uses are on Garlic Bread (page 235), on BBQ'd corn on the cob
and baked potatoes, in mashed potatoes, tossed into cooked
pasta with vegetables for a simple pasta dressing, and so on. I
like garlic butter strong, but I appreciate that not everyone will—
just add more margarine until it is how you like it. As an alterna-
tive and for a less strong garlic taste, roast the garlic first at
400°F for 20 minutes or so until golden and soft, use Poached
Garlic (page 54), or do a cooked and raw garlic combination. The
"butter" will last in the fridge for as long as margarine lasts, so
make a big batch and use as it takes your fancy. Serve garlic
bread alongside any pasta, soup, or chili for a lovely, warm, aromatic addition to your meal.

1. Combine the margarine through the rosemary in a small
   bowl and mix well to combine.
2. Taste and adjust seasonings as required.

GARLIC BREAD

I TEND TO use baguette-style bread but also like to make individual garlic breads from large buns.

Have ready a piece of foil larger than the bread you are using and preheat the oven to 400°F. You can easily use the grill, too, though times may differ and the bread will need watching.

Slice any hard ends off the bread and discard.

Using a serrated knife, slice the bread into ½-inch (finger-width) slices almost all the way through. Leave the bottom crust attached but not too much of the bread, or else the slices will be hard to pull apart when the bread is hot.

Spread the garlic "butter" on each side of each slice of bread while still attached. It is a little fiddly but with care you can separate the slices without ripping them apart. Be as heavy- or gentle-handed as you like with the garlic "butter," depending on your tastes.

Wrap the buttered bread in the foil and bake for 15 to 20 minutes.

Classic Guacamole

MAKES ABOUT 1½ CUPS

**PREPARATION TIME:
10 MINUTES**

2 ripe avocados, peeled
   and pitted

1 shallot, finely chopped
2 tablespoons very finely
   chopped red pepper or
   seeded tomato
2 tablespoons lime juice

Salt, black pepper, and hot
   sauce

THIS IS A very simple guacamole recipe. It comes complete with pretty contrasting red notes and is perfect for all your guacamole needs. To retard browning, place an avocado pit in the center of the guacamole in the bowl, then cover with plastic wrap so the wrap completely touches the surface of the guacamole. This works on the premise that no air contact equals no oxidation, and therefore no browning.

1. In a small bowl mash the avocado with a fork or potato masher to your preferred smoothness.
2. Mix in the shallot through the lime juice with a fork.
3. Taste and season with the salt, pepper, and hot sauce as required.
4. For best taste, chill, wrapped as described above, for 1 hour prior to use.

Green Guacamole

IN MY HOUSE this recipe is known as "Green" Guacamole because it doesn't have the "Classic" recipe's red flecks. If you're a cilantro lover, you're sure to like it. Like Classic Guacamole, this benefits from being stored with the avocado pit in the middle of the bowl and covered with plastic wrap that touches the surface of the guacamole.

2 ripe avocados, peeled and pitted

2 tablespoons finely chopped green pepper
1 tablespoon finely chopped cilantro stalk
1 tablespoon lime juice
1 garlic clove, minced

¼ cup finely chopped cilantro leaves, packed

Salt and black pepper

1. In a medium bowl mash the avocado with a fork or potato masher to your preferred smoothness.
2. Add the pepper through the garlic and mix well.
3. Stir through the cilantro leaves.
4. Taste and season with the salt and pepper as required.
5. For best taste, chill, wrapped as described above, for 1 hour prior to use.

Mushroom Gravy

MAKES ABOUT 1½ CUPS

PREPARATION TIME:
30 MINUTES

3 tablespoons vegan
  margarine

2 garlic cloves, grated
½ medium onion, grated
3 cremini mushrooms,
  grated
½ teaspoon dried thyme
¼ teaspoon black pepper

3 tablespoons chickpea
  flour, sifted if lumpy

½ cup mushroom or dark
  vegetable stock, store-
  bought or homemade
  (page 43)
½ cup plain soymilk
1 tablespoon soy sauce

1 tablespoon nutritional
  yeast

Salt and black pepper

*Please check all packaged
ingredients, as noted on
page 39.

THIS IS A lovely, thick, creamy, and mushroom-y gravy. Although I call for cremini mushrooms, I've made this using an equal amount of button mushrooms, portobello caps (about half of a large cap), and reconstituted dried porcini mushrooms, so use what you have available. Hold the gravy on low heat until ready to serve or make in advance, refrigerate, and reheat if required. Blend it smooth or serve as is. If it thickens too much, add a little extra liquid 1 tablespoon at a time until the desired consistency is reached.

1. Melt the margarine in a medium pot over medium heat.
2. Sauté the garlic through the pepper until very soft, about 5 minutes.
3. Add the chickpea flour to make a roux and cook lightly so just blended.
4. Alternate adding the mushroom stock and soymilk ¼ cup at a time. Add the soy sauce after the first addition of each. After each addition stir well and allow the gravy to thicken slightly before adding the next quantity. After all the liquid is added, cook at a gentle simmer for 5 minutes.
5. Add the nutritional yeast just prior to serving; do not boil.
6. Taste and season with the salt and pepper if desired.

Croutons

PREPARATION TIME:
10 MINUTES

COOKING TIME:
35 MINUTES

NOT REALLY A recipe, more of a general how-to guide, this will have you creating yummy croutons out of leftover or nearly stale bread in no time. There are no set quantities; you need to play it by ear a little, depending on how you like your croutons. I like mine a little chewy, not completely crisp, so I may use a little more oil and cook for a shorter length of time than maybe you would. Play around until you get the right balance for you. Use on soups, salads, pasta, or as a nice crunchy predinner snack.

Leftover bread, at least a
    day old, not completely
    hard and stale but
    getting that way

Olive oil
Herbs as desired
Minced garlic as desired

1. Preheat the oven to 375°F.
2. Cut the bread into uniform cubes (I like mine about ½ inch). Discard any hard crusts.
3. On a rimmed baking pan large enough to fit the bread in a single layer, toss the cubes with the oil and the herbs and garlic as desired. Start with less oil than you think you need and add more if necessary. All the cubes should be lightly coated with oil, but not enough so that they soak it up.
4. Bake for 30 to 40 minutes, until golden and crisp, checking and tossing every 10 minutes to ensure they don't burn so they can be removed from the oven as they reach your preferred level of crispness.
5. Allow to cool on the pan.
6. When completely cool use or store in an airtight container.

Chees-y Crackers

MAKES ABOUT 32
CRACKERS

PREPARATION TIME:
15 MINUTES

COOKING TIME:
10 MINUTES

N in the Dry Chees-y Mix

1 cup all-purpose flour
¼ cup plus 1 tablespoon
Dry Chees-y Mix (page
51)
1 teaspoon baking powder
½ teaspoon salt
½ teaspoon mustard
powder
¼ teaspoon turmeric
¼ teaspoon black salt
¼ teaspoon black pepper

2 tablespoons grated
vegan cheese, optional

¼ cup vegan margarine
2 tablespoons vegan
shortening

5 to 6 tablespoons soymilk

THESE ARE A little pungent, so good for eating by themselves or with soup or pasta. Not saying they aren't good topped with things, too, but you have to match the toppings carefully. I like a slice of tomato, plain. The dough is a little soft but rolls out well. Before rolling out the dough, be sure to cover the board with flour. If you don't want to use a cutter, slice into squares or even into strips and twist into chees-y straws.

1. Preheat the oven to 400°F and line 2 baking sheets with parchment paper.
2. In a large bowl sift together the flour through the pepper.
3. Stir in the cheese, if using.
4. Using a pastry cutter or two knives held together, cut in the margarine and shortening until the mixture resembles coarse bread crumbs.
5. Make a well in the center and add 5 tablespoons of the soymilk. Mix to form a stiff dough. If more liquid is required, add more soymilk 1 teaspoon at a time until the dough holds together when pressed.
6. Press the dough into a ball, then on a lightly floured board, roll to a thickness of about ⅛ inch (or as thin as you can). Using a 2-inch-diameter cookie cutter, cut out the crackers and place 1 inch apart on the prepared sheets. Re-roll scraps for more crackers.
7. Bake for 8 to 10 minutes, or until golden brown.
8. Cool on the baking sheet for 5 minutes before transferring to a rack to complete cooling. Store in a covered container.

Spelt Crackers

IGHT, CRISP, AND neutral-tasting (besides a lovely nutty quality), these are perfect, go-with-anything crackers. If you want to pretty them up prior to baking, feel free to sprinkle with a few seeds, herbs, or even finely chopped nuts. Serve with soup, as a predinner nibble, or even alongside a thick stew.

1. Preheat the oven to 400°F and line 2 baking sheets with parchment paper.
2. In a large bowl sift together the flour through the cayenne.
3. Make a well in the center and add the oils and stock. Mix to form a stiff dough. If more liquid is required, add stock 1 teaspoon at a time until the dough holds together when pressed.
4. Press the dough into a ball, then on a lightly floured board, roll to a thickness of about ⅛ inch or as thin as you can. Using a 2-inch-diameter cookie cutter, cut out the crackers and place 1 inch apart on the sheets. Re-roll scraps for more crackers.
5. Bake for 8 to 10 minutes, until golden brown.
6. Cool on the sheets for 5 minutes before transferring to a rack to complete cooling. When cool store in a covered container.

MAKES ABOUT 30 CRACKERS

PREPARATION TIME: 15 MINUTES

COOKING TIME: 10 MINUTES

1½ cups spelt flour
1 teaspoon baking powder
¾ teaspoon salt
½ teaspoon white pepper
¼ teaspoon poultry seasoning mix, store-bought or homemade (page 52)
⅛ teaspoon cayenne, or to taste

¼ cup canola oil
2 tablespoons coconut oil, melted
3 to 5 tablespoons vegetable stock, store-bought or homemade (page 43)

Cheese and Chives Scones

MAKES 8 SCONES

PREPARATION TIME:
10 MINUTES

COOKING TIME:
15 MINUTES

2 cups all-purpose flour
1 teaspoon baking soda
1 teaspoon salt
Freshly ground black
    pepper

½ cup grated vegan
    cheese
1 tablespoon chopped
    fresh or freeze-dried
    chives
1 tablespoon wheat germ
1 tablespoon nutritional
    yeast

2 tablespoons vegan
    margarine
2 tablespoons vegan
    shortening

1 cup soymilk

IN *QUICK AND EASY VEGAN BAKE SALE* I have a Cheesy Scone recipe that doesn't use a vegan cheese substitute, but since then I have been playing with cheese scones that do contain vegan cheese (usually Daiya, but anything goes), and this is the result. I love these with the chives (fresh and freeze-dried both work perfectly), but for a change I often make the dill variation, which is also super. Great served with soup, but they also hold up well with stews and are even good smothered in gravy like biscuits.

1. Preheat the oven to 425°F and line a baking sheet with parchment.
2. Sift the flour through the pepper into a large bowl.
3. Stir in the cheese through the nutritional yeast.
4. Using the tips of your fingers, a pastry cutter, or two knives held together, rub in the margarine until the mixture resembles coarse bread crumbs. Make a well.
5. Stir the milk into the well; with your hands knead lightly to bring the dough together.
6. Divide the dough into 8 equal pieces, shape into rough balls, then flatten into 1½-inch-high discs.
7. Place on the prepared sheet about 1 inch apart. Bake for 15 minutes, or until the tops are lightly browned.
8. Cool on the sheet for 5 minutes, then remove to a cooling rack.

VARIATION:

CHEESE AND DILL SCONES
    Replace the chives with 1 teaspoon dried dill.

Cornbread Scones

THINK CORNBREAD, BUT in scone format. Super simple to throw together, and with just a bowl and a piece of parchment to clean up, they are way less messy than making cornbread in a skillet or cake pan. Also think super simple to eat, a little crumbly but not as much as cornbread can be. Any recipe in the Chilies and BBQ-Inspired Dishes chapter (page 129) is a good match. These scones are best eaten on the day they are made but also freeze well.

1. Preheat the oven to 375°F and line a baking sheet with parchment paper.
2. Combine the corn through the agave in a large bowl and whisk well.
3. Sift in the flour through the pepper; mix just to combine.
4. Shape into 8 equal portions about 1½ inches high and place on the prepared pan. If the dough is too soft to handle easily or you don't want to use your hands, scoop out with a measuring cup.
5. Bake for 15 to 18 minutes, until golden; cool on the pan for 5 minutes before moving to a rack to finish cooling.

MAKES 8 SCONES

PREPARATION TIME:
10 MINUTES

COOKING TIME:
20 MINUTES

½ cup creamed corn
½ cup water
¼ cup canned coconut
   milk
2 tablespoons canola oil
1 tablespoon agave

1½ cups all-purpose flour
½ cup yellow corn flour
½ cup fine cornmeal
2 teaspoons baking
   powder
½ teaspoon baking soda
1 teaspoon salt
¼ teaspoon chile flakes
¼ teaspoon cumin
Freshly ground black
   pepper

Oregano and Sun-Dried Tomato Rolls

MAKES 4 ROLLS

PREPARATION TIME:
4 HOURS, BUT MUCH
INACTIVE

¼ cup sun-dried tomatoes,
  packed (see Note)
1 cup plus 2 tablespoons
  boiling water

2 teaspoons dried yeast
1 teaspoon sugar

1½ cups white bread
  flour, or 1½ cups all-
  purpose flour plus 1½
  tablespoons vital wheat
  gluten
1 teaspoon salt
2 tablespoons olive oil
1 tablespoon dried
  oregano

1 cup white bread flour, or
  1 cup all-purpose flour
  plus 1 tablespoon vital
  wheat gluten

Olive oil

THESE ROLLS ARE perfect for the middle of winter when you're craving a taste of summer. The pretty orange color and the tomato and herb flavors will make even the dreariest of days seem filled with sunshine. These are also good with dried basil, and are great served with pasta dishes such as Lasagna (page 182) and soups (especially tomato-based) like Triple Tomato Soup (page 66) or Minestrone-Inspired Chunky Fennel and Bean Soup (page 83). You can refrigerate the rolls overnight to complete their rise. In the morning bring the dough back to room temperature, shape, and let rise prior to baking for a lovely warm accompaniment to breakfast or brunch.

1. In a very large bowl, soak the tomatoes covered by the water until the temperature of the water is lukewarm, about 20 minutes.
2. Remove the tomatoes, squeeze out and retain all the liquid, and finely chop.
3. Add the yeast and sugar to the liquid and let stand for 10 minutes.
4. Add the flour through the oregano and tomatoes. Stir 100 times to combine. Cover and let stand for 30 minutes.
5. Add the remaining flour and stir to combine. Turn onto a lightly floured board and knead until the dough is soft and supple and all the flour is incorporated, 15 minutes. If the dough is too sticky, add flour by the scant handful as required.
6. Clean the inside of the bowl and wipe with a small amount of the oil. Add the dough and turn to coat. Cover and place in a warm place to rise for 1½ hours.
7. Punch down the dough, remove from the bowl, and knead on the lightly floured board until supple again, 2 minutes. Divide into 4 equal pieces and form into cigar- or log-shaped rolls about 6 inches long and about 1 inch in diameter.

8. Line a baking sheet with parchment and place the rolls on the sheet. Cover and allow to rise for 30 minutes.
9. Preheat the oven to 375°F while the rolls rise.
10. Bake for 25 to 30 minutes, or until golden and hollow-sounding if tapped on the bottom.

NOTE: If you have oil-packed sun-dried tomatoes, you don't need to soak them. Just ensure your water is lukewarm prior to adding the yeast and sugar.

Puff Pastry Roll-Ups

SERVES 4

PREPARATION TIME:
10 MINUTES

COOKING TIME:
15 MINUTES

One 14-ounce package
store-bought vegan
puff pastry

¼ cup fresh basil or
other fresh herbs to
match the meal, finely
chopped

THIS IS A super way to have something to dip into your soup or stew. It's so fancy yet so very simple! Mix and match the fresh herbs so they complement your meal.

1. Preheat the oven to 425°F and line a baking sheet with parchment paper.
2. On a lightly floured board, roll out the pastry into a large square, as thin as possible. If the pastry comes in halves, roll out each in turn.
3. Sprinkle evenly with the fresh herbs.
4. Starting with the side closest to you, roll the pastry into a tight log shape, enclosing the herbs in the layers. Dampen the edge of the pastry and press to seal.
5. Cut into ½-inch pieces and place them cut side up 1 inch apart on the sheet.
6. Bake 15 to 20 minutes, until the pastry is puffed and golden, taking care not to burn, especially the bases and bottom edges.

Herbed Caramelized Onion Mini Loaves

D ON'T PANIC ABOUT the volume of onions you're chopping! They reduce a great deal when caramelized, and they do get very sweet, so the loaves have a nice sweetish-savory buzz about them. Perfect with chili, stews, and soups, these cute loaves will add a little (more) pizzazz to your meal. Caramelize the onions in advance and hold until required. If refrigerating, bring back to room temperature prior to continuing with the recipe. If you don't have mini loaf pans (a sheet with 8 loaf-shaped indentations), make these in muffin tins; they will make a perfect batch of 12.

1. Heat the oil in a large skillet over medium heat and cook the onions, covered, until soft and translucent, stirring occasionally, about 15 minutes.
2. Turn the heat to medium high and sauté, uncovered, to a golden color with a speckling of brown, stirring frequently to ensure the onions don't stick or burn too much, 7 to 10 minutes. Add splashes of water as required to prevent sticking.
3. Stir in the rosemary and thyme.
4. Let stand in the skillet until cooled to room temperature, 15 minutes.
5. Preheat the oven to 375°F and spray the pans with non-stick spray.
6. Add the soymilk through the oil to the onions.
7. Into the skillet sift the flour through the pepper. Mix just to combine.
8. Spoon the mix into the pans and bake until a toothpick inserted comes out clean, 18 to 22 minutes.
9. Cool in the pans for 5 minutes before turning out onto the rack.

MAKES 8 LOAVES OR 12 MUFFINS

PREPARATION TIME:
40 MINUTES, INCLUDING CARAMELIZING AND COOLING

COOKING TIME:
20 MINUTES

1 tablespoon olive oil
½ large red onion, quartered and finely sliced
½ large sweet onion such as Vidalia, quartered and finely sliced

1 tablespoon finely chopped fresh rosemary, or 1 teaspoon dried
1 tablespoon finely chopped fresh thyme, or 1 teaspoon dried

1¼ cups soymilk
½ cup vegetable stock, store-bought or homemade (page 43)
2 tablespoons olive oil

1 cup whole wheat pastry flour
1 cup all-purpose flour
2½ teaspoons baking powder
½ teaspoon baking soda
1 teaspoon salt
Freshly ground black pepper to taste

Cooking Times List

T O HELP WITH menu planning and good kitchen time management, I thought you'd appreciate a list of the slow cooker recipes by their cooking time. This list does not include the conventionally made To Serve With items or the recipes for ingredient items found in the Basic Recipes chapter.

The recipes indicated with the ☺ symbol are those with a Preparation Time (the actual active hands-on time) of 15 minutes or less—super quick and easy!

3 hours or less

Allergen Awareness Lists

1 F YOU ARE cooking for someone with an allergy, please always check the ingredients list on all the items you buy. The following lists will give you a place to start if you need to watch out for certain ingredients.

Gluten Free

Soy Free

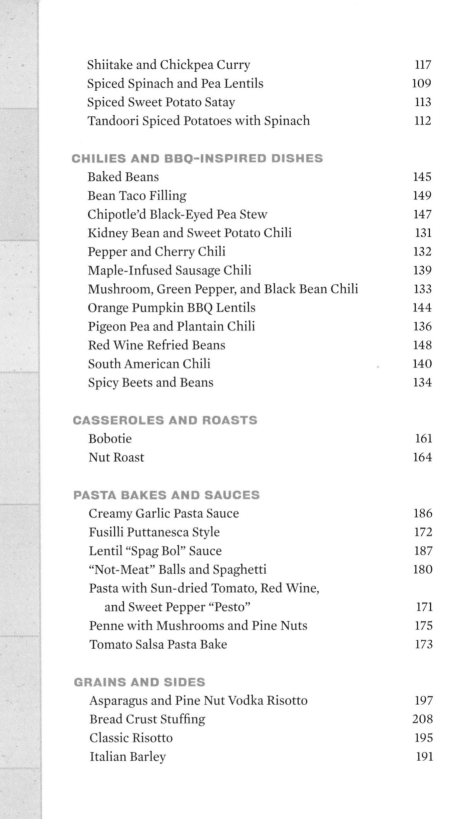

Contains Nuts

Acknowledgments

S O MANY PEOPLE are involved in getting a book ready. It really is a team effort even though only one name goes on the front cover. Working in chronological order (to be fair and to keep things logical) I would like to thank . . .

Matthew Lore, Publisher, The Experiment, New York, for believing in me enough to trust me with book number two. (And number three perhaps . . .)

My lovely and loving family for eating nothing but meals cooked in the slow cooker for months and months. At least I did the washing up.

Karen Jackson and Karen Agabob for the loan of slow cookers so I didn't have to buy extras. These lovely ladies also deserve a further mention (along with Nancy Macdonald and Palo Koorjee) for feeding themselves and their families on the products of my testing. They ate what they were given—and liked it!

My testers: my online international team of committed, helpful, feedback-loaded, variation-suggesting, brainstorming testers. You guys really make the whole testing process wonderful! Following the testers' names are their favorite recipes, if they named one (or more). You can use this list as a starting point when choosing what to make.

IN NORTH AMERICA:

Megan Clarke, Calgary, Alberta

Kelly Cavalier, Ottawa, Ontario {Tandoori Baked Tofu (page 118), Roasted Cauliflower and Carrot Dal (page 111)}

Kim (Veg-in-Training), Lahn, AZ

Debyi Kucera, Prescott, AZ {Lasagna (page 182), Smoky Sour and Sweet BBQ Mushrooms (page 205)}

Lee Ann, CO {Triple Tomato Soup (page 66), Green Seitan Curry (page 126)}

Emily Alves, FL {Lemon Tofu and Beans (page 153), Cauliflower and Cashew Korma (page 116), and Spiced Spinach and Pea Lentils (page 109)}

Kate Lawson, MA {Tempeh Tikka Masala (page 122), Stuffed and Rolled Seitan Roast (page 166), and Green Pasta Sauce (page 185)}

Courtney Blair, Minneapolis, MN {French White Bean Asparagus Stew (page 89), Ratatouille (page 92), and Bean Taco Filling (page 149)}

Tania Osborn, Chapel Hill, NC {Curried Sausages with Apricots, Squash, and Pistachios (page 127), Tandoori Baked Tofu (page 118), and "Not-Meat" Balls and Spaghetti (page 180)}

Monika Soria Caruso, Saxapahaw, NC {Classic Polenta (page 192), Three Bean and Whole Grain Chili (page 142), and Cornbread Scones (page 243)}

Jocelyn, Portland, OR

Jamie Neary (Jamberry), PA {Peasant Vegetable and Sausage Stew (page 97) and Spicy Beets and Beans (page 134)}

Melissa Cormier, Philadelphia, PA {Coffee'd Tempeh Chili (page 138)}

Celia Ozereko, VA {Nut Roast (page 164) and Minestrone-Inspired Chunky Fennel and White Bean Soup (page 83)}

Jamie Coble, Richland, WA {Nut Roast (page 164) and Maple-Touched Chili Brussels Sprouts (page 224)}

IN AUSTRALASIA:

Amy Silver, Auckland, New Zealand {Smoky Chickpea Tofu Pasta (page 176) and [for her husband] Roasted Carrot and Lentil Soup (page 80)}

Theresa Pettray, Queensland, Australia

Penny Tayler, Melbourne, Australia {Creamy Garlic Pasta Sauce (page 186)}

I must make an extra-special mention of two of my sisters who went out and bought themselves slow cookers so they could help me; love you!

Fiona W., Wellington, New Zealand

Linda Findon, New Zealand {Mediterranean Vegetable and Bean Stew (page 95), Poached Garlic and Roast Cauliflower Soup (page 76), and Tomato Salsa Pasta Bake (page 173)}

AND ELSEWHERE:

Liz Wyman, England {Pumpkin and Tomato Dal (page 110) and Red Wine Refried Beans (page 148)}

Thanks and hugs to each of you.

My dad for behind-the-scenes proofreading and pedantically changing the words (which I often then changed back). My mum for keeping my dad able to do so! Also for eating lots of slow-cooked meals on your annual visit this year. Wonder what I'll have for you next time?

Thanks to my brother, Iain, a wonderfully talented chef who gave his feedback and insights, ta muchly. Also, thanks to my sister, Sonia, for just being my sister.

For the inspiration they have given in many ways, thanks to Julie Hasson, Alicia C. Simpson, Tami Noyes, Robin Robertson, Dreena Burton, Taymer Mason, Jennifer McCann, Kittee Berns, Isa Chandra Moskowitz, and Terry Hope Romero.

At The Experiment, the wonderful Molly Cavanaugh and Karen Giangreco, editors extraordinaire, speedy e-mail answerers, and generally lovely ladies! You make the process so much easier! One day we shall meet. . . .

Index

CARLA KELLY is an experienced cook, having started well before the age of ten. As the eldest of five children, she often made baked treats and dinner for her family. She has been a vegan for over seven years and a vegetarian for fifteen more before that, and has developed recipes to suit herself and her family on this journey. She writes the popular blog The Year of the Vegan (VeganYear.blogspot.com) and lives in British Columbia with her family.